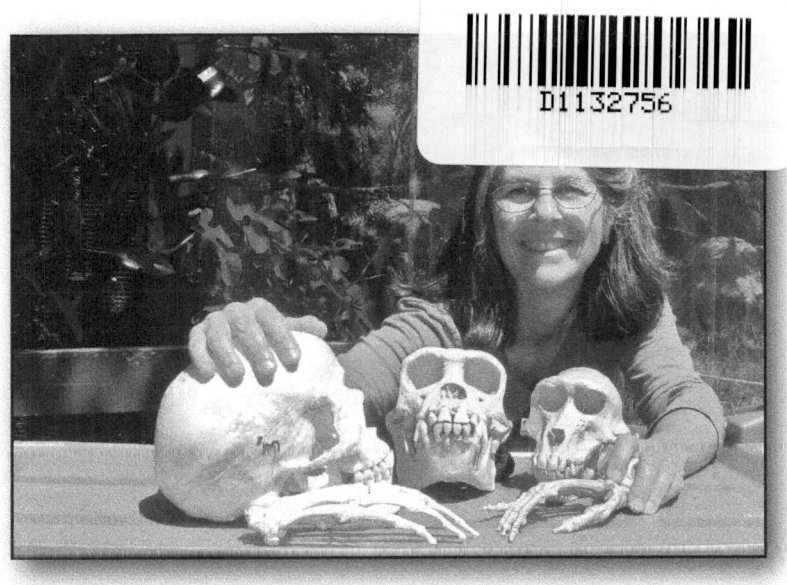

We mammals are curiously preoccupied with social power. You may say you don't care about status, but if you filled a room with people who said that, they'd soon form a hierarchy based on how anti-status each person claims to be. That's what mammals do.

Humans have inherited brain structures that all mammals have in common. We experience happiness when this mammalian limbic system releases neurochemicals like serotonin and dopamine. These "happy chemicals" do not flow all the time. They evolved to reward survival behaviors. When your survival prospects rise in a way that makes sense to a mammal, it stimulates your happy chemicals.

Social dominance promotes survival, so mammals try to raise their status in a herd or pack or troop. Wild animals seek social dominance in ways that are eerily familiar. The field notes of a primatologist are suspiciously similar to the lyrics of a country western song. A biology textbook has uncanny overlaps with a soap opera script. Animal behavior tells us what our own limbic system cannot put into words.

The mammalian brain reacts to the world without using language. It emits neurochemicals instead of verbalizing. That's why our human cortex has trouble making sense of the mammal brain it's attached to. No self-respecting human thinks of himself as a dominance-seeking herd animal, of course. But we want to be happy, and happy chemicals are controlled by the mammal brain. This hybrid brain of ours can finally be understood thanks to an accumulation of research in animal science and neuroscience.

To survive, a mammal must meet its needs and avoid harmful conflict. The mammal brain evolved to choose when to act on the urge to meet a need, and when to hold back and avoid conflict. Neurochemicals ebb and flow as a mammal decides when to hold back and when to assert. Once a mammal sees a safe way to meet its needs, its happy chemicals flow.

Dominance hierarchies emerge spontaneously as each mammal in a group seeks rewards and avoids harm. The frustrations of social hierarchies are not caused by "our society." We are simply heirs to the brain that helped mammals thrive for millions of years.

It's not easy being human with a mammalian operating system. Managing your mammal brain is the challenge that comes with the gift of life. No one else can manage it for you, and you cannot manage someone else's. When you know where your neurochemistry came from, you can stop lamenting human flaws and celebrate how well we do with the mental equipment we've got.

I, mammal

I, mammal

how to make peace with
the animal urge for social power

Loretta G. Breuning, PhD

author of **Habits of a Happy Brain**
and **The Science of Positivity**

Inner Mammal Institute

building power over your mammalian brain chemistry

contact: loretta@innermammalinstitute.org
www.innermammalinstitute.org

also by Loretta G. Breuning, PhD

Habits of a Happy Brain

Retrain Your Brain to Boost Your Serotonin,
Dopamine, Oxytocin, and Endorphin Levels

The Science of Positivity

Stop Negative Thought Patterns
by Changing Your Brain Chemistry

Greaseless

How to Thrive without Bribes
in Developing Countries

Inner Mammal Institute

Get your free 5-day Happy Chemical Jumpstart at:
www.innermammalinstitute.org
Our moods and motivations are caused by brain chemicals
inherited from earlier animals. These chemicals evolved to promote
survival, not to make you happy all the time. You can re-wire yourself
to enjoy more happy chemicals when you know how they work.
The Inner Mammal Institute has plenty of free resources to help.

Dedication

to Donna Meehan
Rosen Method Practitioner

for extraordinary support

Contents

Preface   I'm a Mammal Among Mammals   i

Intro   The Happiness That Dare Not Speak Its Name   1

Chapter 1   The Neurochemical Facts of Life   21

Chapter 2   The Chemistry of Happiness in Mammals   53

Chapter 3   What Social Power Means to Animals   77

Chapter 4   Sex and the Status Hierarchy   104

Chapter 5   Status Seeking on AutoPilot   127

Chapter 6   Self-Destructive Status Seeking   161

Chapter 7   You May Already Be a Winner   187

Chapter 8   A More Perfect World   214

Epilogue   A Mammal at the Movies   237

Bibliography   268

Index   275

Preface

I'm a Mammal Among Mammals

...Knowing the mammal brain helped me
accept the world as it is. That doesn't mean
I paid bribes or joined the Mafia...

I thought people were frustrating until I discovered the mammal brain. Now I know that people are simply heirs to the brain chemistry that causes mammals to seek social dominance.

Every mammal has brain structures that release the chemicals humans recognize as "happiness" (dopamine, serotonin, oxytocin and endorphins). Unfortunately, the mammal brain does not emit these chemicals all the time. It uses them to reward survival behaviors.

Dominance promotes survival in a mammalian herd or pack or troop, and the mammal brain rewards it with "happy chemicals." We don't usually think of animals taking pleasure in status seeking, but research makes it clear that they do.

We humans have the limbic system common to all mammals beneath our big cortex. Once I understood this mammal brain, human antics made sense to me. Given the brains we have to work with, I appreciate how well we do.

Of course, we are different from animals. Our cortex is much bigger. A cortex restrains neurochemical impulses and generates alternatives, so we are more able to restrain ourselves and try something new. But your cortex can't make you happy – it doesn't control the happy chemicals. You can only get them from your mammal brain, and it saves them for boosts to survival as a mammal understands survival.

If you raise yourself up above others in even a small way, your mammal brain notices and responds with happy chemicals. It's not about money. It's about how you stack up against others in your own mind. In nature, animals must measure themselves against others in order to avoid dangerous conflicts. A brain that knows when to dominate and when to submit is more likely to thrive. A brain skilled at making social judgements would get passed on to later generations.

When you feel dominated by others, your brain releases unhappy chemicals. That unpleasant feeling motivates your mammal brain to look for ways to feel better. Mammals stimulate dopamine by finding new rewards. They stimulate serotonin by dominating others. They stimulate oxytocin by bonding with allies in their survival quest. This is easy to see in animals, and that makes it easier to see in ourselves.

I wish I had understood the mammal brain when I was young. I could have made sense of other people, and of my own neurochemical ups and downs. Research on the mammal brain was limited when I was young. But I'm not sure I would have believed the facts if I'd had them. Would I have accepted that my sophisticated cognitions are driven by this ancient limbic system? Would I have acknowledged that my neurochemistry evolved to reward reproductive success? I suspect I would have just sneered "I don't think that way."

My education taught me to blame frustrations on "our society" and its leaders. Once I discovered the mammal brain, I realized that frustration is part of any group, with any leader. People seek support from more dominant group members and feel grieved when these expectations are disappointed. People dislike being dominated and don't notice their own quest for social dominance. Everyone wants the group to meet their individual needs, leaving groups with impossible conflicting demands. The problem is not "our society" but the brain's quest for happy chemicals. Abstract theories about social dominance get created as the human cortex tries to make sense of its own mammal brain.

I am not a status seeker in the usual sense of the word. I don't go to cocktail parties in designer labels to drop the names of A-list people that I lunch with at five star restaurants. But I like happy chemicals and dislike unhappy chemicals, so I have to make peace with my mammal brain.

Happy chemicals are only emitted in brief squirts. We were not designed to gush happy chemicals all the time. ("Designed by natural selection" is always implied.) To get more happy chemicals, I have to advance my survival prospects again. The quest for happy chemicals often tempts people into self-destructive status-seeking strategies. These pitfalls are easier to avoid when you understand your own brain chemistry. But even if I learn to manage my own happy chemicals, I live in a world in which everyone else has a mammal brain. Everyone is looking for ways to stimulate their happy chemicals and avert unhappy chemicals. I am inevitably a mammal among mammals.

Running with Mammals

My awareness of the mammal brain began in one instant in 1995, while I was teaching my International Business class. I was describing Japan's approach to quality when a student raised his hand and asked "Didn't they get this from us?"

I knew he was right, but I didn't want to say so. I knew that the US military initiated quality control programs in Japanese factories during the post-war occupation to help Japan build exports. But I didn't want to say anything positive about the US – especially not the US military. I was in the habit of thinking that Americans are misguided and other countries are inspired. Everyone I knew thought that way. So while a hundred students stood and watched, I searched my brain for a way to answer the question that was consistent with my beliefs.

And then for some reason I noticed myself doing that. I saw myself actively pushing away information I knew to be true. Why would I do that? I'm a person of integrity. I couldn't figure it out in that moment, but the question lingered in my mind. The answer came when I began reading about chimpanzees and baboons. I learned that our primate cousins – monkeys and apes – live in hierarchical groups and spend most of their free time negotiating their status. Suddenly, I got it. I am a mammal. My brain is looking for ways to raise my status. Putting down business and government hierarchies was my way of putting myself up. I could easily overlook this ignoble habit because it was so common in the herd of mammals I ran with.

My awareness of the mammal brain took a great leap forward in 2005, while I was standing in front of a class full of Armenian border guards. I'd been invited to Armenia to speak about my book, *Greaseless: How to Thrive without Bribes in Developing Countries.* The border guards stared at me icily as I extolled the virtues of refusing bribes. I could see their mustaches twitching. When I stopped talking and asked for questions, there was an eerie silence. Finally, one of them asked, "Why are you talking to us about bribes?"

I was talking to them because bribery is routine in their part of the world. Border guards are bribed to turn a blind eye to trafficking in weapons, drugs, and child prostitutes. I was talking to them in the context of a US State Department program to help reduce human trafficking. I was talking to them because they took bribes. But I couldn't say that, so instead I offered, "Nothing will change as long as you say 'everyone does it.'"

"You don't understand our country," a voice rang out. I understood better than he thought. I knew that his job would depend on funneling cash to his boss. In everybody-does-it countries, bribes must be paid for a birth certificate or a death certificate, a driver's license or a wedding license. Even teachers expect bribes, I've learned from those who discretely sought me out after my talks in various countries. From daycare to graduate school, bribing teachers gains advantage and avoids reprisals. Doctors must be bribed, too. I knew that these border guards needed cash to function in their society.

As I formulated a response, animated whispers filled the room. Suddenly the door opened and my Embassy escort walked in. She dismissed the class and guided me to a waiting car.

"What happened?" I asked her.

"They felt like you were accusing them," the young Armenian woman told me.

That answer surprised me because she had translated *Greaseless* into Armenian. She knew what it said. Before we had time to resolve this, our car reached the American Embassy and my problems got worse. The US Foreign Service Officers responsible for my visit were displeased. Some of my talks got cancelled.

It seems everyone was expecting me to blame "the real bad guys" – the top leaders of business and government. It hadn't occurred to them that individual responsibility would be my focus. Blaming those above you in the hierarchy can be so automatic that people don't know they're doing it.

I was certainly not defending Armenia's leaders. They had taken power in a shootout inside the Armenian legislature. They machine-gunned the former prime minister while he was giving a speech on live television. Such violent power transitions are relatively common in everyone-does-it countries. The new governments are typically as corrupt as the ones they replace. Rage against the alphas doesn't solve the corruption problem. It only feeds the cycle of mammalian dominance-seeking.

But resisting the direction of the herd had gotten me into trouble. My status was falling and my unhappy chemicals were surging. Why didn't I just blame "the real bad guys" like everyone else? I had a lot of time to ponder that as I retreated from Armenia in defeat.

I was departing on a 6 AM flight. The Embassy made arrangements to have me dropped off at the airport at 4 AM. They informed me that for a $20 fee I could book an expediter to walk me through the airport formalities. I was thrilled to have back-up at that hour and agreed to pay the fee.

The airport was crowded when the expediter and I arrived. He checked me in quickly and then led me toward a mob of people. He pushed his way into the mob and pulled me behind him. He stopped abruptly and I couldn't see what was happening in front of him. A moment later, he turned around and said "go." I didn't understand what he meant. Then he stepped aside and pushed me toward a small security gate, saying "Have a good trip." In one step, the mob was gone and I was in a peaceful departure lounge.

I took a seat at a coffee shop and expressed my confusion to the traveler next to me. "Did you use an expediter to get here?" I asked.

She nodded.

"Did we bribe our way in?"

"I imagine that's how it works," she said, and introduced herself as a Canadian visiting Armenian relatives. They had taught her the realities on the ground. The fee we paid had probably greased the wheels of the security system.

I started to get frustrated, but then the baboons and chimpanzees I'd been reading about popped into my head. Suddenly, the pieces fit. I saw the airport security workers as dominance-seeking mammals. I saw the border guards and Embassy staffers as mammals. And despite my best intentions, I saw that I am a mammal too. We mammals care intensely about social dominance because our happy chemicals depend on it. And our unhappy chemicals.

Mammals dominate when they can do it without getting hurt. People often take bribes when they can do it without getting hurt. A mammal seizes the dominant position when it can because it's always in the submissive position otherwise. Taking bribes is a double-dip of dominance: once when you demand the cash and again when you spend it.

Mammals are social animals. They find safety in groups and feel threatened when separated from the group. Mammals who live in a bribe-taking group would feel dangerously separated if they refused bribes. The diplomats who hosted me sensed the threat to their careers if they wandered too far from the herd. The mammal brain is always alert for survival threats, and these diplomats had reason to see *me* as a survival threat.

Of course, I was feeling threatened, too. I would not admit that I cared about status, but neurochemical alarms were coursing through my blood. No real threat existed. I'd been sheltered in a nice hotel eating delicious food. I was returning to my safe home and my safe job. My grown children were safe in their homes. Money wasn't at issue because I did not write *Greaseless* for the money. But I was without allies and my status was taking a beating. My brain released unhappy chemicals because a mammal without allies or status is likely to be annihilated. It is likely to be killed by a predator before it succeeds at passing on its genes. I wasn't worried about my DNA being wiped off the face of the earth, but my mammal brain was.

I could have protected myself by sticking with the pack and blaming the alphas. Why didn't I? For some reason, I'd felt a strong repulsion toward bribery since my first encounter with it in 1976. I'd been a United Nations Volunteer in the Central African Republic, and often got hit up for bribes as I rode my motor scooter around the capital city. At first, I didn't know what was happening when police pulled me over. I discussed it with a wide range of people, and most of them said "Just give them money. Everyone does it."

But I couldn't. I had a first-hand view of the corruption problem in my UN job. I was assigned to an international team of economists sent to calculate the GDP. Our project was at a standstill because the dictator kept all financial data secret. Central African Republic was ruled by a "President-for-Life" who later crowned himself emperor. Asking questions about public funds could land a person in prison or worse. On the first morning of my job, the office was abuzz with gossip because the UN population census team had fled the country in the middle of the night. They'd been ordered by the President to inflate their census by 50% – his way of inflating the aid money he put into his pocket. In such an environment, my team dared not ask questions about national income accounting. We simply showed up at the office each day but did no work. This was my introduction to the everybody-does-it mentality. I quit that job and looked for a new career.

As I lingered over my Armenian airport coffee, I wondered why I didn't just follow the group. To the mammal brain, leaving the herd means instant death in the jaws of a lion. That terrible feeling goes away when you join in an "everybody does it." Why couldn't I do that? Then it dawned on me, at dawn in Armenia, that my Mafia roots had something to do with it.

My family is from the historic cradle of the Mafia. My grandparents were born in Sicily, a stone's throw from the real-life town of Corleone, and my parents were raised in the Mafia's New York stomping grounds. We left Brooklyn when I was a baby, and the Mafia was never talked about. But not talking about things is central to my cultural heritage. I had taken to researching the Mafia to help me understand the vacuum in my roots.

I learned that the Mafia is real. In Sicily, these dominators took a cut of everything and crushed resistance with extreme violence. Paradoxically, they seemed to win the hearts and minds of the people they abused – their own people. The reason, I discovered, is that Mafiosi represent themselves as protection from "the real bad guys," which includes everyone outside the local group. In the US, organized crime bullied its way into a huge chunk of the economy. But it convinced people like my parents that talk of the Mafia is just bigotry on the part of "the real bad guys."

Booker T. Washington visited Sicily in 1910, the year my grandfather left. Washington reported his observations in a book called *The Man Farthest Down*. He noticed that the police would stop any Sicilian peasant on the way to sell produce in town and confiscate a fifth of the goods before allowing passage. Washington expressed relief that the descendants of slaves in America did not suffer this problem.[1]

I could have been born into that life. If my family hadn't moved, I might have been dominated by thugs and dismissed it with an "everyone does it." I wouldn't have known that another life was possible. I just barely escaped that world, and maybe that's why I reject the idea of breaking the law in the name of the "good guys." I see how it leads to unchecked mammalian domination.

It's easy to be tolerant of law-breakers in your comfortable living room. But if you were the average Sicilian, you would have lacked flush toilets until the 1960s. Your children would have gotten intestinal worms from soiled water. You would have bought drinking water from a Mafia delivery truck, at a price that would leave you unable to by meat. You would not have benefited from outside aid to

---

1 p.189
Booker T. Washington was half Italian – the "T" stands for Taliaferro, his biological father's name.

Sicily because the Mafia sucked it up. Many parts of the world have similar organized crime systems. A veiled threat of violence is behind every social and economic interaction. The frustration that results tends to fuels the cycle of violent retaliation. People learn to dominate when they can get away with it and submit when that's necessary to survive. The mammal brain is skilled at weighing survival prospects. It scans its world and decides whether lawfulness helps or hurts survival.

On my journey home from Armenia, I thought about the parallels between bribery and organized crime. That got me thinking about the parallels between organized crime and baboon troops. Baboons respect their alpha to avoid getting bitten and scratched. Mafiosi are called "men of respect" in the Italian language. Mammals respect dominators when it improves their own survival prospects.

Baboons and criminals cooperate when it promotes their survival. Mafiosi build bonds of trust with associates who might shoot them in the back of the head at any moment. Animals use tooth and claw instead of guns, but their dominance struggles are suspiciously similar. Monkeys and apes seek alliances with high-status troop-mates, and people seek alliances with dominant individuals. Each mammal brain promotes its survival and its children's survival in the ways it has learned from past experience.

I was astounded by the common patterns in the social habits of monkeys, apes and humans. Species vary but the common core is extraordinary. The field notes of a primatologist sound remarkably like the lyrics of a country western song. A zoology textbook overlaps with a soap opera script, page after page. I wanted to know why. By the time my plane landed back in California, I was determined to find the facts about this common core.

Research on primate behavior is abundant, but scientists from separate disciplines rarely put the pieces together. For example, there are many scientific reports of male apes guarding fertile females, but this behavior is rarely explained. Animals don't know about the sperm-and-egg thing, so why are they so picky about who mates with whom? Animals do not have a conscious, goal-directed intent to make babies with good survival prospects. Yet they consistently act in ways that promote their sperm and their eggs over their troop-mates' sperm and eggs. Something motivates animals to focus their energy on reproductive success. That something is neurochemicals.

All mammals have common neurochemicals. From mice to elephants, a similar limbic system emits chemicals that motivate similar social behaviors. From wild animals like zebras and hyenas to domesticated animals like dogs and cows, mammals engage in similar rivalries in pursuit of reproductive success.

Male and female mammals have well-known hormonal differences, but beneath that they have neurochemicals in common. That's why they have a common goal, but different strategies for pursuing it. Both genders strive to promote their genetic survival, but each gender chooses the strategies that work best for them. A male's reproductive success benefits from maximizing opportunity. A female's success rests on maximizing her children's survival prospects. These differences are only variations on a theme. Males also protect the young, and females also compete for reproductive opportunity. Each gender inherited a cocktail of neurochemicals that mediates these behaviors.

A mammal's neurochemicals continually rise and fall as its genetic survival prospects rise and fall. We humans try to make sense of our neurochemical ups and downs. Our cortex tries to give them meaning. We can only guess since neurochemicals do not speak to us in words. If we knew what our neurochemicals were telling us, we would not like it. By the time we are sophisticated enough to explore our own minds, we've learned to disdain our mammalian impulse to dominate and pass on our genes. But the impulses are there, and the better we understand them the better we can manage them.

Knowing the mammal brain helped me accept the world as it is. I did not start bribing or join the Mafia. I just started taking responsibility for my own happy chemicals instead of waiting for a "better world" to make me happy. People often get the idea that they cannot be happy until the world somehow changes. They continually find fault with the social arrangements they think are standing in the way of their happiness. In truth, no way of organizing the world can keep your happy chemicals flowing. They are only released in short bursts, which is why your mammal brain keeps motivating you to do what it takes to get more of them. This makes life frustrating, but the world cannot fix it for you.

When you understand the mammal brain, you know that people will always care intensely about their status and their children's status. People will react fiercely to status threats, even tiny perceived slights. People will always be mammals.

This is not a book about how people should be. It's about how people are.

It's not about other people's neurochemistry. It's about your own.

As I write, I look out a window at a squirrel in a tree. He flicks his tail, releasing chemicals that communicate his presence to potential mates and rivals. Every time I look out to rest my eyes, he's at it again. The mammal brain never stops doing what it can to improve its survival prospects.

Introduction

The Happiness That Dare Not Speak Its Name

...When a mammal gets the fig or the mate, a burst of happy chemicals is released in its brain...

A farmer taught me the mammalian facts of life. I was touring an organic farm and the owner explained the unromantic truth as he proudly displayed his organic cows. "I rent bulls at breeding time," he said. "They're released into the pasture and the alpha bull pushes his way to the center of the herd. The other bulls start mingling with the cows around the edges. When the calves are born, paternity tests show that 70% of them are fathered by the one alpha."

I was fascinated. I asked the farmer why he rents bulls, since his cows surely give birth to some males. He explained that any males he keeps have to be castrated. Intact bulls are unmanageable on a farm because they fight with each other so much. Only specialists own such dominance-seeking beasts. Everyone else rents.

I wondered about the female side of bovine intimacy, but I didn't ask. The answer came to me when I trained to be a Docent at the Oakland Zoo. I learned that stronger bovines seize the spots at the center of a herd where it's safer from predators. Weaker bovines are pushed to the edges. Suddenly I made the connection. The high-ranking cows at the center of a herd get first dibs on the alpha bull's superior genes. Dominant boy meets dominant girl. The lower-ranking ladies around the perimeter end up mating with the lower ranking bulls. It reminded me of singles trying to get into the hottest nightclub to improve their chances of meeting a "10." I was so excited by my insight into natural selection that I wanted to write to the farmer and share it with him. I restrained myself, however, not knowing how he might interpret such a missive from a lady he hardly knows.

Cows create social hierarchies without conscious intent. Each individual brain simply scans for opportunity while avoiding potentially dangerous conflicts. No social structure is imposed on them, but one emerges.

Mating habits vary from one mammalian species to another. But beneath the diversity lies a common core: status improves reproductive success, so mammals invest energy in status seeking. Human courtship likewise varies widely, but invariably rewards status in one form or another. Reproduction is not the conscious goal for animals or humans. Our brains simply seek happy-chemical rewards. The mammal brain evolved to do this and it does it well.

A mammal is always deciding when to dominate and when to submit. Dominating stimulates serotonin, a good feeling that motivates a mammal to seek dominance again. Submitting triggers the stress chemical, cortisol. But submitting protects a mammal from conflicts that could cause injury. Many apes are missing fingers, toes, or ear lobes due to past conflicts. They quickly learn to restrain their urge for dominance.

Why can't mammals just be equal, a human will surely ask.

Equality is an abstraction. The human cortex can generate abstractions, but the mammal brain concentrates on immediate sensory inputs. An animal sees a piece of food and wants to eat it, but a bigger, stronger individual is nearby. The animal knows the pain he felt the last time he got in the dominant individual's way. (I will use the male pronoun in this book to simplify. Female mammals seek dominance as well as males, we shall see. I will convey behaviors common to both genders by using the male pronoun together with my female voice). An animal can't fill his belly or heal his injuries with abstractions like "equality." He survives by making good decisions about when to go for it and when to hold back.

The mammal brain sizes up the social setting before acting on its urge to feed. In this sense, status-consciousness is more primal than hunger. An animal can survive without any one piece of food, but it cannot necessarily survive a conflict with an angry *alpha* (the biologists' term for the dominant individual in a group). So a brain skilled at sizing up others is more likely to survive.

Animals have no conscious intent to dominate. But when two mammals have their eye on the same fig or the same mate or the same shelter from a predator, they have to work it out. The mammal that gets the fig or the mate or the shelter experiences a surge of feel-good neurochemicals. That etches the moment in his neurons, giving him information useful for meeting his needs in the future. Unhappy chemicals flow when a mammal cedes the fig or the mate or the shelter. The unpleasantness gets etched into his neurons, which helps guide him away from similar experiences in the future.

We mammals long for social dominance the way we long for food and sex. Humans don't think this in words, but our brains seek the happy chemicals that flow when others comply with our wishes. And we seek to avoid the unhappy chemicals that surge when our wants are obstructed.

We are all unique individuals because unique life experience builds unique neural connections. (Neurons do not literally connect, as we will see in later chapters, but this metaphorical expression is standard.) Beneath the individual wiring is a common core. We have common neurochemicals and individual neural pathways that stimulate them.

Happy chemicals alert the mammal brain to anything good for its survival. Each of us plots our individual survival strategy using the neural pathways we happen to have. We don't notice our own neurons and brain chemicals. We only notice the "information" they provide about the world around us. But when we observe animals, this non-verbal mental activity is easier to recognize. We see bulls compete for cows, and cows compete for grazing spots in the center of the herd where a calf can be safer from predators. The brain chemicals that mediate these behaviors are virtually the same, test tube for test tube, as the ones inside humans.

It may be hard to believe that happy chemicals evolved to reward survival behaviors. In modern life, the pursuit of happiness often appears to undermine survival. But when you look at survival from the mammal brain's perspective, it all makes sense. An animal's genetic material survives if it succeeds at mating and protecting its children. Some mammals contributed a lot to the gene pool while others did not reproduce at all. Brains that were better at mating and protecting children were more likely to get passed on. Millions of years of natural selection produced a brain skilled at everything relevant to reproductive success. Social dominance improves reproductive success, so a brain good at social dominance evolved.

In the animal world, higher-status mammals live longer, get more mating opportunities, and have more children that live to pass on their parents' genes. The differences are typically small, but they accumulate over time.

Happy chemicals existed eons before humans began labeling emotions and philosophizing about happiness. Our neurochemicals evolved to do a job, and they have done it successfully for time immemorial. Later, humans evolved a pre-frontal cortex that can anticipate the future. Instead of just accepting whatever neurochemicals come along, our cortex strives to increase future happiness and reduce future unhappiness. But the cortex does not control the happy chemicals. The mammalian limbic system controls the chemicals we recognize as happiness: dopamine, serotonin, oxytocin and endorphins. In order to be happy, you have to coax these chemicals from your mammal brain. That is the challenge of being human.

These crude facts of life can be disturbing. But rejecting the truth about the mammal brain does not make you a better person. On the contrary, you can end up hostile toward your own neurochemical guidance system. We have inherited a mechanism for social relations that evolved long before words and abstract thought. We need to understand it. We gain power over our neurochemical impulses by exploring them, not by ignoring them.

Here is a simple way to grasp the mammal brain's imprint on our lives. First, read the following brief passage about baboons. Then, re-read it substituting the word "Sicilian" every time you see the word "baboon." Now, read it a third time using the name of another group of your choice instead of "baboon." Finally, because you were probably tempted to choose a group you feel animosity toward, courageously choose a group you like and identify with as you give it a fourth read.

Baboons live in tight-knit communities to protect themselves from outside predators. They have a high level of social intelligence. Each baboon knows its rank in the troop's dominance hierarchy, and the rank of each other baboon.

A female baboon inherits her rank from her mother. Female baboons spend most of their time with their female relatives. When they are not foraging for food they spend their time grooming the fur of other baboons – their children, their relatives, higher-status individuals and newcomers who might make good allies when there's conflict in the community. Female baboons are partial to alpha males, especially at their time of peak fertility.

Male baboons get their rank in the social hierarchy by challenging others. Males spend much of their time seeking dominance through intimidating displays. Challenges do not always end up in violence because one or the other baboon backs down. But violence is always imminent as they negotiate their status in the dominance hierarchy. Each group has an alpha male that tries to dominate fertile females. Male baboons will stop at nothing to keep other males away from the females they associate with. And they will fight to protect the children of the females they consort with from violent power-seekers. Male baboons take their grooming seriously because it plays a role in establishing alliances.

Baboons communicate with a number of standard gestures and vocalizations. Words aren't needed. When an individual cries out in fear or anger or excitement, others listen and understand their meaning.

A baboon's brain is always alert for survival opportunities and threats, so it's not surprising that baboons have survived for so many years.

The Private Lives of Mammals

Most mammals live in groups because it protects them from predators. These groups typically have dominance hierarchies. It can be hard to think this way about our furry friends. But an enormous accumulation of research illuminates the mammalian impulse to create social hierarchies. No formal plan or abstract organization is involved. Social hierarchies simply emerge as each mammal brain analyzes social cues in search of safe ways to improve its prospects. The bigger an animal's brain, the more attention it pays to social negotiations.

Humans are mammals, and we negotiate social dominance as busily as our animal ancestors. When two nice people meet, each one strives to establish themselves as the nicer. When two architects meet, both brains evaluate which is the better architect, which has better hair, which has better social contacts. We mammals notice how we stack up against others.

You can say we shouldn't, but the mammal brain keeps doing the job it evolved to do. If you filled a room with people who say they're "anti-status," they would soon create a social hierarchy based on how anti-status they are.

Some human hierarchies are formal and explicit. But social dominance often emerges organically as individuals compare themselves to others. Poets have their social hierarchies, and children have theirs. The hierarchies in government, business, and entertainment often get our attention. But if we look beyond these obvious examples, we can see social hierarchies everywhere. Our minds create social hierarchies because the mammal brain evolved to look for that information.

The mammal brain is always scanning for opportunities to raise its status. It is continually choosing whether to act or to hold back. This constant mental activity rests on an ancient operating system. Serotonin is found in reptiles, mollusks, and even amoeba. Dopamine and oxytocin circulate in meerkats and lemurs. Long before there was consciousness, or secular humanism, happy chemicals were marking improvements in a critter's survival prospects. When we understand our neural inheritance, we understand ourselves.

Beneath our human cortex we have the brain structures common to all mammals, including the hippocampus, the amygdala, and the hypothalamus. This *limbic system* regulates social behavior by releasing neurochemicals. The brain built by natural selection motivates a mammal to do what it takes to keep its DNA alive. Happy chemicals reward a mammal for behaviors that advance reproductive success. Unhappy chemicals, experienced as fear, sadness and anger in humans, warn a mammal of survival threats. Unhappy chemicals motivate a creature to avoid or eliminate the threat, and thus promote its survival.

When your status is threatened, unhappy chemicals surge to alert you to the survival threat. Status threats feel bad because in the state of nature, lower status means lower survival prospects. Your mammal brain cares about status as if your life depended on it because from the perspective of your DNA, it does. You don't consciously care about the survival of your genes, but your conscious mind does not control the neurochemicals.

Animals make social judgements without words, theories, or etiquette books. Brains good at making social judgements were naturally selected for. Over time, brain structures that manage social behavior evolved.

Every mammal has a cortex hooked up to its limbic system, though these range from tiny to extra large. The neural pathways of the cortex build from life experience, and help a mammal adjust the automatic promptings of its neurochemicals. The larger a mammal's cortex, the more it relies on life experience rather than automatic impulses.

Humans have a big cortex and a big capacity to learn from experience. But we cannot short circuit our mammalian limbic system. Our cortex gives our limbic system information to make better decisions, but our limbic system still controls the neurochemicals that link mind and body. Our actions ultimately come from our neurochemical selves.

It's hard to understand your own mammal brain because it does not to report its deliberations to your cortex in words. The verbal conversation you have with yourself is all in your cortex. A human cortex is like a powerful computer running on an archaic operating system. It's like a fancy engine sitting on an old-model chassis. Your cortex is capable of restraining behavior and anticipating the consequences of your actions. But your cortex is only the advisor to the mammal brain charting the course. And the mammal brain sets that course for genetic survival.

Humans use their complex brain to interpret survival in complex ways. But our neurochemicals still take the old view of survival – the view that helped mammals survive for two hundred million years. Our happy chemicals still reward behaviors that would help a mammal keep its genes alive. You may not approve, but if you want to be happy you cannot just ignore a system that has prevailed for two hundred million years.

The mammal brain thrived because it supported group life. Animals that lived in groups found more nutritious food and lost fewer babies to predators. These benefits came at a price, however. Group living means proximity to bigger, stronger individuals who want their own way. A mammal has to make constant trade-offs between its need for the safety of the group and all of its other needs. The mammal brain evolved to make just such calculations. It does so not with conceptual logic but with neurochemicals.

Research in animal science and neuroscience has made it possible for us to understand our neurochemical experience in ways that were not possible for earlier generations. Finally, humans can have a fuller picture of the neurochemicals that make us feel good.

Life would be simple if the mammal brain released happy chemicals when we did things that are good for us. But our old operating system is inclined to reward what was good for our ancestors. It rewards us for raising our status because that brought reproductive success to our ancestors. It's not easy being human with a mammalian platform.

Our brains are inherited from individuals who reproduced. This seemingly obvious statement has important consequences, since some mammals reproduce a lot more than others. Our ancestors were skilled at the behaviors relevant to reproductive success: staying healthy, competing for mates, and maintaining social bonds that protect offspring. As each generation descended from successful reproducers, brains that figured out how to stay strong and negotiate social ties were naturally selected for.

The Sweet Smell of Reproductive Success

Female chimpanzees go for years without having sex. Male chimps are only interested in females that are ovulating, and that doesn't happen during the years a female is carrying and nursing a child. In the meantime, males are more interested in struggling with each other for dominance. A dominant male has a better chance with fertile females when opportunity knocks. In the end, dominants make more copies of their genes. They don't consciously plan this, of course, but brains that prompt such behaviors get reproduced.

A female chimp's brain also focuses where it counts for her genes. She promotes the survival of her children in every way she can find. Sometimes she dominates better fruit trees in order to get better nutrition. Sometimes she makes alliances with bigger troop-mates to get more protection from predators. When she's ovulating, she shuns some males and seeks others in order to give her children the best genes. These skills produce more copies of her brain.

You may not be interested in having children, but your mammal brain stays tuned to everything that *would* promote the survival of your children in the state of nature. Everything that affects the creation of children and the protection of children matters to your mammal brain, from competing for healthier mates to securing the young from predators. Status improves safety and mating prospects, and thus helps spread your DNA. Over time, brains good at status seeking contributed more to the gene pool.

Animals work hard for their mating opportunities. People often think free love prevails in the animal world, but research makes it clear that a mammal's sex life is curiously constrained by social dominance hierarchies. Males don't get the girl unless they build the strength necessary to challenge other males. Females get better paternal genes for their children by running faster than the weaker males, but only the strongest females can do that. Evolution selects for what works, even though it doesn't sound nice to modern ears.

Few people equate reproduction with success today. Modern birth control obscures the link between sex and reproduction that existed for millions of years. Today we are free to think separately about sex, children, and success. But to the mammal brain, the pursuits of love, career, family, friendship, health, security, and status are part of that core drive to promote your DNA. Mammalian neurochemicals respond to everything relevant to competing for mates and protecting the young. Status is simply one facet of that drive.

"I do not think this way," you may insist.

You don't think this way in words. Your limbic system thinks non-verbally by releasing neurochemicals. It reacts to what's good for your DNA regardless of what your cortex is saying in words.

Of course you have free will. Your cortex can override your mammal brain. But your cortex is not in charge the way you might imagine. Your higher logic is always being bathed in neurochemicals. If you ignore your neurochemical reactions to the world, your mammal brain tries to get your attention with an alarm bell of unhappy chemicals. We evolved to honor our own impulses because survival depends on it, from the mammal brain's perspective.

Ignoring your mammal brain is not the path to a good life. Our two brains must work together. This is not easy because the two brains are literally not on speaking terms. The private lives of animals can help us know what our limbic system cannot put into words.

Animals are not always happy. They often die of injuries before their prime. Their children get eaten alive in front of them. They get excluded from the social interactions of higher-status groupmates. But they do not say "what is wrong with the world?" They do not look for root causes and risk-free solutions. Only humans have enough neurons for such abstract thought. Animals simply flow between happy chemicals and unhappy chemicals without the expectation that anything should be different. They simply plot their best course at each moment.

The mammal brain succeeds by repeating behaviors that triggered happy chemicals in the past, and avoiding whatever triggered the unhappy ones. Conscious survival goals are not necessary. The brain simply moves toward what feels good and away from what feels bad. We speak of mammals "striving to pass on their genes" without implying any intention to reach that goal.

Any good feelings emitted by the mammal brain are fleeting. Happy chemicals are quickly metabolized, and a mammal can only get more by advancing its survival prospects again. That's why the mammal brain never stops seeking opportunities to secure its legacy. It is always looking for another shot of happy chemical.

The pursuit of happiness often seems like the opposite of survival in human affairs. That's because we wire up our happy-chemical circuits when we're young. Once we mature, we learn about the unfortunate side-effects of the behaviors that stimulate our happy chemicals. But the mammal brain still seeks happy chemicals in the ways it knows, even when the cortex anticipates the negative consequences. We're often at odds with ourselves because we have two survival perspectives in one brain.

Civilization and Its Discontents

People often compare themselves to others and then feel frustrated. We look for ways to explain those unhappy chemicals. Blaming "our society" is a popular strategy. It's easy to presume that "our culture is bad," "our system is bad," "our leaders are bad," "our health is bad," and "the past century was the worst in human history." Perhaps this millennium will soon be condemned as an insurmountable obstacle to happiness. If you build such patterns into your neurons, you will easily find evidence to fit.

This book proposes an alternative view: nothing is wrong with us. We are heirs of successful survivors. Our brain did not evolve to release happy chemicals all the time. It evolved to release them when something enhances our survival prospects. It releases unhappy chemicals when it sees survival threats. Status ups and downs preoccupy us for this reason. No society can prevent the neurochemical ups and downs that come from the mammal brain's urge for status. Mammals make social comparisons because it helps them seize opportunities to meet their needs while avoiding harmful conflicts with stronger group members. Mammals learn from past social experience – some of it happy and some of it frustrating. This is the naked reality of being a mammal.

Alexander de Tocqueville was a keen observer of the mammalian mania for social comparison. The closer men come to equality, he said, the more frustrated they become over small differences. "It is to these causes that one must attribute the singular melancholy that the inhabitants of democratic lands often display amid their abundance, and the disgust with life that sometimes seizes them in the midst of an easy and tranquil existence."[1]

All mammals get frustrated about status. The more neurons a mammal has, the more information it can store about who is getting the respect and protection that it would like to be getting. Unhappy chemicals result. You can say "I don't care," or "we shouldn't care," but the mammal brain has a mind of its own.

Status makes people happy and unhappy. In short, people care deeply about status. When we hear the word "status," we often relate it to money, titles and possessions. But our animal ancestors show us that mammals cared about social status long before money was invented.

---

1 *Democracy in America* p. 514

People find diverse ways of raising their status and their children's status. Often they use the time-honored mammalian strategy of opposing those they perceive to be above them in the hierarchy, and finding allies in their opposition. Primates are especially skilled at building alliances in pursuit of social dominance. Allies enhance safety and improve your chances of living to reproduce another day. These status-seeking strategies are easy to see in other species and other humans, but they're hard to see in yourself.

In the animal world, aggression is often the key to social dominance. But the mammal brain avoids aggression as much as possible in its quest for status because injuries threaten survival. Humans are likewise inclined to limit aggression because of the risks. Most people avoid direct aggression entirely, and this is a huge accomplishment. Of course, it is tragic whenever an individual dominates by violating others. But this book helps us recognize and celebrate the decline in violence instead of just lamenting the instances that remain.

Humans paradoxically engage in self-destructive behaviors in their pursuit of survival. Our status-seeking strategies sometimes undermine our own well-being. This book addresses the conundrum of self-destructive status seeking. We will explore its roots in the mammal brain's disinclination to un-learn what it has learned from earlier experience. Once your neurons connect a behavior to your happy chemicals, you long to repeat it, even if your cortex knows the behavior is not good for you. Your cortex sees the information but it doesn't control the neurochemicals.

There is no easy way to trigger a constant flow of happy chemicals without side effects. Our brains did not evolve for that purpose. But you can use your cortex to activate new neural pathways for safe ways of giving your mammal brain what it wants.

Ego

When someone openly cares about status, people say they have a "big ego." The word "ego" is often used pejoratively, as if it's wrong to care about status and especially to let it show. This book is not an indictment of ego. Instead, it shows that everyone cares about social dominance. We just act on it in different ways.

Imagine a person who walks into a restaurant and insists on getting "a good table." Their brain has constructed a way of seeing the world that attaches more survival value to one table than another. You may disagree with this person's perspective. But when you walk into a restaurant, the neural circuits you've build from experience light up. You might pride yourself on eating healthier than others, or discovering fine restaurants before others, or getting better value for your money. Your experience built links between social dominance and survival, and you feel good about your survival when you activate them.

We mammals are disposed to pay a real price for status. Sometimes we pay a lot for very small status enhancements. It stimulates our happy chemicals, whether we know it or not. We may groan with dismay when we see others do this – when our neighbors flaunt a new toy or risk their health in pursuit of glory. But when we do it ourselves we don't notice because we never decided to think this way. It's just what the mammal brain does.

People often make sweeping critiques of humanity. They create images of a "better world" that just happens to be a world in which their status is higher. Understanding this appetite for status can help us more than social theories that condemn us for being what we are.

No form of social organization can reach into your brain and trigger a steady flow of happy chemicals. But you can stimulate your happy chemicals and help relieve the unhappy ones by understanding what your mammal brain is looking for.

There is no free happy chemical in nature. Your mammal brain only releases them when it sees an improvement in your prospects. You may not agree with this algorithm but it has been keeping mammals alive for millions of years.

This book limits its focus to the happy chemicals and skips over the unhappy chemicals. One reason is that so much has already been said about the physiology of stress, fear, anger, shame and depression. The second reason is that the best way to manage unhappy chemicals is to turn on the happy ones. However, we will bear in mind that stress, fear, anger, shame and depression are often triggered by the frustrated longing for status, though no one thinks that consciously.

The news is always full of mammals striving to one-up each other. So are history books. These public dominance struggles get so much attention that we may come to think of public affairs as the cause of human frustration. The private neurochemistry behind that frustration is the subject of this book. We'll avoid examples from history and the news in order to stay focused on internal motives. We will use micro-examples from daily life to avoid reinforcing the habit of blaming alphas ("the real bad guys") for our frustrations.

Using neurochemicals to explain happiness may seem like a tautology. Loftier conceptions of a good life. Our cortex may be expert at identifying trade-offs between long-run and short-run happiness. But intellectualizations about happiness should be informed by the scientific knowledge of happy chemicals that research has made available.

Knowing our mammal brain does not mean we should seek happiness by dominating others. It means we can make sense of our neurochemical responses to the world around us. No society can manage your neurochemistry for you. Each individual receives the burden of managing their own neurochemicals as they receive the gift of life.

Outline of the Book

Chapter 1 describes the brain that natural selection created. Our neurochemical guidance system is geared toward leaving a legacy behind when we're gone. That does not mean we are selfish or controlled by genes. It means our neurochemical reward system has a focus that's independent of our conscious intentions. Animal behavior helps us understand this lust for a legacy.

Chapter 2 explores the individual happy chemicals: dopamine, serotonin, oxytocin and endorphins. Their distinct impacts on behavior become clear when we understand their evolutionary purpose. Differences between one person's neurochemistry and another's get a lot of attention, but an evolutionary perspective reveals huge commonalities. The same happy chemicals reward similar survival behaviors across a wide range of species, cultures, and personality types. The chapter describes the specific survival behaviors associated with each of the chemicals.

Chapter 3 shows what social power means to animals. Whenever two mammals meet, each brain quickly assesses the other in order to secure its own safety. Each brain determines whether it is the stronger or the weaker, and then acts appropriately. Hierarchies emerge from such one-on-one status perceptions, without effort or intent. Each individual simply learns from its neurochemical reaction to others as it strives to eat, mate, and protect itself from predators. Animals with more learning capacity have more complex social dynamics because they can store and retrieve more experience with individual group mates. But whether an animal's brain is large or small, status matters because it leads to a larger legacy of surviving offspring.

Chapter 4 shows how sex goes with status in the animal world. We see that status shapes mating opportunities in ways that cut across many species. Higher status males tend to dominate access to more fertile females. Higher status females tend to more assert more mating preferences. Sex motivates mammals to take risks to raise their status. While animals vary widely in their mating systems, they all pursue "better" mating opportunities with great energy.

Chapter 5 describes the mental "AutoPilot" that guides status-seeking behavior. The brain relies on well-trodden neural pathways because electricity flows where there's least resistance. We don't notice our neural pathways because they work so efficiently. We need this neural infrastructure to function, so we are better off knowing where it leads. This chapter makes it easy to see how neural circuits build up from life experience. And it shows how this AutoPilot helps us decide what is good for our own survival.

Chapter 6 looks at self-destructive status seeking. We have all seen people repeat a status-seeking strategy even when it's clearly hurting them. Why would a brain focused on survival repeat self-destructive actions? Because the mammal brain focuses on the survival of its DNA, and because it resists un-learning past survival lessons. Mammals evolved to take risks to keep their DNA alive after the body is gone, so the mammal brain tolerates a little harm in the pursuit of status. The mammal brain evolved to adapt a critter to its environmental niche for a lifetime. It did not evolve to reject its own life lessons. If a person engages in a self-destructive behavior, it's because their neurons linked it to some survival advantage when their brain was most plastic. Resisting those survival habits feels to your mammal brain like a threat to your survival, so it sounds the alarm.

Chapter 7, titled *You May Already Be a Winner* addresses the challenge of stimulating happy chemicals without self-destructive excess. You are already winning more than you realize. The brain automatically focuses on your losses because it's alert for potential harm. The neural pathways representing your past disappointments become well-developed. Your triumphs do not get your attention unless you develop those pathways as well. You can learn to celebrate your wins as automatically as you lament your losses. Your mammal brain wants to leave a legacy. Taking satisfaction in your accomplishments to that end is a skill that allows you to get more happy chemicals from less status seeking. You need not take big risks to stimulate your happy chemicals when you've built efficient pathways to stimulate them with small triumphs.

Chapter 8 explores the desire for *A More Perfect World*. Many people think something is wrong with the world. They believe the world must somehow be "fixed" before they can be happy. The unhappiness caused by our mammalian longing for status is widely disregarded. If you refuse to believe you care about status, some external explanation for your neurochemical ups and downs must be found. People often tell themselves they are unhappy about *other* people's status frustrations. They refuse to be happy until other people's status rises, and see their unhappiness as a contribution. Alas, the happy chemicals you deprive yourself of do not effectively help others. You can be happy in the world as it is and still make a contribution. The first step is to accept that you have an urge to leave a legacy because you are a mammal. You want your contributions to be recognized because that stimulates your happy chemicals. But the world rarely applauds our contributions as much as we expect. Status disappointments trigger unhappy chemicals that color one's perception of the world. When you know that your mammalian lust for status is the cause, you can see past the negativity and find the good in the world. You can be happy despite the disappointment of your perfect-world expectations.

This book has an epilogue called *A Mammal at the Movies*. It tracks the mammal brain's quest for social dominance in a variety of good movies. The link between status and happiness is easy to see on a big screen. The movies chosen are not about status-seeking jerks who deserve their misfortunes, but about people you would like to know. Every human story shows how hard it is to coax happy chemicals out of a brain that evolved to keep promoting its genes.

Many books tell us to "change or die." This book says the opposite. The mammal brain has not changed in millions of years, so we must learn to live with it. We are all going to die, but we can spend our lives celebrating accomplishments instead of fixating on flaws. This book can serve as an operating manual for the mammal brain as it strives to build its legacy.

Studying mammals helped me understand the constant one-upmanship in human life. Mammals helped me see social dominance as part of life rather than as evidence of a crisis. Our frustrations are the normal state of the human brain since it first evolved. The best way to relieve frustration with dominance hierarchies is to see them as our evolutionary inheritance

When a mammal looks at those with higher status, it sees threats to the survival of its DNA. Whether a mammal is at the top or the middle or the bottom, life is frustrating because one's status is always at risk. Yet mammals keep trying to get along with each other because isolation means predator risk, which is more dangerous than losing status.

Humans everywhere care about status because we want those happy chemicals. We are not slaves to our mammal brains because we have some control over where we direct our attention. But the neural pathway of least resistance is harder to avoid than we typically imagine. It's so hard to manage your own mammal brain that people often give up and focus on managing others instead. They condemn the legacy-building of others instead of building their own legacy. Focusing on your own legacy is more satisfying once you learn to accept the inevitable ups and downs.

Chapter 1

The Neurochemical Facts of Life

...Whatever your yardstick of success, you care about it with the intensity of the neurochemicals that drive animals to reproduce...

The term "mammal brain" is used here to denote the brain structures common to all mammals. That includes:
- the limbic system, which is unique to mammals;
- the brain stem (medulla) and the cerebellum, which all mammals inherited from reptiles; and
- a small cortex – size varies, but every mammals has at least a small one.

Only humans have a pre-frontal cortex, so it not included in the mammal brain. Our cortex can manipulate abstractions in a way that smaller brains cannot. Humans have a unique ability to create information instead of relying only on what our senses report. This ability is not located in one spot that can be pinpointed. But it's clear that our large cortex is qualitatively different from the smaller models.

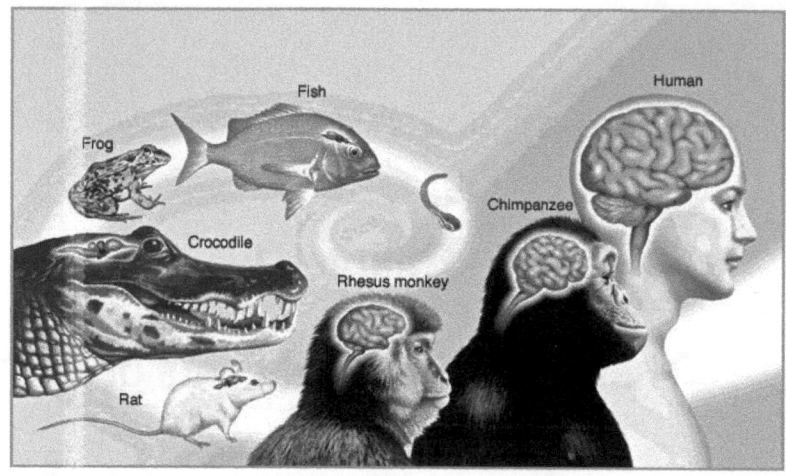

Language is abstract and it takes a large cortex to process. The limbic system does not use language, which is why your limbic system does not tell your cortex what it's up to in words. It reacts to the world non-verbally, by releasing neurochemicals. Your cortex tries to interpret these reactions but it doesn't have the inside scoop.

Your cortex learns about your neurochemistry the way it learns about other things – by observing patterns. If you focus attention on your neurochemical reactions to the world, you can find patterns and interpret them. But it's never easy for a cortex to understand the limbic system it's attached to. Studying animals can help because animals respond to their neurochemicals with less inhibition. Animal behavior patterns have a lot to tell us about what our limbic system is up to.

The first mammals inherited their brains from reptiles and added new features. Reptiles are solitary creatures, without brain structures for making social judgements. Early mammals thrived by living in groups because there's safety in numbers. This strategy was not planned. Survival rates were simply higher among individuals good at tolerating others. Brains good at living with others were more likely to reproduce, and natural selection eventually led to brain structures skilled at managing social interactions. This includes the hypothalamus, the hippocampus, the amygdala, and other structures known collectively as the "limbic system." These structures release the neurochemicals that shape social behavior. Every mammal has a limbic system just above their reptile brain, and no creature but a mammal has one.

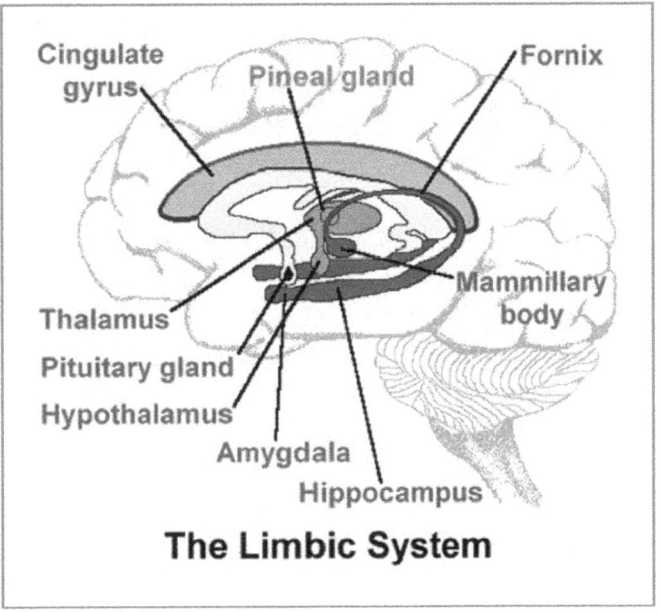

The Limbic System

The limbic system enables a mammal to react positively toward another mammal. A reptile never has a warm and fuzzy feeling toward another reptile. A reptile's central nervous system is always alert for potential predators, but it's not alert for allies. It takes a limbic system to have a good feeling about other members of one's species.

Mammals don't feel equally good about each member of their species. They make social judgements. The limbic system and reptile brain work together, guiding a mammal toward those who stimulate positive chemicals and away from those who trigger threat chemicals. This efficient design has been working for millions of years.

All mammals have a cortex, but some only have a smidgeon. The smaller a mammal's cortex, the more it relies on the automatic neurochemical responses it was born with or learned in infancy. The larger the cortex, the more a mammal can adjust its automatic responses by drawing on stored experience.

Our cortex is about triple the size of our ape cousins' (when the surface area is fully unfurled). An ape's cortex is about triple the size of a monkey's, whose cortex is much larger than a dog's. Yet dogs and monkeys all manage to conduct complex social lives without words and without much cortex. They rely on neurochemicals.

A cortex can generate alternatives to simply acting on neurochemical impulses. Since all mammals have at least a small cortex, all mammals have at least a small ability to restrain an impulse and substitute learned experience. More cortex means more ability to create alternatives to neurochemical impulses. Humans rely so heavily on these complex alternatives that we can overlook the limbic system always working in the background.

Our mammalian neurochemicals are usually categorized into two groups: neurotransmitters and hormones. The ones that stay in the brain are called neurotransmitters, and the ones that cross the blood-brain barrier and circulate in the bloodstream are called hormones. We often hear about hormones in the context of sexuality. This book focuses on the happy chemicals and only addresses sexuality as it relates to status. We will use the more general term "neurochemical" because hormones and neurotransmitters work together in the pursuit of status and happiness.

The imprint of mammalian neurochemicals is all over the record of human history if you look for it. Yet it's widely overlooked, because humans of every time period prefer to explain their behavior in other ways. We prefer not to think of ourselves as status-seeking mammals. But research on animal brains and behavior has expanded in recent years, making it harder for us to avoid the underlying patterns.

Social Dominance in Humans

Humans create dominance hierarchies just like animals. Whenever humans gather, whether two or two million, a hierarchy emerges. Each brain checks out the others for signs of relative strength and weakness.

We humans rank ourselves in myriad ways. Athletes create their social hierarchies, and antique collectors create theirs. Hierarchies based on money get a lot of attention, but people create social hierarchies in everything that matters to them. Consider the distinct hierarchies based on attractiveness, knowledge, physical strength, spirituality or titles.

Each brain is free to create its own hierarchies based on its own values and information. But each brain gathers information by interacting with others, so our social judgements often overlap.

If your status rises within a social hierarchy, it feels good. Happy chemicals flow in your brain when you get recognition from others. You can tell yourself it shouldn't matter, but the happy chemicals are real.

Imagine that you have an award-winning collection of Elvis memorabilia. Your status among fellow collectors soars. Your reproductive success may not be immediately affected because we humans build abstract concepts about reproduction and success. But your happy chemicals respond to the status, and you enjoy it.

Imagine that you win a triathlon. Your brain celebrates with the same happy chemicals that reward reproductive success. In the human world, triathlons might hurt your reproductive success by taxing your body and filling your time. But winning matters to your mammal brain, and it seeks out that feeling.

Alas, bursts of happy chemicals are brief. They evolved to respond to changing circumstances, not to be a steady state. You can get more neurochemical happiness if you advance your status again. Even small advances will do – a momentary reminder of past achievements or future hopes can trigger them. But each new tide subsides, and your brain is soon seeking opportunity again.

Sometimes you fail to win respect, recognition, or status, despite a big investment of effort. Sometimes the status you already have is threatened. Unhappy chemicals flood your system. You may tell yourself it shouldn't matter, but the unhappy chemicals are a real experience. Your mammal brain will look for ways to protect your status to stop the unpleasant feeling.

"Nice" people may say they don't care about status, but they cannot undo millions of years of evolution. Status thoughts enter the mind in spite of ourselves. The mammal brain keeps looking for ways to stimulate happy chemicals and avoid unhappy chemicals. What's a nice person to do?

People often resolve this conflict by telling themselves they care about *other* people's status. You can focus your attention on the status threats confronted by another being or institution to explain your unhappy chemicals. You can strive for an improvement in *their* status. You can stimulate your happy chemicals by dominating on behalf of others, and winning admiration for it. In this way, you can feel good without acknowledging your own appetite for status.

"I don't think this way," you might react. "And I would know it if I did." But your mammal brain doesn't report its survival strategies to your cortex in words. It just releases the chemicals relevant to promoting your prospects as it sees them. It struggles to balance your many different needs. Your need for social alliances often conflicts with your other needs. This problem has no ultimate solution. Your mammal brain simply weighs the options in each moment. It emits happy and sad chemicals as you might use an accelerator pedal and a brake, to steer you toward things that advance your prospects and away from things that threaten you.

You may think others care too much about status. Other people's status seeking is easy to see, while one's own status seeking is easy to ignore. Other people's interest in social dominance gets your attention because your unhappy chemicals alert you to potential threats to your status.

Being human with a mammal brain is so frustrating that nice, educated people often decide that something is wrong with the world. Our frustrations may seem like proof of flaws in the system. But research on primates makes it clear that the same frustrations would have perplexed the first humans that walked the earth, and all of their descendants.

The point is not that we should seek happiness by dominating others. The point is that we do seek happiness, and dominating does stimulate it momentarily. Every one of us struggles to manage this neurochemical contraption we've inherited. It's easy to get frustrated with the mammal in other people, but that just triggers more unhappy chemicals. Neurochemical happiness is more likely to come from accepting our own mammal brain than from demanding that people not be the way they have always been.

Our brain was not naturally selected for happiness; it was selected for reproductive success. Reproducing as much as possible is not the goal of most people today, but our brains evolved at a time when people died before reproducing more often than not. Reproducing was a valid gauge of success, even if it was not a conscious goal.

Birth control technology has made it possible to give up reproduction without giving up sex. Modern humans can choose to put their energy into other ways of leaving a legacy after they're gone.

You might create art, or technology, or a social institution that improves life for future generations. Instead of trying to have as many children and grandchildren as possible, you might invest your effort into a small number of grandchildren who will carry on your values. We learn to define our legacy in unique, individual ways, but we care about that legacy with a common intensity. We are all trying to get happy chemicals from a brain that evolved to reserve them for advancements to its legacy.

Status improves prospects for your legacy, however you define it. That is why status stimulates your happy chemicals. In nature, status brings more and better mating opportunities. This does not sound like a worthy goal to modern humans, so we find loftier ways to explain our lust for status. Many people say they want money so they can give it to a worthy cause. What they really want is the happy chemicals that are stimulated by all forms of "scoring."

We have to live with the brains we've inherited. We cannot demand change in our basic mammalian physiology. The only thing we can change is the neural pathways we connect to our limbic system – and that, we will see, is harder than we expect.

Each individual must manage their own mammal brain. No one can do it for you. You may wish your happy chemicals flowed all the time, but that is not what our equipment evolved to do. We survived as a species because our happy chemicals reward that which we link to survival. If the mammal brain were bathed in constant neurochemical euphoria, we would not be motivated to do what needs to be done.

The neurochemical facts of life are daunting. Your mammal brain is disposed to take risks to get the neurochemical reward. That's because risk-taking is essential to reproductive success. Just surviving is not enough to keep your happy chemicals flowing. Your brain rewards you for finding new opportunities, because that brain kept your ancestors alive.

The True Meaning of Social Power

A male chimpanzee's ability to mate depends heavily on his status in a group. A female chimpanzee's ability to keep her children alive improves when her status improves. Chimps don't care about status consciously. But a male that ignores status is likely to be frustrated, and a female is more likely to see her babies die before they mature. Unhappy chemicals motivate them to do something about it.

Apes invest energy in the pursuit of status. Males schmooze and spar to display their fitness. Females compete for the best foraging sites and the best male attention. Successful status seeking can bring better nutrition, more strength, better mating opportunities, and ultimately more offspring that live to pass on your successful genes.

Animals don't understand genetics, but they often arrive at behaviors that enhance the survival of their genes. For example, monkeys avoid incest. They do not comprehend the risks of incest, and they do not even comprehend paternity in the way we do. Yet their standard behaviors routinely avoid inbreeding. They avoid mating with close relatives by dispersing to another troop as soon as they reach puberty (just the males or just the females disperse, depending on the species). These behaviors don't come from planning and analysis. They're prompted by neurochemicals, routinely and reliably. Over time, monkeys with incest-avoiding behaviors had healthier heirs than in-breeders, and came to dominate the gene pool.

Mammals with status-seeking habits came to fill to the gene pool in the same way. They didn't intend to be status seekers. They simply did what their brains associated with happy chemicals, and those brains were naturally selected for because they triggered successful survival behaviors.

Genes are only part of the dynamic. Dominance-seeking behaviors get passed on through modeling as well as genes. The primate brain is perfectly designed to learn behaviors from others. Special neurons in the primate brain, called *mirror neurons*, prepare a brain to repeat a behavior it observes in others. Young primates learn dominance-seeking behaviors by observing their dominance-seeking elders.

Primates cooperate too, when it brings a survival advantage. The brain focuses on survival, and cooperation is one of many possible survival strategies.

Species have different behaviors because they adapt to survive in different environments. But their diverse survival adaptations are motored by common brain structures. In this book we will see how diverse mating habits have a common core of rewarding status with sex. Bonobos, for example, have gotten attention recently for their apparent "hippie" lifestyle. They reportedly practice "free love," and ingest hallucinogenic herbs. But bonobos also have status hierarchies. Males get their status not from jousting but from Mom. Female bonobos compete for the carnal attentions of the sons of high-status females.

By contrast, savannah baboons oust their sons at puberty and the mother-daughter bond is the primary relationship. Chimps oust their daughters at puberty, and the male-male bond is the primary relationship. The same neurochemical apparatus generates many different cultures as it adapts each species to its environmental niche. But we will see in the following chapters that status plays a central role in each of them.

Humans also seek status in different ways. The word "status" may evoke images of men on yachts and women in jewels. But you may have hitched your neurochemicals to different status indicators. Every scientist knows who ranks in the science world, and every music lover knows who rates in music. Homeless people on a street corner have a status hierarchy and drug dealers on the same street corner have their hierarchy. When humans gather, a status hierarchy emerges, because each brain compares itself to others.

Brain chemicals do not need consciousness to do their thing. We mammals focus on promoting our own legacy without consciously intending to. It's easy to revile the status seeking of people you dislike. And it's easy to glorify the status advancements of those you like. Once we understand how the brain creates this urge for status, we can stop feeling like something is wrong with the world. Humans today are doing what mammals have done for millions of years.

Social Dominance Hierarchies

The mammal brain's genius lies in its simplicity. It releases happy chemicals when it sees improvement in survival prospects, and unpleasant-feeling chemicals when prospects are somehow threatened. With this simple mechanism, it manages whatever comes along.

Happy neurochemicals reward us for scoping out healthy-looking mates and getting their attention. Happy chemicals reward us for making social alliances that protect ourselves and our offspring. Raising one's status in a social hierarchy helps a mammal succeed at getting mates and protection, so happy chemicals reward that too.

Unhappy chemicals flow when a mammal is threatened by a predator or excluded from mating opportunities. When a mammal's status falls, it is more likely to lose out on mating and safety opportunities, so unhappy chemicals respond to status threats too. Unhappy chemicals are warning signals that alert a mammal to the need to do something different. When a mammal acts to stop unpleasant neurochemicals, it thereby improves its survival prospects.

Animals don't philosophize. They simply try to stimulate their happy chemicals and avoid unhappy ones. They don't plan to create hierarchies. They simply submit to those they fear, and dominate those they don't fear. A hierarchy emerges without effort or intent as each individual responds to its neurochemical impulses.

Why does anyone need to dominate, a nice person is likely to ask. Why can't we all just get along? The answer is clear if you take the perspective of the first mammals. Living in groups brought them safety from predators, but things got complicated at feeding time. When a solitary reptile sees a piece of food, it just lunges for it. But if a whole herd lunged at a piece of food, someone would get hurt. The weakest individuals would get hurt. So the weaker individuals protected themselves by hanging back and eating after the stronger individuals were satisfied. This habit made it possible for the weak to live alongside the strong, improving safety from predators for all of them.

Natural selection produced a brain skilled at doing what it takes to survive in a group. Each mammal knows where he or she ranks in the hierarchy. Each brain determines when it is safe to help itself to food and mating opportunities. Humans may be shocked by the idea of animals pushing and shoving at food. It does not fit the idealized view of nature, full of innocence and harmony. But the fact is, mammals have thrived for millions of years by creating social hierarchies, and that is what their brains evolved to do.

Mammals often get along without conflict, thanks to the neurochemical *oxytocin*. This chemical triggers the feeling humans recognize as trust. But we mammals don't trust everyone. That would not promote survival. Our interests are best served by the ability to make decisions about whom to trust, and our brain evolved to make such decisions. Better social decisions mean better survival prospects.

Mammals with bigger brains make more complex social judgements. They shift fluidly between trusting, dominating, and submitting by constantly analyzing their social environment.

The word "dominate" has a bad ring to modern ears, but field biologists needed a term to denote a widely observed behavior pattern. When an animal asserts itself and another animal defers, biologists call it *dominance*. When an individual animal is habitually deferred to by group mates, biologists call them the *dominant*. The dominant may protect or lead group mates at times, and put its own needs first at other times. These roles are not fixed, and the bigger a species' cortex, the more these roles are re-negotiated. Each mammal brain continually chooses between acting on its urges and restraining urges to avoid conflict.

You would not survive for long if you tried to dominate everyone you met. The resulting conflict and injury would hurt your reproductive success. But if you submitted to everyone you met, you might not get the food you need for strength or the allies you need for safety. You might not get the mates you need to keep your DNA alive. Your well-being rests on the ability to make decisions about when to dominate and when to submit.

The word "submit" also has a bad ring to modern ears. Yet submitting is a skill with important survival benefits. Submission helps a mammal avoid conflicts that it would lose. Avoiding injury means living to spread your genes another day. Leaving the group is not an effective way for a mammal to avoid injury because solitary mammals are quickly attacked by predators. Sticking with the group even when dominated is a skill that helps a mammal keep its DNA alive. We are descended from mammals who found ways to live alongside stronger, more aggressive individuals.

Submission promotes survival when an individual is weaker than those next to it. Dominance promotes survival when an individual is stronger. The mammal brain determines which position furthers its well-being at each moment.

More dominant animals end up having more surviving offspring. Dominant males get the girls and keep other males away. Dominant females keep more of their children alive because they seize the safer foraging spots and mate with stronger fathers. The differences are often slight, but mammals pursue them anyway. Dominance-seeking behaviors thus got passed on to a new generation.

The mammal brain is a sophisticated instrument for making those constant little choices between staking one's claim and bowing to the preferences of others. We are descended from individuals who did what it took to meet their own needs and their children's needs. That meant deferring to others some of the time, and seizing opportunity for one's self at other times.

Knowing how an animal makes social decisions gives us a window into our own neural operating system. A monkey does not use words when it decides between asserting and deferring. An ape does not analyze pros and cons the way you do when faced with a complex social dilemma. Our primate cousins do not theorize about the common good or the struggle for individuality. They simply assert themselves when they think they will win and restrain themselves when they think they would lose. This sounds awful to human ears, and we are constantly told not to think this way. But the issue keeps resurfacing because underneath each cortex is a mammal brain that thinks this way.

A monkey decides whether it would win a conflict by comparing itself to another. Mammals that assessed others accurately had more reproductive success. Brains that are good at making social judgements were naturally selected for. The cortex supports success with its skill at extracting information from contrasts. Humans often lament social comparisons without noticing how much their own brain is doing the same thing.

A mammal draws on its past experience when it compares itself to others. Mammals accumulate a lot of experience because they have a relatively long childhood. Mammals have larger brains than earlier creatures, and they need longer childhoods to fill those brains with survival information. A mammal's survival depends as much on its social learning as it does on its learning about food or predators.

Neurochemicals help the mammal brain learn from experience. When a mammal does something that satisfies its needs, a good feeling results, and that etches memory. Happy chemicals create real physical connections between neurons. The mammal brain learns what works because happy chemicals flow when a mammal advances its survival prospects.

Ask Not For Whom the Neurochemicals Flow

If you associate status with spoiled rich people, you risk overlooking the many status hierarchies in your own daily life. Money is only one way that people satisfy their appetite for social power. Let us explore other common strategies.

1. Family

The urge for social power is expressed within families in many ways. Parents care intensely about the status of their children despite great differences in parenting styles. Raising your children's status is a basic form of "reproductive success," though no one consciously thinks about it in those terms.

Every family has status dynamics. Your brain knows from experience which family members tend to get respect and which submit to keep the peace. Some families discuss these dynamics constantly, while in others it's taboo to even mention them. We learn the status dynamics of our own family from experience rather than from conscious intent, so we're not always aware of all we've learned. Yet family is the first social experience stored in your brain, and thus the scaffold on which the brain layers later social experience.

Families exist to help each other meet survival needs, but internal struggles for status within a family are common. Family members can dominate each other with words, or with money, or with aggression, or even with affection. Some families are dominated by an individual who shows extreme, even criminal, disrespect for others. The family dominator could be a person who is strong in the outside world, or weak. Some family alphas dislike the role but find themselves surrounded by individuals who try to get protection by submitting to a leader.

Being born into a high-status family is not the fast track to happiness that people tend to imagine. Children from high-status families can have low status within the family. They must constantly submit in order to retain a place in their high-status world. Their efforts may be scrutinized in a way that leaves them feeling greatly inadequate. Any boost they get from the family name may come at a terrible price, since they risk losing everything any time they do something the family disapproves of. They may seek dominance by rebelling, and that often leads to suffering in other ways. In the end, children from high-status families feel like their survival is threatened just like other mammals, even though they have plenty to eat.

2. Strength

"I can beat him up" is not a respected sentiment these days, but physical strength has been a key to survival throughout human history. A family's combined fighting strength matters intensely where there is so little protection from predators that you have to fight them off at your front door. The physical strength of your family was your only protection from rape and plunder – and from avengers of past rape and plunder – for many of our ancestors.

Where strength is essential to survival, it raises a person's status. Strength is also valued in places where people rarely come to blows or carry a harvest to the barn. Experience teaches us to judge another person's strength in the ways relevant to our environmental niche. Whether you judge strength by a person's workout at the gym or a person's ability to herd livestock, your brain learns to interpret indicators of strength.

3. Honor

Many cultures attach life-or-death importance to honor. In centuries past, men engaged in duels over honor, sacrificing their lives to prevent a drop in status. My Sicilian ancestors kept their women locked at home to preserve their honor. If such measures failed to prevent suspicion from descending upon a lady, the men in the family were entitled – even obliged – to kill her and her suspected defiler in order to protect their "honor." It still works this way in some cultures.

Honor is a matter of survival because it affects belonging to a group. In modern times, your professional reputation is a common example. If someone destroyed your good name as a doctor or a lawyer, you could lose your ability to make a living. Thus, your mammal brain cares greatly about anything that affects your reputation.

Your mammal brain knows that losing the acceptance of the herd means survival-threatening vulnerability to predators. However you define honor in your life, you defend it with all the energy of a mammal trying to ensure its survival.

4. Looks

Physical appearance has a big impact on status because mammals prefer healthy mates and powerful social allies. Good looks convey health to the mammal brain.

An attractive face has no obvious survival function, but humans prefer to be around people with nice faces. Words that come out of a nice face are typically credited with more intelligence, sincerity, kindness, strength and wit. The difference between a good face and a bad face may be just a few millimeters of cartilage, but such differences affect social dominance hierarchies in important ways.

A nice body is equally relevant. We no longer need a strong body to fight our way up the status hierarchy. And we're not interested in reproductive potential most of the time. Yet the appearance of physical strength and robust health still confer status.

Different social groups have different ideas about what looks good. But in every group, small differences in appearance can have a big impact on status. That's why people invest great effort in improving their looks.

5. Education

School gives us experience with social hierarchy at a young age. Different social hierarchies can exist within the same school, reflecting different goals and interests.

People often look to education to raise their status. Sometimes they seek knowledge that will raise their status, and sometimes they simply expect the credential itself to garner respect.

Schools can provide a structure that reflects the real world, showing students that learning can bring future rewards even when it is not "fun" in the present moment. Schools likewise prepare students to respect authorities outside their own family, and to rely on these authorities to resolve problems and conflicts. The educational system is often criticized without appreciation for these accomplishments.

Testing is widely criticized, but the fact is that mammals seek information about those they interact with. People seek information about other people's skills, and testing is one source of it. Some schools' graduates have more skills than others. Those schools acquire status. Students prefer schools that are respected by others, and compete to attend. The competition is intense because reliable skill indicators have survival value.

The need to judge skills is real. When I get a massage, my spinal cord could be paralyzed by an ill-trained massage therapist. I feel safer with someone whose skills were evaluated and certified by a recognized institution. Some massage therapists even get extra certifications in alternative health-promoting techniques. Obviously the skills behind the credentials are what matter, but formal credentials give me information that can help me avoid a survival-threatening encounter with an unskilled practitioner.

6. Religion

Social hierarchies appear in religious and spiritual groups. There are formal titles and rankings as well as spontaneous hierarchies that emerge from the preferences of worshipers. Some religions posit a hierarchy in which all members dominate all non-members.

In a world full of risk and uncertainty, the brain seeks guidance to feel safe. The demand for spiritual guidance creates a supply of people willing to provide it. Spiritual leaders emerge because people want spiritual leadership.

Spiritual leaders acquire alpha status. In some cases they start behaving like typical mammalian alphas, dominating reproductive opportunity for their own interests. Yet, most modern spiritual communities have evolved to the point where leaders promote the welfare of children instead of dominating reproductive opportunity.

Each brain is free to value spirituality in its own way, just as we're free to value looks and fame and politics and even family members in our own way. Many brains choose to construct a status hierarchy around spirituality.

7. Work

Social hierarchies are common at work, and people often look to the workplace for status. As a result, workplace hierarchies get our attention. We notice when people try to dominate at meetings. We get frustrated with our co-workers' status seeking, especially when we perceive them as ingratiating with superiors and disrespectful to subordinates.

Modern workplaces strive to reduce status differences. But when everyone is responsible, no one is responsible, so work groups typically find they need to clarify status relations to ensure that the work gets done.

Office politics is annoying when it raises other people's status. When it raises your own status, however, you may see it differently. You may feel justified in getting a return to all the effort you invested in building workplace relationships. The mammal brain knows that alliances promote survival, and invests in them strategically.

8. Friendship

In your free time, you get to choose your friends. But status plays a role in friendship. We don't like to think so, but it is easy to see monkeys choose friends that advance their status. Monkeys put a lot of effort into sustaining social alliances. They groom each other, share access to resources, and support each other when they are attacked.

Monkeys choose their friends wisely because alliances involve them in conflicts that can get violent quickly. They put special effort into building alliances with high-status individuals who can help them raise their status. And they avoid alliances that may bring harm.

Popularity matters to people. No one will admit that as an adult, but everyone can see the sacrifices people make to be popular. Sometimes we see people sacrifice the truth as they know it in order to preserve and defend their popularity.

Humans seek friends with the kind of status that matters to them. People care about who is "cool" and who isn't, even if they don't put it into words. Friendship rests on the social hierarchies most meaningful to you. Dominance can exist within friendship. But friends negotiate the roles instead of having them imposed by outside hierarchies.

9. Culture

People often blame "the culture" for things they don't like in themselves and others. It's comforting to imagine things are better in some other culture. But when you get behind the scenes in another culture, you find that it is full of mammals with the same problems as in your own culture – sometimes worse problems. For example, some cultures accept domestic violence as inevitable, while others allow each child to start life with the presumption that conflict can be resolved without violence.

The other kind of culture, often called "high culture," also plays a big role in the mammalian quest for social dominance. Cultural pursuits such as art, music, and literature provide opportunities for self-expression, community, and insight. But like any gathering of humans, they become laden with status hierarchies. Culture provides opportunities for social dominance without the damage that goes with some other dominance strategies. A proliferation of cultural hierarchies allows more human mammals to feel dominant without hurting anyone.

10. Politics

Politicians who raise your status trigger your happy chemicals. Politicians who threaten your status trigger your unhappy chemicals. To win your support, a politician must appeal to your status urge without explicitly acknowledging that you care about your status. We blame politicians for disappointing our expectations without regard to the reasonableness of our expectations.

People invest great effort in politics because it can boost status so much. Politics is the gateway to government status. Governments establish official status hierarchies, with formal rankings and prerogatives. The power of government officeholders is effectively limited by politics, as rivals continually check each other's dominance.

Cynicism about politics obscures the deeper problem of government. Life is insecure, yet we expect governments to fix it. Governments help solve life-threatening problems by building consensus around potential solutions. Consensus is hard to achieve among large groups of self-interested mammals. Politics helps build consensus among competing alliances, and thus helps us survive.

In nature, almost all mammal groups have leaders. Mammals expect their leaders to protect them. When baboons are threatened by a lion, they climb a tree until the alpha fights it off. Wolves and chimps follow their alpha when hunting and foraging. Humans usually expect protection and leadership from political leaders, be they government officials or tribal equivalents.

Some people feel frustrated by politicians, but they feed their own frustration by focusing their attention on political figures. Monkeys in the wild spend more time gazing at their leaders than at other monkeys. Monkeys in a laboratory study exchanged food for the chance to look at photos of their leaders. The mammal brain focuses on leaders because they're relevant to our quest for social dominance.

Mammals topple their alpha when they see weakness or abuse. Animals sometimes cooperate to oppose bad leaders. Once an old leader is gone, another individual asserts dominance. Strength and seniority play a role in determining this status. Social alliances play a larger role among mammals with larger cortexes. The routines of human politics are staples of the mammal world.

Humans often try to raise their status by challenging the status of existing leaders. Finding fault with leaders seemed to be the primary focus of education when I was in the academic world. Critiquing the government seemed to be equated with being an educated person. Intellectualized opposition to authority obscures the fact that young mammals everywhere oppose their elders in order to establish their own place in a hierarchy.

People often look to politics to relieve the uncomfortable feeling of being dominated. But it only provides a brief spurt of happy chemicals. Soon, they return to whatever feeling is supported by the neural pathways they happen to have built from their life experience. Your mammal brain can always find someone who is dominating you if you've learned to experience the world that way. Politics can be a way to explain the constant one-up and one-down feelings that are part of every mammal's life.

11. Fame

In every human group, a few people seem to get more than their share of the attention. Attention is the ultimate scarce resource. This motivates people to make huge investments in pursuit of fame. We are all free to decide how much of our lives to invest in the pursuit of fame. But we cannot make that decision for other people. We have to share the world with people who care about fame.

The human mind responds to familiar faces. When you see a famous face, your mind perceives the person as an intimate because their face is so familiar. But when you give your attention to a famous person, it is not reciprocated. Famous people are giving their attention to other famous people, not to you. Long before television and movies, primates focused their attention on the individuals others paid attention to. People in every culture choose to give their attention to "celebrities" of significance to them.

12. Money

Billionaires often worry about how they stack up against other billionaires. Our feelings about money depend on whom we compare ourselves to. You may feel bad if you have less money than your parents or sibling or spouse or friend or neighbor, no matter how much you have. And you might feel good about your status if you have more money than those who are significant to you, whether you make a lot or a little in absolute numbers.

Most people say that money can't make you feel good. Yet they often continue to focus on earning more money, depriving themselves of time for other pursuits. They don't make the trade-offs they say they want because the mammal brain perceives the potential status threat from having less money.

Money can be its own hierarchy, or it can be used to raise your status in any of the preceding categories. It can improve your attractiveness and help you gain recognition in culture, politics, religion, academia, sports, or business. Money can buy symbols of status in the hierarchy of your choice.

People often expect money to bring the feeling of freedom from dominance or the relief of past feelings of subjection. They are often disappointed, because the task of earning money requires a lot of submitting to others. You can earn good money without feeling dominant. You might think more advancement will solve the problem, but you end up submitting more to others to advance your career. An unrewarding cycle can result.

No amount of money can guarantee alpha status on every social hierarchy in this list. You can always find someone who has something you don't have if your mind looks for it. Unlimited status goals leave you feeling poor no matter how much money you have. The only escape from this trap is to learn to feel comfortable when you're in the subordinate position.

13. Crime

Some people seek dominance in ways that violate others. Human groups strive to prevent aggressive dominance seeking. But we are all biased judges of when others have violated us and when our own self-advancement efforts violate others. Human groups create formalized justice systems to solve this problem. We need explicit rules and enforcement mechanisms because humans can beat, kill, steal or rape to satisfy their urge for dominance.

Some individuals violate the rules of their group. These law-breakers often form alliances with each other to promote their own interests. Status hierarchies emerge within those alliances. Making alliances with law-breakers can raise your status in many ways, which tempts people to do it.

Crime is often excused with the presumption that a person has to feed their family. But many criminals accumulate far more than is necessary to eat. Few acts of aggression are caused by the immediate need for food. Aggression brings a feeling of dominance that the mammal brain likes. People learn to restrain their aggression by anticipating the consequences. Many criminals have highly developed social skills in certain areas, but they have not built the skill of restraining the urge to violate others.

Right and Wrong, Good and Evil, Fair and Unfair

When another person helps you advance your status, you are inclined to see them as fair and good. It's only human.

When another person threatens your status, you're inclined to see them as bad or evil. The brain is not an objective machine. It evaluates things in relation to its own well-being. This bias annoys us in others, but it is easy to overlook in ourselves.

We aspire to objectivity, and often transcend a narrow focus on our own interests. But our mammalian bias is real, whether we perceive it or not. Becoming more aware of our individual subjectivity can help us be more objective. We can only benefit by knowing how our urge for status colors our judgment. Ethics and morals are just words unless a mammal brain puts them into action.

There *is* a difference between right and wrong, but no individual is a reliable judge of it. We are inclined to feel "wronged" by any setback to our own interests. We don't see the neurochemicals that bathe our conceptions of ethics and morals. Each brain sees the world from the perspective of its own needs and desires. It's easy to notice other people's mammalian biases. That's why discussions of ethics and morals often focus on what other people should do. Telling other people what is right gratifies the urge for social dominance. Moral superiority is an effective way to raise your status. It's easy to see this strategy in others. In one's self, it just seems like "goodness."

The mammal brain evolved for life in groups. Bonding with a group stimulates the happy chemicals. Unhappy chemicals warn a mammal when it strains its group bonds. Every group of mammals determines which behaviors to tolerate and which to reject. Animals decide this without words. Each critter simply moves toward or away from another, as their neurochemicals flow through the channels they built from their past experience. Underneath our higher abstractions, humans do the same thing.

From the largest public institution to the smallest clique of friends, human groups are always rewarding some behaviors and resisting others. Each individual interprets the group's feedback to plot his own survival strategy. Our neurochemicals guide us according to the neural pathways we have built for them from life experience.

Mammals continually shift between cooperating and competing. The mammal brain discerns which strategy best meets its needs in each circumstance. This book is not a prescription for how mammals *should* act but an exploration of how mammals come to settle on certain actions.

Every mammal figures out when they benefit from dominating and when submitting best promotes their survival. This urge to dominate we inherited is neither all good nor all bad. It can be used for good or bad. It can lead people to make great contributions to the world, and to protect children from harm. But it can also lead to evil. The outcome depends on the neural circuits each person builds from their accumulated experience.

Each person develops a sense of right and wrong by processing feedback from the environment. To the mammal brain, the behavior that gets the cheese is right and the behavior that doesn't get the cheese is wrong. This doesn't mean mammals are always selfish. In some situations, a mammal can get the cheese by trusting or aiding its pack-mates. Experience teaches the mammal brain when to trust, when to assert, when to defer, and when to protect. Each brain learns from the rewards it experienced in the past.

As we promote our survival in the world, we are inevitably surrounded by others who are promoting theirs. Our own goal seeking is often frustrated by the goal seeking of others. The daily play of one-upmanship can be hurtful, but it also spurs efforts to solve real problems.

The moment one mammal brain encounters another, it scans for cues about relative strength. Each brain scans for the information it needs to decide if it should submit to survive. Say a dancer meets another dancer. Each brain ponders its relative strengths and weaknesses. Who has better legs? Who has better moves? Who gets better party invitations? The mammal brain goes there. It's easy to condemn this in others and ignore it in one's self.

The urge to dominate drives mammals to take risks. Many good things result from this risk tolerance. People protect those who are weaker than they are. People triumph over difficult circumstances and find solutions they did not expect. The mammal brain is always weighing risk of acting against the risk of doing nothing and having its DNA wiped off the face of the earth. You may not care about reproduction, but your mammal brain strives non-verbally to avoid the risk of dying without a legacy. Paradoxically, this explains the self-destructive behaviors humans are sometimes inclined toward. Your mammal brain will engage in risky behavior if your past experience built a neural link between that behavior and the advancement of your legacy. Chapter 6 explores this problem in depth.

Rage Against the Machine

We often get frustrated with the mammalian dominance hierarchies in our lives. To your mammal brain, those above you in the hierarchy are threatening your life because they are impeding your chances of passing on your genes. They trigger your unhappy chemicals, and you can easily conclude that your happiness depends on opposing them.

But opposing dominants does not assure happiness. It might raise your status and trigger a brief spurt of happy chemicals. Soon, however, you are likely to be back where you started, frustrated about your status and looking for something to do about it.. You might seek a new splash of happiness by embarking on a new campaign against those you feel belittled by. Yet a big investment of effort may leave you feeling frustrated.

The best way to free yourself of status frustration is to understand why your brain creates it. Status disappointments feel life-threatening to your mammal brain because in the animal world they truly are. A mammal's DNA is wiped out forever if higher-ranking individuals get the mates and the safety from predators. Your mammal brain seeks status because you are descended from those who scored in the reproduction game.

Your mammal brain focuses on your well-being, but it defines that in its own way. Other people's brains are focused on their well-being. They define it differently because each mammal brain is shaped by its unique experience. Of course, each brain has certain experiences in common. We all start as vulnerable children and come to understand the true extent of our vulnerability as we mature. We all fail to get some of the rewards we seek, and see rewards go to others.

We all feel the consequent frustration;, and wonder if something is wrong with the world.

Each bull's legacy is threatened by the other bulls. No bull thinks this consciously, but its neurochemicals surge when rivals appear. Your neurochemicals also respond when others pose a threat to your legacy, even though you would never consciously think that. Your mammal brain equates threats to your status with real survival threats. Unhappy chemicals flow because that motivates mammals to do what it takes to spread their genes. Natural selection built a brain that motivates us to care about our status.

Our world is full of status hierarchies and reading the news often focuses our attention on them. You may have strong neuro-chemical reactions to the news. But focusing on the strangers in the news distracts us from the fact that the people we interact with directly are also mammals disposed to one-upping each other. Our focus here is not to blame the people on the public stage for the behavior patterns common to all mammals. We are better off learning to see those patterns in everyone than blaming them on the alphas in the news.

Success

You probably don't measure success by the spreading of your genes. But when you know how animals pursue reproductive success, you may find their strategies surprisingly familiar. Animals continually check out each other for fertility indicators in ways not too different from the humans impulse to check out others. Animals promote the status of their children in ways that resemble humans who obsess over their children's SAT scores. Animals get mating opportunities by improving their status, and humans do too.

Your definition of success depends on the neurons you've connected to your happy chemicals. Things relevant to reproductive success in the state of nature get your mammal brain's attention, even if you've been sterilized or live in a monastery or already have many grandchildren. Your mammal brain zooms in on reproductive success factors: your health, your looks, your status in relation to others, your safety, and the safety of children. You may not care about keeping your genes alive, but your ability to feel successful depends on mammalian factors because the mammal brain controls your emotional chemistry. This does not mean you would feel good if you had a lot of babies, because your cortex has built up circuits with additional information. But if you follow *only* your cortex and ignore your mammal brain, you are not likely to feel good no matter how successful you are. You have to define success in a way that makes peace with your mammal brain. And that starts with understanding it.

In nature, males and females have different strategies for reproductive success. Male mammals tend to rely on a quantity strategy, whereas a quality strategy works better for females. The strategies overlap, but the distinctions have importance.

A female mammal must invest so much time in each child that she can only have a limited number of children in her lifetime. Her success depends on her ability to keep each child alive until it mates. She does this by getting the best nutrition possible, the best protection from predators possible, and the best paternal genes possible. High status helps her do all these things.

Male mammals, on the other hand, succeed by getting as many mating opportunities as possible. The main obstacle to this strategy is other males. Becoming strong enough to scare away other males is thus an effective path to success. Another effective path to reproductive opportunity is developing bonds of trust with females or other males. Social alliances tend to increase the quantity of mating opportunities.

Of course male and female strategies overlap. Females compete with other females for the best mating opportunities. Males invest effort in keeping the young alive. This book focuses on the commonalities among mammals rather than the differences, Therefore, we will use the term "reproductive success" to refer to both the mate-seeking (quantity) strategy and the child-protecting (quality) strategy.

The mammal brain never stops seeking reproductive success. As soon as a mammal meets its immediate survival needs, it invests its effort into raising its status. An animal cannot put reserves into a bank account or a warehouse to help meet tomorrow's needs. When it has extra energy, it puts it into raising its status instead. In an uncertain world, achieving status today can help meet survival needs tomorrow. Survival and status are the same thing to the mammal brain because status improves chances of having surviving descendants.

Modern birth control has given us the freedom to define success in different ways. We can have sex without investing energy in children. We are free to invest our energy into other personal legacies. But whatever your yardstick of success, you care about it with the intensity of the neurochemicals that drive animals to reproduce. All the survival energy of nature gets invested into your status goals because the same neurochemicals motivate it. If you want more happy chemicals and fewer unhappy ones, you have to please your mammal brain.

This book is certainly not advocating reproduction as the standard of success. The earth is crowded and there are many other ways to leave a legacy. But understanding our instincts toward reproductive success help us understand why we care about status despite our best intentions.

What Love Has To Do With It

Love is obviously linked to sex, and also to happiness. But truth be told, love is also linked to status. No one likes to admit it, and no one intends to love in this way. But people typically fall in love with someone who raises their status. The exceptions prove the rule: when a high-status person falls in love with a low status person, the romance often helps the high-status person resist the domination of their family, thus raising their status in the way that matters to them. And a person who does not want children still falls for a Mr. Big or a Miss Nubile who's ideally suited for making high-status kids.

Love is a big dose of happy chemicals. A big neurochemical spurt is the mammal brain's response to a big boost in its genetic survival prospects. When you meet someone who improves your prospects in a way that's meaningful to you, the neurochemicals are your brain's way of motivating you to make a big investment of effort.

Love is not one happy chemical but a cocktail of them. That multiplies the reward. The brain rewards love so abundantly because the things we do for love are so crucial to reproductive success. Sex is only a small part of the story. Love motivates people to do what is necessary to find a mate that enhances their legacy. However you define your legacy, your mammal brain zooms in on a potential mate's relevance to it. When you see that special someone, your mammal brain sees an extra-large boost to your legacy, and gives you an extra-large shot of happy chemicals. Love is an extra-large link between status and happiness.

Let us look at the happy chemicals individually to see how they reward survival behaviors.

Chapter 2

The Chemistry of Happiness in Mammals

...The alpha monkey needed deference to stimulate his serotonin...

...The dopamine was not a response to the sweet juiciness itself, but to the pleasure of getting more than expected...

The brain chemicals that make us feel good emerged from the harsh life-and-death struggles of our mammalian ancestors. This is the shocking truth about human emotion. Each of our feel-good brain chemicals has an explicit survival purpose. This chapter describes the purpose of endorphins, dopamine, serotonin and oxytocin.

The brain only releases happy chemicals when they're needed for a specific job. That's why we don't always have as much of them as we'd like. Knowing the job each happy chemical evolved to do leads us to the reasons we care about status despite ourselves.

In this chapter, we will simplify in order to clarify. We will look at the happy chemicals individually, though they typically work together in daily life. We will omit the neurochemistry of unhappiness and focus only on the feel-good chemicals. We will also overlook the sex hormones, since they do not specifically trigger the experience of happiness. With this sharp focus, the link between status and happiness will be easy to see.

Mammals evolved brain systems that release good feelings in response to other beings. Our reptile ancestors never felt good about others. Mammals evolved positive neurochemistry because it promotes survival. But there's no survival value in feeling warm and fuzzy toward all mammals all the time. Survival depends on making good choices about whom to feel safe and contented with. The mammal brain evolved the ability to discern the best response to others at each moment.

Smaller-brained mammals focus on judgements immediately relevant to food, mates, and predators. Even those decisions are more complex than they seem. An animal risks predator danger when it's out seeking food, so the need for food is always weighed against potential predator risk. As brains get larger, they increasingly weigh the social dimension, which complicates things immensely. Social ties bring protection from predators but they also bring competition for food and mates. A brain that can calculate all the angles of each situation is a sophisticated instrument indeed.

The brain makes these judgements by turning neurochemicals on and off. Happy chemicals are the body's way of saying "this is good for you; get more of it." The chemicals are triggered by electrical impulses traveling along neurons. Our neurons start developing their capacity to carry electrical messages from the moment we're born. Each time your happy chemicals are triggered, they build up neural circuits that can trigger them again in the future.

Humans pursue happiness in ways that are different from other mammals. Animals mostly repeat behaviors that produced good feelings in the past, while humans are more prone to innovate. Humans can imagine new paths to happiness by mentally manipulating past experience. We can subordinate short-run happiness to goals we expect to bring more long-run happiness.

Animals do not analyze and conceptualize about happiness. They don't wonder what's wrong when they're not happy. Humans get frustrated with the way things are because we have enough neurons to contrast present experience with peak moments of the past, or with an imagined future. When happy chemicals sag, we notice, and we want to do something about it instead of just waiting for happiness to come on its own.

The human cortex excels at finding patterns. Your pattern-seeking ability helps you figure out what it takes to get your happy chemicals flowing. Sometimes you're right – you extract patterns from your past that do indeed lead to happiness. But sometimes you're wrong, and you end up with unhappy chemicals despite your best pattern-seeking efforts. Your cortex cannot control the happy chemicals; it can only decipher their patterns. These patterns are often bewildering because they evolved in a world so different from our own.

Your neurochemicals are attuned to what's good for your DNA, in the environmental niche you were born into. They're not tuned to your higher vision of yourself. For this reason, the quest for happy chemicals can lead a person down paths that are not in their true long-run best interest. Their cortex often sees the problem. Inner conflict results when the mammal brain prompts behaviors that the cortex sees as harmful. The mammal brain often wins because it controls the happy chemicals. When we understand these chemicals, we gain leverage with our mammal brain.

Endorphins

We often hear about the "endorphin high." Turning on the endorphin faucet might seem like the key to happiness. But once you understand why endorphins evolved, it becomes clear that a constant endorphin high is not a realistic life strategy.

Endorphin chemicals block the perception of pain. That may sound good; but if you were high on endorphins all the time, you wouldn't take your hand off a hot stove. You'd walk on a broken leg. You'd volunteer for abuse. In the long run, you'd be worse off. That's why endorphins are only released in those rare instances when blocking pain has immediate survival value.

For example, a mammal attacked by a predator needs to block pain in order to escape. If an animal stopped to nurse a wound, it would be killed instantly. Instead, the pain of the wound triggers the release of endorphins. This produces the sensation humans recognize as euphoria. It enables a mammal to run to safety despite injuries. Soon, the endorphin wears off and the pain is felt.

Pain is necessary because it informs us that an injury needs attention. Ignoring pain does not promote survival. Oblivion has survival value only as long as it takes to escape an immediate threat.

Mammals that escaped from dangerous situations lived to pass on their genes. We've inherited an endorphin system because our ancestors succeeded at escaping danger, not because they were high all the time.

Sometimes a prey animal fails to escape. When a gazelle is eaten by a lion, it dies in an endorphin haze. This is not a happy thought, but it underscores the fact that endorphins did not evolve for partying.

The human brain releases endorphins when it receives physiological pain signals. But inflicting pain on ourselves in order to feel endorphins is obviously not in our long-run best interests.

A "runner's high" appears to be an exception to this rule. Running, if done properly, causes enough pain to trigger endorphins but not so much as to damage the body. This activity is prized because safe ways to release endorphins are so rare.

This phenomenon can lead to abuse. Some people run to the point of hurting themselves to get the endorphins. Starving one's self can also have this effect. Various forms of self-injury likewise trigger pain and thus endorphins. People have to hurt themselves to trigger neurochemical euphoria because it evolved to be released only when we're really hurt.

Endorphins are not triggered by emotional pain as they are by physical pain. It would be nice if a broken heart triggered endorphins the way a heart attack does, but our ancestors did not evolve that feature. This is probably a survival benefit, because pain is information. Most of the time it's better to learn from pain than to obliterate it. But euphoria is more enticing than the opportunity to learn from emotional pain. That explains the appeal of opium and its derivatives, which are chemically similar to endorphins. Mood-altering quests exist in every culture because of our propensity to generate emotional pain.

The brain evolved to feel pain because that alerts us to dangers we should avoid. Pain is so fundamental to survival that reptiles evolved it long before mammals existed. Pain is feedback that helps a creature mend its wounds and correct its course. We evolved to interpret pain, not to mask it with constant happiness.

Pain originates in the reptile brain. Imagine a lizard sunning itself on a rock. You might think it's the picture of happiness, but the lizard's brain is actually focused on lethal danger. Every minute the lizard is out in the open, it risks annihilation in the jaws of a predator. But if it stayed hidden under a rock, it would die from hypothermia. A lizard limits the life-threatening risk of sunning by doing it only when absolutely necessary. The pain of being cold prompts the lizard to come out, and when the pain stops it goes back under the rock. Its brain is skilled at monitoring its body temperature and sunning only as needed to survive. The central nervous system of a reptile is a marvel of efficiency.

Pain is the mechanism this system relies on. Low body temperature triggers a lizard's release of a neurochemical that is equivalent to pain in humans. The lizard suns until the pain stops. It is not having fun yet; it is monitoring internal pain signals in order to survive.

Every mammal inherits this central nervous system from our reptile ancestors. The reptile brain has no ability to feel happiness. Its success lies in its ability to trigger a full body mobilization to escape from pain. Reptiles have been great survivors because their brains are so efficient at avoiding pain. But a reptile is not happy when it succeeds at escaping from pain. It simply goes back to what it was doing before the pain, which is scanning for pain.

A lizard does not get frustrated about being on alert for danger all the time. It does not think "something is wrong with a world that would squash me to bits." Reptiles don't feel pain about "the state of the world" or abstract disappointments. They don't have enough neurons for abstract thought. Reptiles react to sensory inputs without building complex mental images of their world. Organisms function with as few neurons as possible because neurons consume a lot of energy.

Humans nevertheless evolved a massive stock of neurons We use them to avoid *potential* sources of pain as well as imminent physical pain. We have made our lives safer by anticipating dangers and preventing them. But we can't stop. We react to social disappointment as if they were survival threats. We thus create emotional pain that endorphins do not relieve. We feel anticipated pain with no natural way to relieve it.

Oxytocin

Mammals like the company of other mammals because of the chemical *oxytocin*. It's known as the "bonding chemical," and humans experience it as the feeling of "trust." Mammals do not consciously set out to bond. They engage in bonding behavior because it triggers oxytocin which feels good.

A sheep releases oxytocin when it is with its flock. If a sheep cannot see at least one other flock mate, it panics by releasing cortisol. Cows do the same. Re-connecting with the group stops the cortisol and stimulates the oxytocin. The survival value of this mechanism is clear, since predators tend to pick off animals that separate from the herd. Oxytocin rewards a mammal for sticking with the herd, and that helps it survive.

Reptiles don't have the bonding chemical. Young reptiles don't attach to their parents – they leave home the moment they're born. Reptile parents don't watch their children grow up.

Without a group, reptiles have no help monitoring for predators. A mammal shares the task of scanning for predators with a group instead of being alone in its vigilance. A mammalian herd or pack or troop functions as an extended alert system. When any one mammal senses an approaching predator, it reacts in a way that the others recognize. A mammal with a herd thus has better survival prospects. Being in a group allows a mammal to lower its guard a bit, and that feels good.

Mammals that lived in groups were naturally selected for. In other words, mammals that preferred company were more likely to pass on their genes. Brains that prompted mammals to stay with the pack were more likely to reproduce. Brains evolved to prompt affiliation by releasing pleasant-feeling oxytocin when a mammal bonds with others.

Oxytocin is the neurochemical reward for sustaining social bonds. A surge of oxytocin feels good, so a critter is motivated to do what it takes to repeat that experience. Oxytocin has many profound roles in humans: it is released during orgasm by both genders, it triggers labor and nursing in women, and babies release it when they are held. In each of these manifestations, it helps a body feel safe in the company of another individual.

Oxytocin is best understood through its impact on animals, since words don't get in the way. Mammals release oxytocin at birth, and more oxytocin is stimulated when a mother licks or holds her child. This motivates a newborn to cling to its mother, which helps protect it from wandering off and getting eaten. A mother mammal cannot guard her child every second, so a child that clings is more likely to survive than a child that casually wanders away. The bonded child is more likely to live until puberty and pass on genes for bonding.

Monkeys and apes stimulate oxytocin with an activity that researchers call "grooming." For hours a day, monkeys and apes pick bugs and debris out of each other's fur. The skin contact is known to release oxytocin. The giver experiences it as well as the receiver, though to a lesser degree. Researchers have extensively studied who gives and who receives, who initiates a grooming and who commands one. The research provides great insight into primate status hierarchies, as we will see in the following chapter. Grooming builds social alliances that help primates survive. But they do it because it feels good. Natural selection favors what works.

Animals can be picky about whom they bond with, and animals with bigger brains are pickier. Monkeys have a big enough cortex to remember each individual troop-mate. Their oxytocin responds to each individual according to the relevant stored experience. Trust feels good, but trusting those who are likely to disappoint you does not promote survival. A bigger brain helps a mammal make better decisions about where to put its trust.

If a mammal is at the bottom of its troop's hierarchy, abused by one and all, the bonding power of oxytocin keeps it from leaving. In nature you rarely see a mammal live by itself, and for good reason. Solitary mammals have poor survival prospects. They get eaten before they have time to reproduce. Brains good at bonding, even under duress, are the ones that have remained in the gene pool.

Cats are often thought of as an exception to the social nature of mammals. However, it is important to remember that domestic cats evolved to bond with humans instead of conspecifics. Feral cats do live in colonies, and lions do hunt in packs. Tigers are one of the rare mammals that do not have social lives. They are adapted to environments where they have no natural predators, and where food is scarce enough to require dispersal to avoid conflict.

Another rare example of a mammal without a group is a deposed alpha. Baboons and chimps sometimes ostracize an alpha once they depose him. Researchers have used this opportunity to observe the outcome. But they quickly lose sight of deposed alphas, despite great efforts to track them. The animals may quickly succumb to predators once alone, and researchers speculate that depression also plays a role. Blood tests reveal depressed serotonin levels in alphas who lose their status. This may reduce their ability to fight off predators.

Primatologists often report sightings of "immigrants": monkeys or apes who live alone on the outskirts of a troop while trying to gain acceptance. These are typically hardy males seeking access to fertile females. Often they try to dominate the males of the troop. By going it alone they lose oxytocin, but when they dominate they gain serotonin. Let us see how serotonin adds to the neurochemical steering mechanism.

Serotonin

We hear a lot about serotonin in connection with depression, but we rarely hear of its specific physiological function. Its easier to understand this chemical, whose happy effect on humans was discovered by accident, if we take an evolutionary perspective.

Serotonin is found in every creature, down to the simplest organisms – even amoeba.

More surprising, the digestive system has more serotonin than the brain.

These clues lead us to the reason serotonin brings a sense of security. Animals look for food when they feel hunger, but when a predator is near an animal restrains its foraging in order to survive. Once the predator warning signs are gone, an animal finally feels safe to go out and satisfy its appetite. Serotonin is the green light. It's the all-clear signal that tells an animal it is safe to go ahead and satisfy its wants.

Let's see how this works with amoeba, where things are simpler. Our one-celled ancestor doesn't have a brain, but it does turn neurochemicals on and off in a way that motivates behavior. It turns on the cortisol when it picks up a danger cue, and that prompts it to quickly change its course. When no danger is perceived, an amoeba turns on the serotonin and forges ahead in pursuit of food. The serotonin prepares it to digest any food it finds. Thus, the one chemical has two functions: it conveys the decision that it's safe to venture out and it prepares the body to receive food. Just how a one-celled animal makes a "decision" requires a bit more explanation.

Amoebas, like humans, take in information from their surroundings. The little protozoan does this by constantly allowing tiny samples of water to penetrate its cell membrane. If a sample reveals a high concentration of foreign matter, the one-celled animal interprets that as potential danger, and starts wiggling in a new direction. But if it finds a low concentration of matter in the water sample, it sees that as potential for food. The amoeba releases serotonin and moves full steam ahead. Serotonin means happy sailing in the expectation of food.

Obviously the little blob doesn't think this way explicitly. But that's just the point – serotonin works without explicit thinking. For a simple creature with only a few behaviors, a few neurochemicals do all the "thinking." Cortisol is the signal that a change in course is necessary to avoid harm. Serotonin is the signal that it's safe to go forth and satisfy your needs.

Serotonin had been found to play a curious role in the behavior of locusts. A locust generally avoids other locusts, but serotonin transforms them into swarm creatures. Locusts produce serotonin when they get jostled and stimulated by fellow locusts due to overcrowding. Once their serotonin is triggered, they seek each other out, creating a pestilent swarm in pursuit of food. Serotonin makes them sociable when solitary food seeking cannot satisfy their needs.

This helps us understand the feeding problem of mammals living in groups. Each mammal constantly chooses between satisfying its urges and restraining itself to avoid conflict with bigger, stronger troop-mates. The mammal brain reduces complex social dilemmas down to the same basic decision tree as an amoeba: either forge ahead and meet your needs or change tack. The mammal brain releases serotonin when it looks safe to go ahead and satisfy its needs.

If two mammals lunge for the same bit of food, the smaller of the two is more likely to get injured. The bigger, stronger one is more likely to be safe when it lunges, so having more serotonin promotes its survival by getting more food. For the smaller, weaker mammal, less serotonin promotes survival by avoiding injury. Thus, high serotonin improves survival prospects for relatively stronger individuals, and low serotonin promotes survival for relatively weaker individuals. This may sound "unfair" from a human perspective, but it's important to understand from an animal perspective.

Mammals seem to have higher serotonin levels when they rank higher in their group's hierarchy. You might presume that high serotonin levels cause high status, but research points in the opposite direction. High status seems to cause the high serotonin. In a landmark study, Michael McGuire and colleagues placed a one-way mirror between an alpha vervet monkey and his subordinates. The alpha could see the troop but they couldn't see him. The alpha made the usual dominance displays, but his subjects didn't respond with submission gestures. They just ignored him because they didn't see him. Each day of the experiment, the alpha's serotonin level fell lower and lower, and he showed signs of great anxiety. His high serotonin level was apparently sustained by the submission displays he was accustomed to receiving. He needed the deference to stimulate his serotonin.

The higher serotonin of alphas should not lead to the presumption that serotonin causes aggression. Here again, research points in the opposite direction. Serotonin seems to inhibit aggression and make a primate more sociable. Low-serotonin individuals are more inclined to aggressive outbursts than high-serotonin individuals.

Low-status monkeys are more likely to be violent, according to a body of research on impulsivity. This makes sense when we recall the connection between serotonin and food. A low-status monkey needs to avoid fights with bigger guys, but he also needs to eat. When a low-status monkey is truly hungry, restraining his aggression no longer has survival value. He needs to lunge at food despite the risks. Research shows a link between low serotonin and quick, impulsive anti-social action. A monkey with little status and little serotonin is less inclined to restrain its impulses. Impulsivity also helps a low-status monkey to reproduce, as we will see in Chapter 4.

An alpha primate has good reason to be calm. He can count on getting first crack at the best food. (Female alphas dominate female hierarchies in similar ways, but one gender pronoun is here used for simplicity.) An alpha greets others with a dominance gesture, but as soon as he gets the expected submission gesture in response, he knows he will not have to fight. He can relax and be one of the gang. Indeed, he becomes friendlier and more trusting than low-status primates, who have reason to be more guarded.

High serotonin makes primates calmer and more sociable. That is why the dominance-submission rituals typical of primates lead to alliances more than to conflict.

The picture is complex, however. In one study, chimps experimentally dosed with serotonin became very assertive and raised their status in the group. Researchers woke up one morning to find that an especially assertive chimp had been executed by his mates. He'd gotten so uppity that they killed him in a gruesome manner reminiscent of organized crime. It seems that the artificial spike of serotonin administered by the experimenters triggered confidence faster than the unfortunate chimp could refine the calm sociability that naturally develops with dominance.

Food is the link between serotonin and status. High-status primates have more serotonin and get more food. But they need more food because they are expending more energy in the pursuit of power. Low-status primates get less food and have less energy. But they expend less energy dominating others, so they need less food. Dominance seeking carries the risk of expending more energy than you take in. The status seeker risks his survival if he can't get enough food energy to keep dominating.

What came first? High serotonin? High energy? High status? High food supplies? Researchers found that chimps' serotonin levels rose when they were presented with an abundance of food. This reinforces the idea that serotonin helps a primate adapt to its circumstances. When one has more food, one is more assertive because there is more energy to spare. Low serotonin causes a poorly-fed primate to conserve energy instead of fighting for food. This helps him survive on less food. Stronger individuals are more likely to win food fights, so they can risk more energy-expending challenges. Thus, we see again that high serotonin improves survival prospects for a strong primate and low serotonin improves prospects for a weak primate. The neurochemical helps mammals adapt to the physical and social environment they find themselves in.

Serotonin creates a sense of well-being. It tells a primate that it has enough extra energy to push ahead, to do more and be more. A primate understandably wants more of this feeling. But there's no easy way to get it. We did not evolve to boost our serotonin by over-eating because an overweight primate would be too slow to escape from predators. We did not evolve to get it by constantly dominating because careless aggression provokes a dangerous loss of social support. We did not evolve to have high serotonin at every moment, but to fluctuate between high and low serotonin according to the survival constraints of the environment. There's no natural way to shortcut the serotonin system that evolved over the ages, which is why the pharmaceutical solution is so popular.

Dopamine

A burst of joy is the feeling we associate with dopamine. But it's not the joy of sitting on the couch. It's the joy of attaining a reward. A runner surges with dopamine when he sees the finish line. A chimp surges with dopamine when he is within arm's length of a piece of fruit high up in a tree. Dopamine supplies the burst of motivation that keeps a mammal exerting until its needs are met.

Monkeys exert for an amazingly long time in efforts to crack open a nut. Wildcats stalk prey for extremely long stretches. Apes persevere in pursuit of insects, and dogs persevere in pursuit of bones. Dopamine keeps mammals going until the prize is in hand.

The miracle of dopamine has been clarified only recently. The old view was that dopamine signals a reward. The new consensus is that dopamine signals the *expectation* of reward. The significance of this shift becomes clear if we go back to the famous dopamine-crazed mouse of the 1950s. At that time, researchers stuck an electrode into a mouse's hypothalamus and gave the mouse a lever to electrically stimulate itself. Soon, the mouse spent the whole day pushing the lever. It took no interest in food or sex. It would have died of thirst if the experiment had continued.

The electrode was triggering dopamine. Originally, researchers interpreted this finding in terms of pleasure. They presumed the mouse was too preoccupied by pleasure to stop for mundane needs. But why would the brain define pleasure in such a way that it rejected food and sex? Why would a brain define pleasure in a way that leads to its death? A fuller explanation was needed.

Recent research suggests that dopamine triggers the expectation of pleasure. The poor little mouse was pushing the lever in the expectation of a big boost in well-being. This is akin to the excitement you might feel when making reservations at a five-star restaurant. The pleasure of anticipation is different from the pleasure of delicious food in your mouth or nutrition in your intestines. You enjoy the expectation.

The mouse kept expecting a reward even when no reward came because dopamine signals imminent rewards. Instead of revising its expectations, the mouse opted for the joy of dopamine and pushed the lever again. Such behavior is astonishingly reminiscent of addicts, who feel miserable yet remain focused on the next dose, expecting it to bring the anticipated bliss.

The distinction between expected and actual rewards is subtle but important. I remember observing the difference when I gave my nine-month old child her first taste of ice cream. We were sitting in an ice cream shop surrounded by people licking cones, and I realized that this meant nothing to her. I was excited, thinking "you're gonna love this." But even as I lifted the spoon to her mouth, she had no expectations. Then she tasted the ice cream. At first she had a look of intense concentration. She had no experience with food that's cold and suddenly disappears. But she found it so rewarding that she quickly begged for more. With a look of intense concentration, she panted and flailed to get more from me the instant she would swallow a spoonful. Her brain identified it as something important because of the concentrated fat and sugar.

Fat and sugar are hard to come by in nature. They are very relevant to survival because they supply great boosts of energy. A mind that pays careful attention to concentrated energy sources is more likely to survive. Dopamine is the body's way of highlighting that information. Dopamine gets our attention because it feels good. It rewards you for going after the fats and sugars that are rewarding to your body. Primitive foragers remembered the location of foods high in fat and sugar without analyzing the nutritional benefits and plotting out maps. Their brains simply released dopamine when they tasted these foods, and that effortlessly built neural connections to all the relevant details. The pleasure of eating nuts and berries caused their brains to store the survival-relevant information. In the future, their dopamine would start flowing as soon as it recognized familiar signs of being near the nuts or berries.

My young daughter learned to associate the sight of people licking cones with the pleasure of ice cream. The dopamine released when she tasted ice cream bridged all the neurons that were firing at that moment. Pleasurable experiences stimulate the brain to store relevant information because in the state of nature, pleasurable things are typically good for you. That's why dopamine causes both learning and pleasure. In modern life, pleasure is not always our best guide to survival. We have access to more fat and sugar than is good for us. We try to restrain ourselves, using knowledge of long-term consequences to build new neural circuits. But it's hard to resist the lure of dopamine.

Researchers have learned that dopamine spikes when a reward is greater than expected. This was cleverly demonstrated by a recent experiment that varied the rewards given to monkeys for performing a task. First, the monkeys were trained to expect leaves as a reward. Then the experimenters started rewarding them with juice. The monkeys' dopamine levels soared. The concentrated sweetness of juice is much more rewarding to a monkey than the bitter leaves that comprise its natural diet.

But after a few trials with juice, the dopamine response ceased. The monkeys had learned to expect the juice. It no longer made them "happy" in the shot-of-dopamine sense of happiness. Clearly, the dopamine was not a response to the sweet juiciness itself, but to the pleasure of getting more than expected.

When my daughter tasted ice cream, it was more rewarding than she expected food to be. Dopamine is the mammal brain's way of saying: "Wow! This really meets your needs. Remember it." The dopamine flow paves a trail of neurons. It etches the details of the unexpectedly rewarding experience into your brain, connecting all the neurons activated by that experience.

To be precise, these are not literal connections. They are improvements in the responsiveness and efficiency of those neurons. Electricity flows more easily along neural pathways so developed, which guides you toward more of the reward in the future. The next time you see juice boxes or ice cream cones, your dopamine-induced neural circuits effortlessly alert you to the presence of a reward.

The juiced-up monkeys experienced a drop in dopamine because their brains had learned to *expect* the juice. The dopamine had simply finished doing its job because the juice contained no new information about rewards. We humans likewise lose that dopamine feeling about a familiar pleasure when it "gets old." We don't realize that the dopamine has simply finished doing its job.

Dopamine fuels a football player doing a victory dance at the goal line. His joy signals the expectation of a reward. The points are not the *expected* reward since he has already scored them. He is dancing because his brain expects some other reward, such as living the life of a football hero once the game is over. He may be anticipating the respect of his peers, an increase in material resources, and an abundance of mating opportunities. Past experience taught him to expect these rewards. Now that they seem within reach, his dopamine circuits are triggered. These circuits have fueled him through the grueling practices. But now he anticipates even more reward than he'd expected, so he's releasing more dopamine.

Imagine a mother doing a victory dance when her child gets a high SAT score. She is experiencing a sudden rush of dopamine. Her reproductive success rests on the child's long-term security. Of course, she does not think this consciously. But her brain has already linked SAT scores to her children's status. Everything relevant to reproductive success is a big reward to the mammal brain.

Imagine a child at a spelling bee. He has invested many hours memorizing spelling words, motivated by dopamine and the expectation of a reward. Something in this child's past experience taught him to associate spelling with high rewards. He may have gotten more attention than expected from a teacher or parent after scoring well on a prior spelling test. That triggered dopamine, which built a neural circuit linking spelling success to above-average rewards. This dopamine circuit will fuel hours of memorizing spelling words in the future.

A marathon runner invests in grueling training before he gets to the finish line. An opera singer builds skill for years before becoming a respected performer. These efforts are fueled by dopamine because the brains of these individuals have somehow linked these pursuits to real rewards. And we can be sure they are expecting rewards relevant to a mammal, whether it's better health, better mates, or higher status, because that's what turns on the dopamine. Each mammal's life experience builds circuits that guide them toward survival-enhancing rewards in the future.

Experience teaches us which actions are likely to be rewarded with higher status. Your brain will not turn on the dopamine for a status-seeking opportunity unless it has a real expectation of achieving it. I might wish for a Nobel Prize in Economics or an invitation to recite poetry in Carnegie Hall. But I do not truly expect to get them, so I am not inclined to invest the effort it takes to achieve them. Which is to say, I have not built circuits that would trigger dopamine during long hours of effort in economics or poetry in expectation of huge rewards.

If you tried to become a rock star for decades and only had doors close in your face, you'd eventually lose that dopamine feeling when you looked at your guitar. A new circuit would eventually tell you *not* to expect a reward. Yet you might build another dopamine circuit when some new experience gives you a more-than-expected reward.

Romantic love is mediated by dopamine. The distinction between romantic love and other kinds of love is dopamine. Romantic love is fueled by the expectation of extra-large rewards. You expect from the beloved an extra-large contribution to your survival prospects, however your mind has come to define them. Usually, you don't know how your mammal brain has defined your survival needs, which is why you fall in love with a person without consciously knowing why. Your mammal brain simply gushes dopamine when it expects that your survival needs are about to be met more than usual.

On the surface, love may not seem to be about survival, but it's the mammal brain's view of survival that gets the dopamine going. A partner who looks vigorous or who promises security is highly rewarding to a mammal brain. Of course, the expectations we bring to our mating choices vary widely. But our romantic triggers overlap a good deal. When you receive the attentions of a healthy looking, high-status person of the right gender, your dopamine circuits are likely to light up. You have reason to expect an improvement in your DNA's survival prospects, even if that's not what you seek.

Love has a chase aspect that is curiously reminiscent of the "finish line" role of dopamine. That explains the oft-noted phenomenon of love fading once the finish line has been crossed. The ebb and flow of dopamine can lead to disappointment and cynicism. We would feel better about love if we understood the different neurochemical components. There's a dopamine-fueled goal-oriented component, and an oxytocin-fueled trust-oriented aspect, and a serotonin-fueled security aspect. These feelings run together when love is new. When we sense that "something changed," the dopamine is gone. You already expect the juice so there are no extra rewards.

The chase aspect of love has a bad reputation, but the dopamine it triggers alerts us to valuable information. Finding someone you can really trust is difficult, and if you expect them to protect your children it's even harder. You invest effort in the search and when you find such a person, it's like finishing a marathon or winning a prize. The dopamine makes sure you stay focused on the reward.

Dopamine is the excitement of believing you are near the finish line, just about to have the reward. Oxytocin and serotonin are the reward itself. Once you have a secure relationship, your brain no longer needs to anticipate having it. You no longer need the dopamine because you are already at the finish line. Once you have the reward, your mammal brain efficiently starts searching for the next way to boost your survival prospects.

Dopamine is not champagne – it's the sense that you can start icing the champagne. Without dopamine, life doesn't feel rewarding –

even a perfectly secure life. It's not surprising that people seek artificial ways to stimulate their dopamine system. Cocaine and amphetamines activate dopamine receptors.

When I was young, "dope" was the common word for drugs. Artificially stimulating your dopamine system gives you the feeling that you are just about to score a big reward, even if you are doing nothing to make that happen. Artificial dopamine gives you the feeling of scoring a touchdown without ever being in training. It gives you the feeling a monkey has when it cracks open a nut after struggling with it for a very long time, and prepares to pop that nut into its mouth. Drugs give you the joy of rewards without the bother of learning to crack the nut.

Addictions seem to be rooted in the dopamine system. Addictions begin with an experience that causes a huge rush of well-being. The brain remembers that rewarding feeling and seeks to repeat it. The addict expects to get that feeling from the next drink or the next fix or the next smoke. But the next one never triggers as much dopamine as the first time. The brain already "learned" to expect that reward, so it is motivated to try again. Repeating the unhealthy habit leaves a person feeling worse, and their urge to feel better activates the feel-good circuit their brain has already built – the addictive habit.

Dopamine supplies the extra spurt of energy we need to keep going until our needs are met. Our body evolved to release its reserves only when the finish line is actually in sight. Dopamine feels so good, however, that it's natural to want it all the time. If you could release your reserve tank any time, it would feel good in the moment, but your tank would be empty when you really needed it. Dopamine did not evolve for the purpose of giving us constant happiness. It evolved to help us persevere in meeting our needs. If we could feel dopamine all the time, without actually meeting real needs, we would not be better off. We would not be skilled at meeting our survival needs.

Why Status Brings Happiness

There's no fast, easy way to get more happy chemicals out of your mammal brain, even if you understand it. You can't get more endorphins without hurting yourself. You can't get more dopamine without constant pursuit of bigger rewards. You can't get more oxytocin without putting more trust in your herd mates, and we all know the downside of trusting the herd.

That leaves serotonin. Getting respect from others releases serotonin. With so few paths to happiness, it's not surprising that the serotonin path has its attractions. People end up caring about social dominance more than they'd like to because the alternatives are so limited. Few people go to the extreme of seeking dominance through direct aggression. We usually learn at a young age not to expect rewards from that strategy. It gets one excluded from most social groups. Instead, people often seek social dominance by investing effort in accomplishments they expect to be rewarded by the respect of others. When others recognize and respect us, serotonin flows, even if we don't know why. The brain records the experience and strives to repeat it. You may not know why you are motivated to seek status in a particular way. But your neural circuit is real, whether you "know" it or not.

We start building expectations about rewards as soon as we're born. By the time we're five, we have built a lot of neural circuits about the rewards we can expect from the world around us – the social world as well as the physical world. These early circuits guide the experiences that follow, even though we're not aware of them.

As we move through life striving to create a legacy, we rely on the neural pathways we have. That means your mammal brain is relying on lessons you're not aware of in pursuit of goals you're not aware of. No wonder we have such a hard time figuring out what turns on the happy chemicals.

Animals don't seek happiness explicitly. Their happy circuits simply respond to the information reaching their senses.

In the animal world, your status rises when you do what feels good. For example, when a chimp gives and receives a grooming, it creates social alliances that raise its status and at the same time it enjoys oxytocin. When a chimp pursues delicious food, dopamine flows and the nutrition makes it stronger which raises its status. When a chimp dominates others, its serotonin rises and so does its status.

Doing what feels good works for animals. Their instincts are a pretty good guide to survival. Natural selection created a pretty good product. It doesn't work perfectly, to be sure. Animals see their children get eaten alive. They get clawed in the face and their wounds get infected. They get excluded from reproductive opportunities and even feeding opportunities. They also deplete the resources of their ecosystem. Animals don't respond by questioning their instincts. They don't condemn "the system." They just try again.

Animals are not happy all the time, but they just keep trying. They keep sticking with the group-mates that trigger oxytocin. They keep foraging for the food that gives them strength. They keep scanning for opportunities to dominate and to escape from being dominated. Animals trust the guidance they get from their neurochemicals instead of trying to improve themselves or resist their instincts. It works for them. Doing what comes naturally leads them to raise their status, release happy chemicals, and create copies of their DNA. If their impulses lead to trouble, animals deal with it when the trouble is upon them.

Humans want more. We anticipate problems that could undermine our future happiness. We anticipate improvements that could increase our future happiness. We humans are not satisfied with whatever happiness just happens to flow. We want to make happiness happen, now.

Social status among humans is different from the status dynamics of cows or wolves or monkeys. Yet the similarities are striking if you look closely. The following chapter describes mammalian social dominance behaviors in more detail. You will see how our common neurochemistry leads to behaviors that are eerily familiar.

Chapter 3

What Social Power Means to Animals

...Animals seek dominance the way humans seek a cushion of security for a rainy day. If food becomes scarce in the future, the mammal who attained dominance will get more of it. . .

This chapter shows explicitly how animal seek social power, and how it improves their survival prospects.

When two mammals meet, they check each other out. Whether it's two grizzly bears or two poodles or two administrative assistants, each brain is calculating the best way to act around the other. If a mammal encounters a stronger individual, it quickly exercises self-restraint because it wants to keep itself safe. Encountering a weaker individual is more relaxing. The mammal brain knows that a weaker individual is not likely to attack. Instantly scanning others for signs of relative strength helps a creature survive. This scanning for danger is prompted by the self-protective reptilian part of the brain. But reptiles don't have enough memory to recognize allies. The reptile brain sees all moving things as either predators (if they're bigger), food (if smaller), or potential mates (if they're similar in size). A reptile tries to eat, mate, or run from things without making fine distinctions. A mammal's life is dizzyingly complex is comparison.

A mammal cannot automatically eat smaller critters because they could end up eating their own children. A mammal cannot flee all bigger individuals because their alpha can be an ally and protector. And a mammal cannot find willing mates without lots of preliminaries. Mammals started out with the social judgement of a reptile and added onto it. They evolved the extra brain power necessary to distinguish friend from foe. Mammals can recognize the sight and smell of group mates and link this information to their efforts to meet their survival needs.

But even group mates are not always safe to be near. Mammals come to blows regularly despite their enduring bonds. They bite and scratch those who get in their way, and the resulting wounds can be fatal. Violence is avoided most of the time, but it is always imminent. So a mammal learns to assess social situations before he relaxes. (Once again, female mammals engage in dominance behaviors as well as males, but the neutral "he" is used throughout.)

If a mammal deems himself weaker than the individual in front of him, he makes a submission gesture such as crouching and lowering his eyes. Showing the stronger one that he has no aggressive intent promotes the weaker one's safety. Mammals are careful to avoid conflicts they might lose. It promotes survival.

When a mammal believes he's stronger, he makes a dominance gesture such as standing erect and vocalizing. If the other responds with a submission gesture, the dominant mammal knows he can lower his guard. This ritual is the core of social hierarchy. A mammal learns the dominance and submission gestures of his group by the time he's an adult. These gestures range from subtle to dramatic, but their meaning is widely understood. Charles Darwin described these behaviors in 1872 in his *Expression of Emotions in Humans and Animals.*

Dominance-submission rituals prevent violence because they reward the probable winner without a fight. These rituals also promote bonding because the dominant relaxes, and then the subordinate relaxes a bit too. Getting the formalities out of the way first seems as natural to animals as it does to humans.

Status hierarchies develop because fear creates memory. Each mammal knows whom he fears and whom he doesn't fear, and a hierarchy emerges. Individuals good at sizing others up quickly were more likely to survive and pass on their genes. Over the generations, mammals handed down brains skilled at assessing others the instant they meet.

Status hierarchies make it safe for weaker individuals to live alongside stronger group mates. A weaker mammal benefits greatly by living with a group. He may not get first crack at the food, but he gets far more protection from predators. Stronger mammals sometimes risk their own safety to defend the group, so the strength they get from eating first benefits all.

Internal conflict must be avoided for mammals to enjoy the benefits of group life. Conflict is difficult to prevent among animals with no verbal skills and an immediate survival focus. Status hierarchies are the conflict-avoiding solution that evolved.

Mammals with small brains make simple status distinctions. They merely conclude that they are weaker or stronger than the individual in front of them. In general, they fight each other once and take a lifelong place in the social hierarchy based on the outcome.

Larger-brained mammals tend to change rankings more often because they are capable of updating their memory to reflect recent challenges. Bigger cortexes allow a mammal to recognize individuals and even to infer each individual's strength relative to third parties. Large brains enabled mammals to renegotiate their place on the social hierarchy instead of having a permanently fixed status. Sometimes they do it with physical aggression, sometimes with the threat of aggression, and sometimes they cooperate and build alliances. Their extra neurons support complex social dynamics.

Animals bite and scratch when they think they can get away with it. But they keep the biting and scratching to a minimum because they are good at predicting the outcome of conflicts. They arrange things according to what everyone knows they can get away with. Most humans learn they cannot get away with raising their status through physical aggression. We look for other ways to raise our status. Our brains look for information about what will work and what will not work. That is exactly the job the mammal brain evolved to do.

Humans get along with each other fabulously in contrast to the conflict among our mammalian ancestors. It may not seem like it because we have zero-tolerance expectations that are often disappointed. The human world is so safe that we can interface with thousands of strangers on the streets without getting attacked. Humans are so restrained that when we meet, we both take the submissive position by shaking hands. Shaking is a submission gesture because the open hand communicates the absence of a rock and thus the absence of aggressive intent. Most people learn to seek dominance without aggression, and that improves our quality of life tremendously. If we compared human conflict to our animal ancestors, we'd appreciate the success we've had in restraining conflict.

The point is not that mammals are naturally violent. The point is that mammals are naturally able to restrain their aggression when they see that it's in their own interest.

Mammals thrived by getting along with others. But they did not get along by becoming selfless altruists. They did it by becoming good judges of opportunity, able to shift fluidly between asserting and deferring. Each individual is constantly deciding which social behavior best promotes their own reproductive success at each moment.

Animals don't care about money or titles. They don't join clubs or plan for the long run. But this chapter shows that animals invest effort in the pursuit of status.

Snooty Cows

Cows wrangle for social dominance in ways you would never guess from looking at them on a pastoral hillside. The social dynamics of cows were brilliantly depicted by Vance Packard, pop sociologist of the 1950s:

Cow Society is even more snooty than New York's 400. Every single cow in the herd has her place. Toward all cows who are above her on the social scale, Gertrude is respectful. She will always step aside to let her social superiors be first at the watering trough. But toward all cows who are below, she is a little despot.

In every herd there is a top queen. She may not be the prettiest or biggest--in fact she may have only three teats or have a lame leg--but she still runs things her way all the time. Every other cow in the herd is a humble subject.

She wins her position as dowager queen by being the toughest, buttingest cow in the herd. To be queen she had to butt it out with every cow. These butting contests can be fierce, but usually they are half butt, half bluff. The cow that backs down never again challenges the winner. Thus the cow dowager, unlike a human dowager, does not have to lose nervous energy wondering whether her subjects are plotting to unseat her.

...(T)he queen of them all has many interesting prerogatives. She has first crack at the best grass in the pasture, and gets the choicest milking stall. When the herd goes walking, she leads the way. And when the herd has to go through a door or gate, the subjects all stand respectfully aside while the queen goes first. Cow No.2 in the social order usually goes second,

and so on. Last cow in the barn is the dope, who has been outbutted by every other cow.

A newcomer in the herd must butt it out with every cow to settle her position. If she outbutts the ruling queen, the queen is deposed, and often takes it very badly.... [1]

Packard goes on to describe the dramatic downfall of one such queen:

She had never kicked in all her well-mannered queenly life; now she exhibited a ferocious skill at kicking backward, forward and to either side. She charged her handlers, wrecked her stall, smashed a milking machine and sent a milker to the hospital. To the end of her days--and they were numbered--she remained hopelessly insane, all because she had lost her regal place in cow society.

Cow status is closely linked to reproductive success. The alpha cow claims the safest position in the center of the herd, where it is least likely to be attacked by a coyote. Each cow tries to push its way to the safety of the center, and the weakest cows are left arrayed around the unprotected perimeter. A calf born to a low-ranking mother is more exposed to predators than a high-born calf.

When a hungry coyote spots a herd of cows feeding in a field, it will only eat one of them. A cow is safe as long as it's not that one. Status is clearly central to a cow's success.

When a young cow reaches adulthood, it fights every other cow once. The outcome of those fights determines its status for the rest of its life. The same status tournament plays out when an adult cow joins a new herd.

Cows don't think of status conceptually. They don't imagine the overall hierarchy. Their brains simply store a fear reaction to individuals who have beaten them in the past. The neurons that recognize the stronger cow are connected to the neurons that trigger

---

1 *The Human Side of Animals* p.197-99

the fear neurochemical. Recognizing a weaker cow, by contrast, triggers calming neurochemicals like serotonin and oxytocin thanks to the neural connections built from past experience.

Cows don't have enough neurons to keep learning new reactions to others. They rely on the neural wiring they've already created. A dominance hierarchy emerges from those behaviors and doesn't change much.

Monkeys have a lot more neurons and more ability to build new connections between them. So it's not surprising that monkeys do a lot more tussling over their status. Monkeys challenge other members of their group whenever they think they can win. They don't do it too often because they can get badly injured, which hurts reproductive success more than it helps. They bide their time and build their strength. When a monkey does challenge and win, every monkey in the group updates their mental data base to reflect the new dominance hierarchy.

Primatologists often speak of female monkeys "inheriting" their mother's status. On the face of it, this seems absurd, as if human customs are being projected onto animals. Yet research consistently finds daughters ending up with their mother's status. If primates challenge the status hierarchy, how could this outcome occur? The reason, research suggests, is that social dominance behaviors are learned. A daughter learns social skills from her mother, so she usually lands in the same place.

"Inherited" Status

Female monkeys have to earn their status in the troop once they reach adulthood. They learn to do this literally at their mother's knee. A riveting depiction of this social-climbing dilemma is presented by neurobiologist Dario Maestripieri's observation of a young rhesus macaque female he calls "Tequila":

The integration of young macaques into the adult dominance hierarchy is not an automatic process, but requires work. The problem is that adults are larger and stronger than juveniles and very unwilling to let anybody enter the dominance hierarchy above themselves, regardless of who their mothers are. Rhesus infants enjoy a period of temporary immunity from adult-like aggression in the first three or four months of life, when all the other monkeys think they are cute and are willing to put up with them (but may also harass and kidnap them, as we shall see). When this immunity ends, infants start getting threatened, slapped and bitten just like everybody else. All of a sudden, infants become particularly vulnerable to aggression because they are small, weak, and inexperienced, and because you can be sure there is somebody in the group who has some beef with their family....

The day Tequila had the idea that she could boss her aunt Lola around, she started paying close attention to what happened every time her mother interacted with another adult. She started a file on every adult in the group and recorded in her mind who was afraid of her mother and who wasn't, who her mother treated with respect and who she didn't care for, who won the fights and who lost them.

From then on, every day and many times a day, Tequila tried to pick a fight with Lola. She would get in Lola's personal space, threaten her, and then scream her head off to get her mother's attention and help. At first, Lola was just annoyed by Tequila's behavior. Obviously she wasn't afraid of Tequila and wasn't going to show this ill-mannered juvenile any sign of respect. She knew, though, that if she gave Tequila the beating she deserved, there could be trouble, so she just tried to act indifferent. When Tequila was very pushy, Lola would threaten her and even slap her. Tequila, however, was very persistent and became better and better at screaming at Lola and getting others interested in her show. The time finally came when Lola was worn out by this constant harassment and gave *in...All Lola had to do was to show Tequila a sign of fear, and one day, when she just couldn't take it anymore, she did just that....*

Tequila moved on to the next victim, repeating the entire process with all of the adults who ranked below her mother. Eventually she was incorporated in to the adult dominance hierarchy with a ranking just below Yvette's [her mother]. [2]

You can see from this story that primates pursue status as an end in itself. Status is not just a means to an end such as meat or sex. Primates seem to strive for dominance in the abstract even when there's no immediate resource at stake. And they seem to do it the way their mothers do it. Such early learning shapes males as well as females, although males typically go on to learn additional skills from other males (except for male bonobos, who continue to rely on Mom). The following chapter on sex and the status hierarchy explores male status in more depth.

Animals are always acting on their knowledge of status. For example, when a group of baboons stops to rest in the savannah, the highest-ranking baboon takes the best seat. Everyone knows which seat is best – it is the most comfortable seat and it has the most commanding view of potential predators. Everyone knows who should get the best seat. A baboon will be bitten and scratched if he goes for a seat desired by a higher-ranking baboon. He could go for it anyway. An occasional, judicious challenge to the status quo might be survivable. But a baboon who simply ignores the dominance hierarchy will not last long. Mammas don't want their babies to grow up without social awareness. Mamma's genes only get passed on if she prepares her youngsters to avoid conflicts they can't win.

How can animals teach their children the niceties of social status without language? The recent discovery of mirror neurons makes it clear. The mammal brain learns from observing the behavior

---

2 Macachiavellian Intelligence pp.54-57

of others. When a young mammal watches others, special neurons are activated that build circuits for reproducing the behavior.

Mirror Neurons

Neuroscientists in Parma, Italy, made a monumental discovery in the 1980s while studying the brain waves of macaque monkeys. They were monitoring the activation of a monkey's motor neurons as he grasps a peanut. One day they had finished working with a monkey but hadn't turned off the monitors yet, and they accidentally noticed their screens lighting up with activity when the monkey *watched* a researcher pick up the peanut. The act of watching apparently activated the same electrical pattern that occurred when a monkey executed a grasp himself, though at a lower intensity.

The intuitive idea of "monkey see, monkey do" was suddenly manifest in electrodes and computers.

The researchers were stunned and went on to discover that particular neurons specialize in this mirroring activity. They introduced the term "mirror neurons" and found that about ten percent of the neurons in certain regions of the macaque's cortex had this function.

Now it seems that all primates, including humans, have a mirror neuron system. Even song-birds appear to use mirror neurons to learn the unique tune that attracts a mate of their own species. Mirror neurons facilitate the social learning essential to reproductive success.

No conscious intent to teach or learn is necessary for a young mammal to pick up the behaviors of others. The mammal brain comes equipped to learn by watching. The brain absorbs the behavior patterns it sees without awareness that it has learned. We learn simply because activation of a group of neurons stimulates them to connect to each other. A cluster of neurons repeatedly triggered at the same time becomes an efficient pathway in the brain.

We rely on these established neural pathways because electricity flows where there's least resistance. When an electrical impulse is triggered in your jungle of neurons, it does not hack a new trail if a superhighway is nearby. Our automatic reliance on well-worn neural pathways will be explored in depth in Chapter 5.

A young monkey sits in its mother's lap for years and watches her social interactions. It sees whom she fears and whom she trusts. The young monkey learns to associate fear or trust with certain individuals because repeated activation builds those neural circuits. Without thought or effort, a monkey learns to be deferential around every monkey above Mom in the social hierarchy, and to expect deference from monkeys that appear to have lower status than Mom.

Mirror neurons explain the mystery of mammalian childhood. Mammals take far longer to mature than other classes of animals. All that time spent with Mom is used to wire a young brain with the knowledge in Mom's brain.

The bigger a mammal's cortex, the longer it remains with Mom. A big cortex does not promote survival unless it's filled up with survival-relevant information. Otherwise, extra neurons are a liability because so much energy is necessary to keep them alive. A creature has to work harder to supply his neurons with warmth and glucose, so survival rests on getting his money's worth out of them.

Long childhoods are also a liability from a survival perspective. Investing more time in each child limits of the number of offspring a mother can have, and magnifies the cost of losing a child to a predator. Long childhoods must have a significant survival benefit to offset these costs. That benefit is the opportunity for a juvenile to mirror and store the knowledge embodied in the behavior of surrounding adults. Primates have long childhoods because it takes time to build neural circuits for the behaviors essential to their reproductive success.

Conscious effort is not necessary for young mammals to build circuits for finding food and getting along with others. They simply watch and play. In the end, each mammal reaches adulthood knowing what is known to others in their group, including the ins and outs of status.

Zoo animals usually have low reproductive success. Their health is optimized by teams of veterinarians, but zoo animals tend to lack the social behaviors necessary for reproduction. Surprisingly, their mating skills fall short as well as their parenting skills. Most zoo animals grew up in relative isolation and thus did not have the social experiences that stimulate learning. This highlights the degree to which essential survival behaviors are learned from observing group mates.

Raising A Well-Adjusted Mammal

A piglet born can be born in a litter of ten to a mother who has only eight teats. From the moment of birth, the piglet must compete for survival against its own siblings. Video clips of suckling pigs make it clear that each brain is seriously motivated to meet its own needs. They do not wait for the milk to come to them.

If a piglet is slightly weaker than its siblings things quickly get worse, because all of Mamma's teats are not created equal. The teats closer to a mother pig's heart have a higher fat content. A piglet who falls behind will get less fat, and soon fall further behind. Mamma doesn't intervene. Her genes are more likely to survive if some of her offspring become as strong as possible so they can make it in a world full of predators.

Each piglet struggles for a better position in the food chain in order to advance its survival prospects. To human ears, this may seem cruel and unusual. The point is not that mammals should deprive their siblings of food; the point is that the mammal brain evolved to confront real survival risks from the moment of birth. We humans want every individual to survive, no matter how weak. But beneath our urge to help others is a core drive to help ourselves.

Nature is more brutal than most people realize. Most mammals die before they achieve reproductive success. When you add up all the newborns who die before puberty plus the adults who die before breeding plus the parents whose offspring all die before they reproduce, it's clear that keeping your DNA alive is no simple feat. Success requires not only ensuring your own survival, but equipping your children to survive once you're gone. Reproductive success rests on the survival skills of your children.

Cooperation is a survival skill that mammals increasingly employed as their brains grew larger. It takes a bigger brain to anticipate the benefits of joint action. Primates have relatively large brains and they are good at calculating when to cooperate. Their long childhoods provide ample time to learn this skill. But cooperation is not learned by renouncing self-interest or the urge for dominance. Cooperating is an extra tool in the mammal brain's pursuit of its own survival.

People often think peace is the state of nature, and the quest for status is an evil of civilization. But animal behavior makes it clear that the pursuit of dominance is the state of nature; civilization offers peaceful ways to channel the mammalian urge for dominance.

Everybody Knows Everybody

When two baboons fight, their troop-mates look on knowing the relative rank of each combatant. After the fight, each observer understands the outcome and reconfigures the status hierarchy in their mind. No one imposes a hierarchy on a baboon troop. Status emerges as each individual does what feels good and avoids what feels bad.

A baboon can always choose to challenge a more dominant individual rather than submit. His brain evolved to make this choice. It weighs the expected rewards of an action against the anticipated danger. These expectations of risk and reward come from the circuits he has built from past experience. Years of learning enable a mammal to restrain its urges when self-assertion is likely to be dangerous.

Experience builds circuits that enable a mammal to sustain social bonds and seek status at the same time. As primatologists Cheney and Seyfarth explain it:

> *Perhaps because the benefits to be derived from high rank do not usually outweigh the potential costs of a serious fight, overt challenges to the existing hierarchy are rare. Although a low-ranking female will unhesitatingly cuff a high-ranking juvenile who is attempting to take her food, she will do so only after ensuring that none of the juvenile's relatives are within earshot. Nonetheless, beneath the peaceful, orderly hierarchy lurk individuals – and indeed whole matrilines – just waiting for an opportunity to disrupt the social order.*[3]

The latent impulse to establish dominance relations is familiar to many dog lovers. As soon a dog becomes aware of another dog's presence, it starts negotiating the rankings. Dogs seize the opportunity to dominate if they think it's safe to do so. People are often surprised to see a small dog trying to dominate a large dog. In the wild, a small dog would learn the limits of its ability from feedback – the pain a bigger dog would inflict. But if the small dog was raised by a human who acted submissively toward it, its expects to dominate and it acts on that expectation.

The mammal brain's quest for dominance has been illuminated by Cesar Millan, TV's *Dog Whisperer*. Millan grew up on a farm in Mexico, where dogs labored alongside humans. He saw dogs

---

[3] *Baboon Metaphysics* p.69

calmly following his grandfather's lead in doing the farm work that was necessary to survive. But he observed dogs on neighboring farms testing each other and aggressively fighting for dominance.

Millan dreamed of training dogs in Hollywood when he grew up. Arriving in California, he supported himself as a dog groomer. There he first encountered neurotic pets. These dogs had no work to do and were constantly pampered, yet they were strangely aggressive.

The problem, he realized, is that city people act submissively toward their pets. They seek affection rather than labor from their dogs, which makes pet owners reluctant to be authoritative. A power vacuum results, and the dog's natural urge is to fill it.

A dog's brain tells it to either follow a leader or be a leader, Millan explains. When no one is asserting authority over a dog, it asserts itself. If you don't act like the alpha, your dog presumes he is the alpha. And a dog sees aggression as an integral part of this role, since the alpha's job is to herd and protect the pack. Most pet owners do not realize they are acting submissively toward their dog because they don't understand the dog's view of dominance-submission rituals.

Millan became a consultant to people whose lives are dominated by neurotic pets. He shows them how they are causing the neurotic behavior. First they give the dog the impression that it's the pack leader, and then they discipline the dog for the aggression that's a normal part of being a pack leader. To make matters worse, pet owners follow up the discipline with lots of affection, which re-activates the dog's idea that it's the dominant. That precipitates another round of aggression and discipline. The dog becomes neurotic because it can't make sense of the social reward system.

The mammal brain is always looking for clear information about dominance relations in order to promote its own survival. A dog doesn't get clear information if it sees humans flip between dominance and submission in no systematic way. Dog owners who refuse to take the dominant position literally drive their dogs crazy.

Millan's views have been criticized. People mistakenly think he is advocating aggression toward pets. He continually explains how to dominate without aggression, a behavior he calls "calm-assertive." He teaches pet owners to reward their pets for "calm-submissive" behavior. Neither party is aggressive when dominance relations are clear. The mammal brain wants to know who the leader is, and is agitated when status relations are unclear. Millan's insights are relevant to well-intentioned parents who are unwittingly submissive toward their children and end up with aggressive, neurotic offspring.

Every mammal is born with the capacity to be both a dominant and a subordinate. Unlike bees, which are born into the aristocracy or the working class, a mammal can take either role depending on the circumstances. The mammal brain comes equipped to choose behaviors according to the feedback of its environment. Some behaviors get rewarded, and the rewards are neurochemicals that fuse lasting neural connections. Young neurons connect more easily than old ones, which supports the proverb that "you can't teach an old dog new tricks."

The mammal brain is always making social calculations as part of its effort to survive. For example, when a monkey sees a luscious piece fruit high up in a tree, he makes a quick decision about the branches' ability to hold his weight, and he also infers his troopmates' likely reactions to his taking the fruit. Social learning is part of the automatic survival focus.

Humans continually make social calculations as well, even young children. I remember offering juice to three-year olds in cups that were identical except for different colors. One child immediately declared, "I want the red cup." That forced the other child to make a decision. He could assert himself or avoid conflict. Is the reward worth the risk? How well can he predict the outcome? His mammal brain evolved to gather and analyze such social information. As an adult, I was tempted to tell the children that the color of the cup doesn't matter. But as a mammal, I know that it's unpleasant to be dominated.

Status and Reproductive Success

Imagine a group of female chimpanzees out foraging for food. They come upon a wonderful patch of berries. But not all foraging spots are created equal. Some spots have more berries than others. Some spots have more protection from predators. Every chimp would like to be in the spot at the center of the group in front of the densest patch of berries. There she would have more nutrition faster, with less effort, and she would be safely surrounded by her troop-mates while feeding. But only one lady can be in that best spot. And only one lady can be in the second best spot, and the third.

If each lady made a beeline for the best spot, conflict would erupt. Weaker chimps are more likely to get injured in conflicts. So each chimp learns which troop mates are stronger than herself, and refrains from picking a foraging spot until the stronger ladies have picked theirs. Every chimp learns which group-mates she should defer to in order to avoid conflict, and which group-mates can be counted on to step aside. Thus, a social hierarchy forms without anyone intending or directing. Each individual is simply doing its best to meet its needs and stay safe.

The ladies that get the better foraging spots tend to be better nourished. As a result, they tend to have better-nourished babies and more of them. Status seeking improves reproductive success.

I saw a heart-wrenching example of this on a nature video. A group of macaques were feeding on lotus roots in crocodile-infested waters. Most of them gathered on a large floating patch of lotus leaves, but they didn't all fit. The lowest-ranking monkeys were left to feed alone on dispersed plants that were vulnerable to crocodiles, or do without that meal in order to survive.

The narrator focused on one nursing mother who desperately needed the food despite the risk. Macaques need to eat often, and nursing mothers have huge nutritional needs. The camera zoomed in on the mother nervously scanning the plants from water's edge. She leapt to an isolated patch and held her vulnerable baby while trying to gather food. The mother survived this meal, the narrator tells us; but her prior child died from malnutrition and keeping this one alive will be a formidable challenge.

Social hierarchy did not begin with the money economy. It began with the fact that two mammals could not be in the same place at the same time. One spot offers more nutrition and safety from predators than another, and the mammal that gets it is more likely to keep its genes alive.

Predators are the biggest threat to a mammal's reproductive success. Predators target juveniles because they're easier to catch. Zebras evolved stripes because striped juveniles blended in with adults and were thus harder for predators to target.

Humans are very conscious of predator threat. Just one predator in a city of millions will have every parent guarding their child anxiously. Very few humans actually lose children to predators, however, so it's hard for us to appreciate how real the threat was to our mammalian ancestors.

Reptiles have lots of babies because so many get eaten by predators. They spend no energy parenting or getting attached to their offspring. Reptiles go off and pursue their own interests as soon as their eggs hatch. Lizard parents only hang around long enough to eat any hatchlings that are below par. Newborn lizards start running the instant they break from their shells. A parent stands watch and gulps down any laggards as the new generation scurries off to seek its fortune. Recycling the energy into a new brother or sister promotes survival better than letting it linger and attract predators.

Fish don't even hang around until their eggs hatch. They stand by their eggs until they're fertilized, and then swim off to do their own thing. Trees send their seed into the wind and never know what mighty oaks develop. Most seeds die before growing into trees that carry on the progenitor's DNA.

Mammals changed all of this. Mammals have very few offspring and do their darnedest to ensure that every single one of them survives. Mammals guard newborns constantly until the young are strong enough to escape predators. The bigger a mammal's brain, the longer it guards each offspring. Investing so much in each child is a risky reproductive strategy. A female ape loses many years of her reproductive life when a child gets killed. A lizard would have had thousands of descendants in that time.

A female mammal puts her eggs into very few baskets. Her reproductive success rests on her ability to protect these children from predators. One proven strategy for doing that is to make friends with high-status males who are willing to provide protection.

Friends in High Places

Nursing mothers need a lot of food, so they must go out and forage often. Foraging with a baby in tow is risky because it slows a mother's ability to escape from predators. Even if the baby escapes attack, the mother's death typically precipitates the death of the baby. Orphaned juveniles get some care from group-mates, but the odds are against them.

Mother monkeys try to leave their infants in the care of others and go out foraging alone. Leaving baby with sisters, cousins, or aunts is one way to do this, but researchers have noticed that these relatives are not always as vigilant as necessary. Females who recruit males to protect their children have measurably higher success rates.

This explains why female monkeys and apes invest effort to build alliances with strong males.

Baboon research provides interesting data on females' efforts to develop exclusive friendships with males. Female baboons seem to initiate relationships after they give birth by offering groomings to the male of their choice. They choose the highest status male available and follow him around, approaching him and picking specks out of his fur whenever he allows it.[4] Higher status males make better protectors because they have more proven fighting ability. Thus, females have good reason to compete for the attentions of higher status males.

These friendships are not what you'd expect. No sex is involved. The male babysitter is not sexually interested in the mother as long as she is nursing. A lactating female does not ovulate, and male primates (except for bonobos and humans) seem disinterested in sex when the pheromones of fertility are not in evidence.

Researchers interpret these friendships as a sort of courtship activity. Males develop a familiarity with a female in the expectation of being favored when the time is right. Any advantage gained is small, however, because these relationships end as soon as a female is done nursing. Once she's back in circulation, the male dominance hierarchy still applies.

Male-female relationships outside the mating season are not common in the animal world, but larger-brained mammals do invest effort in these relationships. Research shows that they have real survival value for all involved. Cheney and Seyfarth explain:

> *Playback experiments have shown that males recognize the screams of their female friends and respond preferentially to their cries of distress. Perhaps as a result, when a potentially infanticidal male arrives in*

---

4 *Baboon Metaphysics*, p. 59. This research was done on southern African baboons, which are typical of most baboons species, but unlike the northernmost Hamadryas baboons.

the group, lactating females with male friends experience significantly lower glucocorticoid [stress] levels.

...Once the infant dies or is weaned, the friendship ends abruptly...Males do, however, continue to defend the now independent juvenile, and if the juvenile is orphaned the male will often take over the role as the juvenile's primary adult companion. Indeed, over time a male's successive friendships transform him into a Pied Piper, and he is accompanied wherever he goes by a troupe of tumbling and twirling youngsters. For an old, slow-moving, low-ranking male, it is as good a way as any to finish out his years.[5]

Female chimpanzees are typically more "promiscuous" than female baboons – that's not my judgement but biologists' classification. Practically speaking, that means a dominant male chimp is less able to enforce exclusivity over a fertile female than an alpha baboon is. A male chimp's sperm has plenty of competition on the road to reproductive success. A male chimp who builds an alliance with a female has a better shot at immortality.

Researchers have observed male chimps offering meat to their female companions. Meat gives a female the strength she needs to nurse and protect her child. Extra meat makes her milk more nutritious, which makes her baby grow faster, allowing her to have another child sooner. A higher status male has more meat to offer the ladies in his life. And females remember these allies when fertility time finally arrives. Once again, status promotes reproductive success.

A male's relationships with females helps him climb the male dominance hierarchy. When there's conflict among males in the troop, females often cast the deciding vote. That is, females line up with their male allies and help intimidate their male rivals. Typically, the male with the most groupies wins.

---

5 *Baboon Metaphysics* p. 60-61

Alliances help female primates protect their babies from predators. Mothers with more alliance-building skills end up with more surviving children. But sometimes the predator threat comes from a member of the group itself. That calls for additional survival strategies.

In-group Predators and the Quest for Status

Researchers have been surprised by the level of internal violence in monkey and ape troops. Infanticidal alpha males threaten young primates, as do bullies of both genders. Young mammals need protection from other members of their species as well as from hungry carnivores.

Infanticide is shocking but well documented among monkeys and apes. New alpha males appear to kill infants in order to terminate nursing and make females available for new pregnancies. An alpha male is in a hurry to pass on his genes because he might be overthrown at any moment. If females were not fertile during his reign, his long struggle to the top would have been for naught. If a female is nursing another male's child, it's a wasted opportunity from the new alpha's perspective. Of course, he doesn't consciously think that; he just acts on his impulse to kill those infants, and his genes get reproduced.

It would be counter-productive for an alpha to kill a child that was his own. Research shows that infanticide occurs only in situations where there's an extremely small chance of paternity. Animals do not comprehend paternity in the factual way that humans do, but males tend to engage in infanticide only when they encounter females with whom they've had little prior contact. For example, a male lion or gorilla stumbles upon a poorly guarded family and takes over.

Things get more complicated among chimps and savannah baboons, where new males tend to rise in the hierarchy more gradually. Research suggests that infanticide only occurs when a relative newcomer to the troop becomes alpha. The same practice has been observed in mice, which is striking because the first primates evolved from mouse-like ancestors.

Cheney and Seyfarth provide a moving description of infanticide from the mother's viewpoint:

Female baboons defend their infants vigorously against real and potential threats, sometimes leaping and biting any male that attempts to attack them. Many males, though, are relentless in their pursuit, stalking females for months and waiting for an opportune moment to grab the infant in a drive-by attack.[6]

For females, the safest way to avoid losing your baby is to mate with the alpha. But that only works as long as he rules. If he's deposed before her infant is weaned, the child is at risk. That puts extreme pressure on Mom to forecast political developments in the male hierarchy in order to ally herself with the winner.

Different coping strategies have emerged in different species. Female chimps seem to hedge their bets, mating with any male likely to take power and any male likely to offer protection against infanticidal attacks. Female gorillas and lions tend to ally themselves with the perpetrator of infanticide – he proved to be stronger than their last protector and thus can be expected to provide better protection for her next child. Within all these variations, the common theme is that brains good at understanding social dominance are more likely to keep their DNA alive.

Sometimes females are the perpetrators of in-group violence. Kidnapping is an extreme example:

6 *Baboon Metaphysics* p. 59

The alpha female in this group was an old and mean female named Annette, who had a passion for infant kidnapping. She...had no milk to offer and...was very rough with these babies...Rhesus babies may be made of rubber, but if they don't drink their milk often, they will die of starvation or dehydration. After many hours in Annette's hands – sometimes a whole day or longer –the baby was at serious risk, so animal caretakers had to intervene...Annette learned that the best time to kidnap babies was on the weekend [when] animal caretakers were not around...

Since then I have seen hundreds of other infant kidnappings... [They] always puzzled me. Although the infants' mothers were obviously bothered by the kidnapping, they never tried to forcibly take their infants back....Instead, they would follow the kidnappers around and patiently wait for them to let go of their infants...[T]he kidnapper was higher ranking than the mother and she would have kicked her butt had the mother tried anything. 7

Sometimes, violence is caused by the simian equivalent of neighborhood bullies. The following macaque incident shows how a sign of weakness tends to provoke attack. In this case, the weakness was caused by a medical procedure:

Buddy had not fully recovered from the anesthesia when he was first reintroduced into his group. The others could immediately tell there was something wrong with him. He wasn't running as quickly as usual. He didn't respond to a threat with a submissive signal. He didn't run back to his mother seeking protection.

...He was weak and vulnerable. The behavior of other monkeys changed swiftly and dramatically – from friendliness to intolerance, from play to aggression.

...The bully bites Buddy's arm. Buddy screams in pain and runs away. But he is slow, too slow. The bully quickly catches up with him and

---

7 Maestripieri, *Macachiavellian Intelligence* p.125-26

bites him again, this time on the ear. More screaming. Two other adolescents – Buddy's playmates is one of them – and an adult female run toward Buddy...they are all over him, barking and screaming, grabbing his arms and face, and biting his fingers and tail.

...Buddy has spent every day of his life in the enclosure with all the other monkeys. They eat the same food...they cuddled him when he was an infant...Yet, that day, if the researchers had not taken Buddy out of the group, he would have been killed. His mother and aunts would have tried to protect him, but probably to no avail.

Buddy's vulnerability became an opportunity for others to settle an old score, improve their position in the dominance hierarchy, or eliminate a potential rival for good.[8]

The researchers put Buddy in a separate cage, and in two hours he was fully alert and back to his old self. They returned him to his troop, and this time he defended himself well enough to avoid getting bullied:

His playmate and another adolescent walk up to him and grab him. He grabs them back and the three of them wrestle...[H]e inadvertently bumps into a young infant and knocks him down. Immediately the infant's mother arrives, picks the infant up, and threatens Buddy with a stare and a wide open mouth. Buddy shows his teeth to the mother and raises his tail, exposing his genitals to any other monkey who might be behind him...No one pays attention to him now.[9]

Buddy had to display the dominance behaviors expected of him in order to avoid being a magnet for would-be dominators. Status is not something fixed; it is constantly negotiated and re-negotiated. A

---

8 Maestripieri, *Macachiavellian Intelligence* p. 2-4

9 Maestripieri, *Macachiavellian Intelligence* p. 3

primate needs tremendous social intelligence to survive. It takes years to build this social knowledge. A mother helps however she can. The better her child navigates the social hierarchy, the more likely her genes will survive.

In good times, status differences have only a slight effect on reproductive success. But even small differences accumulate over millennia, each generation inheriting the genes and the model of the higher-achieving mothers.

Why Mammals Are Social Climbers

Animals seek dominance the way humans seek a cushion of security for a rainy day. A mammal may have plenty of food today, but anything can happen tomorrow. Animals can't do much to improve their future survival prospects. They can't eat more today to protect themselves from future food shortages because the excess weight would slow them down when running from predators. They can't store extra food because it spoils or gets stolen (with rare exceptions). The main thing a mammal can do today to improve its security for tomorrow is to convert surplus food energy into social power. If food becomes scarce in the future, the mammal who has built up strength and dominance is likely to get more of it.

Mammals are not purely selfish. When collective strategies promote the survival of their genes, mammals use those. The mammal brain does what works. It constantly interprets its surroundings and plots the course that enhances its welfare. It coordinates three different brain systems: a reptile brain that scans for danger, a limbic system that scans for allies, and a cortex that scans for similarities between the immediate situation and stored experiences.

A mammal that's too aggressive is likely to get killed by rivals and their allies. A mammal that's not aggressive enough is likely to lack food and mates and safety. A mammal skilled at modulating its behavior to the social dynamics of each moment is more likely to thrive. The genius of the mammal brain is its ability to strike a balance between individual needs and social bonds.

A mammal's survival rests on its ability to make judgements about others. It must decide when it's safe to assert and when it's better to defer. People say it's not nice to judge, but good social judgement is essential to survival when you're a mammal among mammals.

Every mammal, even a dumb cow, can see the link between status and survival. It's simple neurochemistry. Feel-good chemicals flow when a critter meets its needs, and dominating helps it do so.

In the human world, the rewards of status are often quite subtle. In the animal world, the rewards for status are typically more tangible, such as food, safety, and sex. Let us now turn our attention to sex, the ultimate mammalian reward for status.

Chapter 4

Sex and the Status Hierarchy

...Before mating, every species has some preliminary qualifying event. The males of most species make great sacrifices for any reproductive opportunity that comes their way...

We have all seen images of two deer locking antlers while a fertile female stands by. Deer fight to the point of serious injury because immortality is at stake. The winner always gets the girl. What does she see in the brute?

A female deer wants the strongest male so her baby will have the strongest genes. When suitors joust in front of her, she gets all the information she needs.

There are other ways for female mammals to weed out the weaker progenitors. Female squirrels simply run away from their male suitors. Only the fastest male squirrels get the girl. The strongest female squirrel can escape all but the strongest males. Her children thus benefit from the strongest genes. Female elephants likewise qualify their suitors by running away. Both genders invest great effort in these chases for reasons we can only speculate about.

Every mammal is the product of its ancestors' mating choices. When Darwin spoke of natural selection, he was more focused on the competition for mates than the competition for food. Successful food-seeking only promotes survival for a day, but successful mate-seeking promotes survival for a generation. Biology teachers have tended to downplay the conflict over fertile females because it can be hard to discuss in a high school classroom. So we tend to underestimate the degree to which sexual selection is the engine of evolution. The fact is that some individuals contributed a lot more to the gene pool than others.

Mating behavior is produced by happy chemicals and sex hormones working together. These chemicals produce the feeling that you *must* have Mate X to be happy, but you could do without Mate Y. In this chapter, we will focus exclusively on the status aspects of mate selection. In the mammal world, status is both the means and the end: your status is the means to getting the attention of Mate X, and status helps explain why Mate X has caught your fancy. Of course, no human would consciously embrace this cynical view of mating behavior, but the following up-close and personal look at animals' mating choices shows a pattern that's too consistent to ignore. Sex and status go together in the mammal world.

This chapter explores diverse animal mating strategies, including harems, male rivalry and pair-bonding. Within all the variety is a common pattern: sex is the reward for status, be it the quantity or the quality of mating opportunities.

Mammals are quite particular about their mates. They don't run off with just anyone. All this pickiness ends up improving an individual's prospects of keeping their DNA alive. The mating market gets sorted out without words because the mammal brain evolved to make social judgements.

There is no free love in the animal world. If there were, more babies would be born than an environmental niche could support. Many babies would die, and the whole species would be at risk if it overloaded its ecosystem. Successful species have evolved behaviors that lead to fewer offspring but higher survival prospects for each one. Mate selection is one of those behaviors. Before mating, every species has some form of preliminary qualifying event. These events influence which sperm fertilizes which egg and thus which mammals get born.

Biologists use the term "tournament species" for mammals that joust to determine status for mating purposes. Male tournaments may look like they're just display, but research shows that they are often ruthless ordeals that sap a huge chunk of a male's energy and body weight. Losers get nothing for their trouble, and even winners get injured. In the wild, injuries are not patched up by vets and zookeepers; they may bleed, fester, cripple and kill a guy, or weaken him to the point where he's soon picked off by a predator. In short, the males of most species make great sacrifices for any reproductive opportunity that comes their way. Any male can refuse to participate, but then he won't pass on his DNA. We have inherited our brains from individuals who played and won in the reproduction game. A male who failed to reproduce cannot be our ancestor.

For the ladies, the tournament system also has its advantages and disadvantages. To humans, it may seem that the system restricts a girl's freedom of choice. But tournaments have curious advantages for females. They give every girl her species' equivalent of the captain of the football team. Every girl gets a guy who fought for her.

A scientific explanation of these benefits is known as the *sexy son hypothesis*. Serious biologists coined the phrase to underscore the reproductive math. A male mammal can have a large number of offspring in his lifetime if he becomes an alpha, but a female's reproductive potential is much more limited no matter how high her status. She nurses each newborn for such a long time that she can only have a few in a lifetime. So how can a female's reproductive success match a male's? She can give birth to a son who grows up to be an alpha, thus making many copies of her genes. And the best way to have a son who's a big stud is to select a father who's a big stud.

I first learned the ins and outs of mammalian mating in France. In the Loire region is a primate zoo known as the *Vallé des Singes*, literally "Valley of Monkeys." There I heard a sweet young zookeeper explain the lifestyle choices of savannah baboons. She described the alpha baboon's tendency to monopolize the females. "The group doesn't mind," she said, "because when a lion comes around, they all climb up a tree and don't come down until the alpha chases it away or dies trying."

I was confused. Was she saying that low-status males never get to have sex? Ever? Maybe it was my French, but the more I thought about it, the worse it seemed. So I went to ask her privately when her talk was over, straining to find French vocabulary to express the delicate matter.

Her answer was, "Low-status males do have sex, but they will not be fathers."

That confused me even more, but I couldn't come up with a follow-up question in French. I consulted a textbook as soon as I got home, and that's how I learned the finer points of primate angling and wrangling. It seems that dominant baboons allow middle-ranking baboons to consort with females, but not when a female is actively fertile. The whole male status hierarchy revolves around the subtle distinction between fertility and pre-fertility. Male primates, with the exception of humans and bonobos, are only interested in sex when females broadcast their fertility with visual and olfactory signals. Females generally start broadcasting a few days before the big moment. Mature males of experience perceive the difference between the preliminaries and the real thing, and they don't come a-courtin'. This creates a small window of opportunity, and ambitious younger baboons seize the day. Female primates often accommodate them, eager to build goodwill with the leaders of tomorrow.

Older male baboons do what they can to block these advances. The more fertile the female, the more effort the old guard expends to chase younger males away. As a young male starts to rise in the dominance hierarchy, he becomes harder to chase away. So young males spend years building their strength and their social alliances. A male must be on the winning side of a lot of fights before he ranks high enough to be in the pecking order on actual fertility days. If he becomes especially powerful, he will be able to chase away other males on those days, and then his DNA is slated to win the genetic sweepstakes.

All these complications remind me of the celebrity dating gossip I see in magazines on supermarket checkout lines. But the competition for mating opportunities is only one piece of the reproductive puzzle. Reproductive outcomes depend as much on the subtle daily choices that shape a primate's health and social bonds as it does on the obvious act of consortship. And neurochemistry mediates these daily choices. The sexual politics of animals has an oddly familiar ring because the same neurochemicals create the same complications. Happy chemicals reward a mammal for everything relevant to reproductive success, and that includes strength-building, child-protecting and social climbing as well as mate-pursuing.

We humans think twice before we act on our neurochemical impulses. Indeed, we usually think more than twice. Animals are less inclined to restrain their impulses because they have fewer neurons to re-channel these urges. Animal "just do it" while humans have enough neurons to create poetry or neurosis instead. Animals can't tell us why they do what they do, but animal research can. The research reveals a strikingly consistent pattern: sex and status go together. When animals invest effort in status seeking they are rewarded with mating opportunities.

And You Thought Your Parents Were Judgmental

A National Geographic video I saw shows two male zebras viciously attacking each other, whacking heads and hooves and every other part they can mobilize. A young female stands by. Suddenly the males stop fighting and one trots off with the maiden. You might presume the two combatants are young lads, but a narrator explains that one of them is Dad. His daughter just reached puberty and was about to wander off from the herd with the young buck at her heels.

Dad is not against his daughter mating, the narrator carefully explains. He is against her mating with a wimp. His DNA is at stake. His daughter will have only so many offspring in her lifetime, and they need to survive for Dad's DNA to survive. He doesn't consciously think this, but he makes sure his daughter saves herself for the best possible candidate. A young male zebra has to strut his stuff to win over a girl's father.

Mammals have complicated sex lives because mating behaviors that work in an ecological niche are naturally selected for. A striking example of this is the sex life of wolves, or more precisely the lack of it. Wolves live in harsh environments where births must be kept to a minimum to keep the species alive. An interesting form of birth control evolved to meet this constraint. No wolf gets to have sex except the alpha pair of each pack. The alphas make sure of this with jealous guarding. The top dogs viciously attack the lower-status wolves at the merest hint of behavior that violates this code. The alpha male bites any male who goes near a fertile female. And the alpha bitch attacks her female pack-mates if they go near a male. These attacks stress the females to the extent that their hormone levels drop and they don't ovulate. This makes the world safe for the alpha female's children.

Every wolf is born with a full set of reproductive equipment. But instead of reproducing, most of them spend their lives working to support the children of the power couple. They die without heirs unless an individual builds enough strength to challenge the alpha or start a new pack. Lower-ranking wolves could fight the power whenever they want, but their survival instinct tells them to avoid getting bitten.

A pair of young wolves could run off alone. Nothing is stopping them. But without a pack, their survival prospects are poor and their love child's prospects are worse. Hunting works best with a group, so most wolves stick with the pack despite the asymmetry. It's not surprising that some wolves opted to scavenge in human settlements and become "man's best friend." Wolves evolved into dogs as newborns attached to humans rather than to pack-mates.

Wolves never decided to create a totalitarian system. The system emerged spontaneously as each individual brain sought happy chemicals and avoided unhappy chemicals in whatever ways possible in their environment.

The mammal brain is always alert for ways to give its own offspring the competitive edge. The result is rivalry among females as well as males. Female chimps, for instance, have been observed interrupting matings between the alpha and another female. They don't label it "jealousy" and they don't know about genes, but the neurochemical urge to dominate prompts the behavior without such rationales.

Wahoo Contests

Male baboons intimidate each other with loud cries that experts call *wahoos*. A wahoo contest allows male rivals to resolve matters without bloodshed. A wahoo displays a male's strength and thus his potential to win a fight if challenged. One party to the wahoo contest usually backs down, so their respective ranks are settled without injury to either party.

Avoiding injury is critical to reproductive success. The longer a male lives, the more chances he has to reproduce. A male that can intimidate others without having to fight thus achieves a reproductive advantage.

But faking it is not an option. If dominance could be achieved with wahoos that were not backed by real fighting strength, big-mouthed phonies would get the girl. The next generation of baboons would then have weak fathers rather than strong ones, and the troop's survival prospects would decline. Neighboring troops would seize their women and their fruit trees, and predators would eat their children. Natural selection would eliminate any species that based its tournaments on anything but authentic indicators of fighting strength. Scientific research confirms this:

Wahoos satisfy all of the criteria for a classic competitive display. They are extremely loud, low-pitched calls that can be produced only by large, fully adult males. They are costly to produce not just because of their loudness and low pitch but also because males give them in long bouts, often as they race through the group or bounce through the trees, leaping from branch to branch. A wahoo display is therefore an exhausting demonstration of a male's stamina and coordination. And lest there be any doubt that wahoo displays are surrogates for actual fighting, male baboons often engage in wahoo 'contests'...The contest continues until, one by one, the males drop out, exhausted. Usually, only one of the most dominant males is left calling at the end.

While the wahoos of a young, vigorous, high-ranking male are thunderously loud, intimidating calls, the wahoos of older males are weak, hoarse waughs with little hoo left at the end... Males of very disparate ranks seldom engage in wahoo contests, presumably because subordinate males can assess, through their rival's wahoos and behavior, that they are outmatched and that discretion is the better part of valor. Escalated fights between males of very different ranks are therefore rare, occurring only when the contested resource is extremely valuable: meat, a sexually receptive female, or an infant threatened by infanticide. By contrast, wahoo contests involving males of similar rank –whose wahoos sound more alike – occur at high rates. They are longer, occur for unpredictable reasons, and are more likely to escalate to physical fights and wounding. [1]

In many species, male competition revolves around "displays" rather than actual fights. But these displays somehow embody the skills and traits essential to reproductive success. Conflict is inherent in the fact that only one sperm can fertilize each egg. The conflict can be resolved in many ways, but all of them reward traits and behaviors that promote survival. Natural selection makes sure of that.

Sneaking Off with Strangers

If a lady routinely consorts with the same crowd, inbreeding will eventually weaken her offspring. A lady who consorts with strangers gives her children the advantage of "new blood."

The benefit would be small if those strangers were weaklings. But a lady can be sure that any stranger lurking on the periphery of a troop's turf is robust because it's a jungle out there and surviving alone takes character. Adventurers are likely to have just the qualities a mother wants for her children.

Researchers notice female primates making efforts to hide these relations. They have documented couples selecting locations outside the alpha's field of vision, acting with haste, and hushing their typical vocalizations. They clearly anticipate rebuke from the alpha, and leering field researchers have indeed documented the revenge of cuckolded alphas.

---

1 Cheney and Seyfarth, *Baboon Metaphysics* p.52-54

Why do females risk dangerous liaisons when they could easily stay home and party with the elite of their troop? Genetic diversity is not a conscious objective, but incest-avoiding practices must be naturally selected for because they are so common among mammals.

Inbreeding is a risk that every species must manage. A female mouse risks consorting with her own son, who joins the ranks of available bachelors two months after she gives birth to him. Most mammals prevent inbreeding by expelling their young from the group when they reach puberty. Some species cast out their adolescent males and others expel their young females. These behaviors evolved without intention or comprehension. Inbreeders simply bred themselves out of existence, leaving cross-breeders to inherit the earth.

Adolescent primates have reason enough to go off and live with strangers. Young males are typically shut out from female companionship by the older males, and young females are sometimes dispersed by way of kidnapping.

Even with these pubescent troop transfers, a gene pool can become inbred over time. If the alpha fathers a lot of children, his descendants will have a lot of consanguinity. Primates have developed an additional strategy for giving their offspring good breeding. Reputable biologists call it *sneaky mating*.

Research suggests that this sneaking around reduces the risk of infanticide. When a new alpha male takes over a troop of primates, he has incentive to kill babies that are not his own. But if a new male has already been welcomed by females of the troop, he tends to be less infanticidal if he rises to dominance. Somehow his intimacies restrain him from killing infants that have some chance of being his own. Preventing infanticide promotes a female's reproductive success more than anything else she could do. She lacks the strength to resist a homicidal alpha directly, but with strategic maneuvers she can make sure her genes dominate in the end. Animals cannot understand their maneuvers empirically; they do what their neurochemicals prompt and natural selection does the rest.

How do female primates choose their secret lovers? Research suggests that females have an uncanny ability to scan for partners who are a little different but not too different. Looks and smell are the basis for these judgments. Mammals focus more on looks than on hormonal scents as their brains get larger. At the very point in evolution that fertile female primates developed external genital swellings, the brain region that processes sight took over portions of the brain region that processes smell. Brains good at seeing fertility signals were more likely to get passed on.

Perhaps this helps explain the human focus on looks. The face plays a huge role in human mate selection even though faces have no obvious reproductive role. Some insight into this behavior comes from the ape species most attracted by faces – the orangutan.

Good Lookers and Rapists

Female orangutans are always on the lookout for a certain kind of male. He has large flaps of skin hanging from his cheeks. These flaps may appear ugly or comical to humans, but they attract female orangs for a good reason: only a dominant male has them. Survival in the jungles of Southeast Asia is so difficult that only a rare few male orangutans manage to accumulate enough extra fat to make the flaps. They are a good indicator of the right stuff.

But things get complicated in the lonely treetops. Young males with no flaps are interested in girls but girls are not interested in them. These guys are not likely to develop flaps for another decade, and they are not content to just wait around. Instead, they become rapists. To understand this unfortunate adaptation, we must know more about the ecological niche it adapts to.

Food is sparse in Asian rain forests where orangutans live. A huge territory is necessary to meet the nutritional needs of just one of these shaggy red-haired apes. Dispersing widely thus promotes survival more than living in groups. In short, orangutans are loners. The females do not live in the communities typical of other primates, and the males are drifters. They play the field, literally.

Male orangutans spend their lives swinging from tree to tree in search of mating opportunities. As they arrive in each new tree, they make loud calls to announce their availability to the local ladies and scare off potential male rivals. Each guy has his usual circuit, but it's a territory larger than he could defend.

When female orangs hear the call, they come and check the guy out. If they like what they see, they mate with him. They judge him instantly by looking at the flaps on his jowls – the bigger the better. Research proves that this is a smart move, because a male orang does not develop flaps unless he dominates a territory. A jowly male is a worthy supplier of genetic material.

Field biologists have found that male orangutans mature in two stages. At the "sub-adult" stage, around age eight, a male develops the ability to reproduce, but not the "secondary sex characteristics": the flaps, long fur, and the huge size of a dominant male. These visual signals are a fast easy way for female orangs to determine a stranger's status, since they don't have the familiarity that ordinarily comes with group life.

Social dominance works differently when individuals live far apart from each other, but sex revolves around status just the same. Subadult males don't challenge mature males directly. Dominance is more a matter of attrition. When a subadult finally comes to dominate a turf, his facial flaps grow suddenly.

Researchers were amazed to find that flaps don't develop when a male lives near another male, yet they develop quickly when a male has exclusive dominion over a certain territory. It's as if his neurochemicals were saying "this jungle ain't big enough for the two of us, and I ain't leavin.'"

Females are only interested in dominants. When a female sees a stranger who's not up to her standards, she runs off to the higher branches of the trees. Those branches only support the weight of females because they are smaller than even the young males. But the spurned young male sometimes pursues the fleeing female and tries to coerce her. A female who isn't fast enough to escape may be overpowered by a subadult male. Her babies get fathered by the wrong stuff. Stronger, faster females get to have babies fathered by a dominant male. Thus, dominance brings reproductive success for both males and females.

The risk of conflict motivates orangs to keep widely spaced from each other, and that helps avert malnutrition. Orangs have adapted the standard mammalian neurochemistry to the survival constraints of their environment.

Most primates do not grow flaps when they achieve dominance. Most do not rape. But all primates have their ways of recognizing the "best" mates and investing energy in competing for them. As higher primates relied more on the visual cortex, individuals with a sharp eye for good-looking mates ended up contributing more to the gene pool. Apes skilled at visually checking out potential partners were favored in the reproductive sweepstakes over apes that could only smell opportunity. And so visual acuity evolved.

Reciprocity: You Scratch My Back

As primates grew larger brains, their reciprocal strategies grew too. Males began appealing directly to females instead of going head-to-head with the patriarchy. Male chimps are known to appeal to females in ways that are familiar to humans. To put it frankly, chimps in the primeval forest have been found exchanging meat for sex.

The motives for this exchange are not obvious. Let's begin with the female perspective. A female takes a risk when she mates with a gift-giving male because the alpha male could retaliate against her or her children. This tells us that meat is a strong motivator for her. It turns out that a mother's protein and fat consumption influences the size of her newborn's brain. Meat is scarce in the jungle. Insects supply survival amounts of protein, but meat can boost nutrition significantly. Over time, females who attracted meat-bearing gentlemen callers wound up with bigger-brained children. This delicate transaction may be the very engine of human evolution.

Now let's consider the male perspective. A low-status male chimp has a hard time getting meat. Male chimps hunt in groups that dole out their kill in rank order. An alpha male can always grab meat from other males and they don't resist. A low-status male ends up with a smaller share of meat, and he needs the nutrition himself if he's to build up his fighting strength. Is he better off sharing his meat with a female or eating it himself?

In truth, it must be reported that a lot of begging goes on in primate communities. When a male returns from the hunt munching on a piece of meat, females beg persistently. Ovulating females beg most enthusiastically. To some extent, males share meat in order to be left in peace to eat the rest.

Reciprocal exchange is not necessarily an explicit transaction. Two individuals may have a very casual interaction without conceptualizing the future. But if they interact repeatedly, neural pathways for trust gradually build. Trust circuits motivate sharing without a conscious intent to give and get. An ape simply releases oxytocin in the presence of another ape. Networks of familiarity can develop alongside the formal status hierarchy.

Such reciprocal bonds are not driven by meat alone. Grooming and babysitting are popular alternative forms of giving. Offering to groom is a well-documented primate strategy for cementing relationships. Female baboons who experience the death of a close female relative are observed to respond by initiating groomings with new partners. Grooming typically reflects the status hierarchy, but it is also a tool for raising status. Young males groom older males to accelerate their climb up the dominance hierarchy. Young females groom older females to build support.

Primate grooming is not always reciprocal. A lower-status individual often grooms a high-ranking individual without getting an immediate return. But the groomer gradually develops an ally in case of future conflict.

When there's open conflict between two primates, the winner is typically the one with the most allies. When a baboon or chimpanzee gets into a fight, it makes a distress call that the others recognize. Cheney and Seyfarth documented this selectivity by recording individual calls and playing them back to individual group mates. They found that baboons respond to the calls of those with whom they have developed longstanding bonds of reciprocal exchange. Primates do not risk their lives to protect just anyone, but they rush to protect individuals with whom they have spent a lot of time grooming. When you spend a lot of time around an individual, you create neural pathways that register their alarm call instantly.

Monkeys and apes seem to have an amazing ability to keep track of the favors they owe and are owed. My parents did the same thing when I was growing up. I noticed them keeping track of gifts given and received in order to maintain reciprocity. This custom is widespread in traditional societies. Animals manage to do it without explicit cognition. Repeated contact simply creates neural circuits, and behavior follows.

Researchers find that fertile females favor males that repeatedly groomed them in the past. Monogamy is rare in the primate world, but repeated grooming develops into neurochemical attachment. When a primate receives a grooming, its brain links the good feeling of oxytocin to the individual grooming it. Oxytocin circuits condition a primate to expect this good feeling when it sees that individual.

The hard data on grooming show that much of it occurs among males. Lower-ranking males tend to groom higher-ranking males. The resulting bonds help males cooperate while hunting or defending their territory from neighboring troops. Higher-ranking males do not need to groom others because they have the strength to win conflicts. Weaker males initiate groomings to build good will with the males that dominate food and sex. This gives a low-ranking male a choice of strategies for advancing his reproductive prospects. He can build muscle, court the male power structure, and/or court ladies directly. A brain good at choosing the best strategy at each moment is likely to get passed on.

Love and Monogamy as Success Strategies

Relationships can be brutal for monkeys. A male might provide meat and babysitting to a female only to see her favor others come mating time. An alpha male can spend days guarding an estrous female, only to lose the match during a moment when his attention is elsewhere. Disappointment triggers unhappy chemicals, which prompt the brain to look for an alternative.

"Love" is one alternative that evolved. If a partner only has eyes for you, your DNA has an advantage. Getting another to fall in love with you is a great reproductive strategy. Chimpanzee researchers occasionally find such *consortships* – exclusive bonds that last the whole length of a female's ovulation. That isn't long-term from a human point of view, but such exclusivity is rare among chimpanzees and bonobos. Researchers eagerly analyze these trysts for answers to the big questions of life. From the far end of a telescope it looks like love, but let's look at a mundane neurochemical explanation.

Female chimps usually mingle with the alpha and the high-ranking males of the troop during their fertility periods. But researchers occasionally find a female chimp sneaking off with a lower-status male. Top-ranking males tend not to engage in exclusive consortships because their status in the male hierarchy is at risk while they are away. Why would a female go off with an underling and give up the chance to raise her standing with the ruling clique? Why would she give up the chance to beg many males for meat and hide silently with one beau on the outskirts of the troop's range, exposed to the risk of attack by raiding parties from neighboring troops? Inquiring minds wanted to know, and they got research grants to find out.

They found some evidence of coercion, and some evidence of dopamine and oxytocin. Researchers are still trying to discover why those happy chemicals get triggered. What makes this particular mate so special? A female may be attracted by a scent that's different from hers. It seems to mark the male as genetically diverse. Did the male with the right smell just get lucky? Researchers are hotly pursing this apparent end run around the status hierarchy.

In any case, chimpanzee consortships do not last. After a few days, the couple goes back to the way they were. A male chimp isn't predisposed to "babysit" for his own flesh and blood. Lasting pair-bonds are rare among mammals, except for the few species whose brains naturally produce high levels of oxytocin.

Monogamy is the norm for a few oxytocin-rich mammals, including one ape: the gibbon. But even mating for life doesn't stop gibbons from focusing on dominance. They simply treat it as a couples activity. Their relationship is an alliance to raise their dominance together. They start working at it first thing every morning.

Gibbons make loud calls for a half hour when they wake up every morning. They jointly scream their heads offs to scare other gibbons off their turf. Then, Mr. and Mrs. Gibbon start patrolling in case other gibbons failed to get the message. Their children join in these enterprises.

Trouble in paradise is never far away. When other gibbons hear the duet of a mated pair, they judge it. If the sound is not strong and well-coordinated, neighboring gibbons interpret it as a weakness. Unattached singles enter the family's domain. Soon, Mrs. Gibbon may be starting a new family with another man. When the intruders are female, Mrs. Gibbon quickly attacks if she sees them approach her mate. Scientists have found high levels of aggression in the female gibbon. Her children's survival depends on keeping all the territory's nutrition for them rather than sharing it with the other woman's baby.

Once again, sex and dominance go together.

Matriarchy and Patriarchy

Some mammalian groups are male-dominated and some are female-dominated, but both genders are status-conscious. Patriarchal and matriarchal primates use different means to the same end: to manage the potential conflict that emerges from each individual's pursuit of reproductive success. Let's look at a matriarchal ape, the bonobo, and a patriarchal ape, the gorilla, to see how each system links sex and dominance.

Bonobos, the most recently discovered ape species, are a close cousin of chimps and humans. They are the only species other than humans known to engage in sexual activity when the female is not actively fertile. Bonobos appear to rub genitals in situations where humans would shake hands, exchange business cards, or say "excuse me." But even with almost unlimited reproductive opportunity, bonobos care plenty about status.

Female bonobos work their way up the hierarchy by developing close, often intimate bonds with higher-ranking females. Male bonobos get their status from their mothers. Female bonobos apparently compete to have their babies fathered by the sons of high-status females. Males don't fight because their mothers do their fighting for them.

I experienced some of this for myself on a trip to the San Diego Zoo. Very few zoos in the world have bonobos, and I was excited to be able to see them. When I got there, only a handful of bonobos were on exhibit. The keeper explained that she had to split them up into two groups because when two females got together they would violently attack a male. Researchers in the remotest forests report the same tendency for pairs of females to attack males. The presumption that bonobos are peaceful because they are matriarchal is erroneous. The mammal brain asserts when it sees that it can win.

Scientific knowledge of bonobos is limited for may reasons. Their natural habitat never expanded beyond a tiny spot on the south bank of the Congo River. (All chimps originate from the north bank.) Access to this region has been restricted by human warfare for much of the past few decades. In addition, bonobos are highly avoidant of human contact. Researchers are eagerly seeking more information on bonobos. Yet it's already clear that even with virtually unlimited mating opportunities, they create status hierarchies and struggle to get the "best" mates.

Gorillas are almost the opposite of the sociable bonobos. A male gorilla dominates his family completely, but they live in isolation rather than in large dominance hierarchies. Male gorillas cannot get along; they avoid conflict by avoiding contact.

Gorillas have the mating system commonly known as the *harem*. Gorilla experts don't like this term. They'd rather call it a nurturing female community where males are under-represented. Whatever you call it, it's plain that the alpha gorilla exerts absolute dominion over his brood.

Gorilla experts often try to rehabilitate the gorilla's bad image. They emphasize the nice-guy aspect of the silverback, the term for the dominant male that refers to his gray hair. It is true that papa gorilla is a vegetarian who often plays with his children and is hardly ever violent. But he becomes violent instantly if others don't submit to him completely.

I had a chance to witness this dominance at the Denver Zoo. I was standing in front of the gorilla enclosure and a docent came over and narrated the action for me. He pointed out a gorilla that I will call the "spinster aunt." She was introduced into the group at an older age, he said, and has always refused to consort with the patriarch. In the wild, this wouldn't happen. The silverback would rule. But the spinster aunt grew up in captivity without being socialized properly. She spurned his advances and the silverback responds to the indignity by harassing her constantly. I saw her sitting very far from him. Every few minutes he'd lunge a few feet toward her, and she'd move to a new spot to maintain the same huge distance between them. Every few minutes, the same dynamics would repeat. He never attacked her while I was there, but he renewed the threat with an intimidating gesture again and again. She remained in a constant state of vigilance that I would not have understood if it weren't for the docent.

Female gorillas do not bond with other females the way primates typically do. And a gorilla harem has no defined territory. In short, nothing holds the social unit together except the silverback's absolute power. He quickly threatens a subordinate or intruder who fails to defer. If that doesn't bring immediate submission, he escalates to his iconic full-scale rage. He rarely has to fight because other gorillas submit. This leaves him a lot of free time to play with the children who are most certainly his.

A gorilla's kids leave home at puberty. Sons leave to find their own females rather than compete with Dad. Daughters must leave to prevent incest. This delicate dilemma was explained to me by the Denver Zoo docent.

He pointed to an adolescent female and explained that in the wild, gorillas always give away their daughters by her age. A father gorilla literally ambles through the forest looking for a good family. When he finds one, he brings his whole family to a nearby clearing. The other patriarch, always interested in acquiring another wife, brings his family to the clearing to scope them out. Both families spend the day there, though they keep a large distance between them. At the end of the day, one family leaves without their daughter and the other family leaves with a new fertile female. It seems uncannily similar to the widespread human practice of arranged marriage.

The docent told me they can't arrange this in the zoo because their enclosure is too small for two silverbacks to tolerate each other. The Zoo was scrambling to find the daughter a new home to eliminate the risk of incest that wild gorillas have somehow learned to manage.

A gorilla patriarch guards his females constantly when he's not giving away a daughter. He has good reason – other males abduct any female they can safely get their hands on. When a strange male approaches, a silverback unleashes his chest-thumping threat gesture, and if the intruder doesn't leave he immediately escalates. This is no hollow threat. He will kill a rival who doesn't withdraw immediately. Sometimes the intruder is stronger than the patriarch. Then, in a drama that rivals Shakespeare, the intruder kills and eats the silverback's children and becomes the new patriarch. The females switch their allegiance to the new guy, who has the proven strength to protect their next baby. Mothers do what it takes to promote the survival of their offspring.

Abducting females is a mating strategy that humans have practiced up to the past millennium. Genghis Khan had a large harem which he added to via the abduction method. This approach to mate selection was not uncommon in his ecosystem, and men guarded their women carefully to prevent abductions.

In traditional societies, a man with more power accumulated more wives. There was nothing to buy in the distant past, so status was expressed through the number of people you dominated. This caused a shortage of wives for young males. The new generation had to build their strength until they could abduct a woman or two of their own as their elders weakened. Lots of men died in the conflicts, but females shared the men that remained. Any man who survived the status conflict was assured of reproductive success.

This system is remarkably similar to the mating system of the very first primate species, the mouse lemur. These creatures look more like mice than humans, so their mating habits might not seem relevant to us. But on closer inspection, the mouse lemur has some eerily human traits: fingers like ours instead of claws, and eyes that face forward stereoscopically like ours. More important, the mouse lemur has a much larger brain than a mouse. It bears relatively few children and invests heavily in each one, just like us. The mouse lemur is the mother of all primates, so its dating and mating habits have something to tell us about the link between status and reproductive success.[2]

Mouse lemurs live in large colonies of women and children. Male "bachelors" live around the periphery. The female status hierarchy is organized around matrilines, each girl ranked by the status of her mother's family. Boys leave the nest at puberty to live solitary lives except during mating season.

Once female hormones fill the air, male lemurs quickly change from docile to aggressive. They begin a frenzy of conflict with other males that continues for days. The last man standing gets most of the girls. The aggression unleashed by their sex hormones consumes so much of their energy that males lose about a third of their body weight during mating season. Between seasons, while the females are busy gestating and nursing, the males rest and rebuild their

---

2 To be precise, the mouse lemur is the closest living ancestor to the now-extinct first primate.

strength for the next round of combat. It seems like a crazy way to live, but everyone does it in the lemur world.

Male mouse lemurs do not build lasting bonds with their communities. They travel from one group to another, seeking a place where their chances of rising in the ranks are best.

It's easy to see echoes of this core pattern in the rest of the primate world. The competition for mates was built on violence in the distant past, but less violent ways of competing for status and mates gradually evolved.

Sex and Survival

In nature, reproduction is serious business. A huge percentage of newborns die because survival threats are daunting. Mammals lose fewer children than earlier species, and the larger a mammal's brain, the fewer children it loses. Status hierarchies are nature's way of reducing the loss. They help each individual create the strongest possible children and give them the strongest possible protection.

Reproduction takes a lot of effort in the mammal world. Child-bearing requires a huge investment from females, and rivalries of one sort or another require a huge investment from males. All this effort improves the odds of baby mammals being born to parents capable of protecting them.

Mammalian neurochemicals link sex and status. Males seek status because sex is the reward. Females prefer sex with high-status mates because their children's survival is the reward. These strategies don't come from formal logic. They come from brain chemicals that evolved through natural selection.

Chapter 5

Status Seeking on AutoPilot

...Teens value what mammals value: qualities relevant to success in the mating game. Teens respect peers who have lots of allies, take risks with confidence, and are attractive as mating partners,...

This chapter shows how the mammal brain shapes our understanding of the social world without our awareness.

Monkeys choose their social allies carefully. A monkey can see that some troop mates will be able to help him more than others. He sees that alliances can be dangerous because your allies expect you to defend them when attacked. So monkeys make shrewd assessments of their associates. They do it automatically with neural circuits fused by life experience.

Your parents were choosy about their social allies, and so were your grandparents. Their status-seeking strategies may have irritated you. You may have vowed to live differently. Probably your parents felt the same way about their parents. Young minds look for ways to accelerate their rise in status. Young mammals oppose old alliances and create new ones. New generations celebrate new status markers. Each generation feels righteous in its motives. We never imagine ourselves creating new alliances for the purpose of accelerating our own rise. We never imagine that we are seeking status on Automatic Pilot.

But our unhappy chemicals get triggered when our status prospects seem bleak, and we are strongly motivated to "do something" about it. You don't intend to seek dominance, but you long for the happy chemicals.

When you get the respect of others, your happy chemicals flow. Your mammal brain learns from the experience. It stores the related details, which prepares you to get more respect in that particular way in the future. The mammal brain automatically learns information associated with your neurochemical ups and downs. We will see in this chapter that neurochemicals are like paving that transforms faint neural trails into neural superhighways. Your neurochemical experiences build the AutoPilot that guides you toward ways of stimulating your happy chemicals and avoiding unhappy chemicals in the future.

"Automatic" sounds like a bad thing, but this chapter shows that AutoPilot makes life possible. We must do routine things on automatic because it saves our limited higher capacity for things that matter most to us. Of course we are more than our AutoPilot because we can override it and analyze alternatives. But some automatic processing is essential for survival, so we should know how it works.

Each mammal is born with a brain prepared to learn what is necessary to survive in its environmental niche. Social knowledge is as important to survival as knowledge of the physical world. We build a mental model of the social world the way we build one of our physical surroundings. This chapter shows how mental models of the social world are constructed and how they promote survival.

You Mean I've Been Speaking AutoPilot All These Years?

Our mental models are made up of real physical changes in the brain. Your AutoPilot comprises the physical changes that you built up from your unique experience. Neurochemicals automatically cause learning in the brain, so experiences that triggered your neurochemicals in the past made an important contribution to your AutoPilot. You seek status on AutoPilot because status triggered your neurochemicals in the past.

The clearest evidence of our need for AutoPilot is the fact that we have ten times more neurons going from the brain to the eyes as we do from the eyes to the brain. That means *your brain tells your eyes what to look for.* Your eyes are not passively taking in whatever is there. They zoom in on information that your past experience recognizes as important. Your brain is so good at activating templates from past experience that you don't even know you're doing it. You do it automatically.

Electricity flows effortlessly through the neural pathways you built up from experience. Electricity is triggered when the external world reachers your senses. That electricity flows where there's least resistance. It finds less resistance in the neural pathways you've activated before because experience makes neurons more efficient. Your old pathways light up easily when new inputs are similar to old patterns. You are not a prisoner of your old circuits. You can re-direct electricity to new and unpaved pathways if you make an intense conscious effort. This is what it means to over-ride your AutoPilot. But our capacity for such effort is limited. Once you focus it in one place, everything else you do at that moment is on AutoPilot.

Your ready-made neural pathways guide you through the social world as well as the physical world. You have built up expectations about people just as you have learned to expect that water is wet and knives are sharp. When you interact with people, electricity flows into the circuits you built from your past social interactions. Your AutoPilot tells you which behaviors are likely to get respect from others. It tells you which status hierarchies matter and which status cues to notice.

You don't recognize your expectations about the social world because they are so...automatic. It's easier to see other people's automatic expectations simply because they're not what you would have come up with. The popular wisdom is that we should not have preconceptions. This is foolish because only a newborn could look at the world without preconceptions. Survival would not be enhanced by looking at the world like a newborn. Relying on our stock of experience is how we survive. When you try to reject the expectations that come to you automatically, your mammal brain feels like you are threatening your own survival.

The world constantly bombards the senses with more detail than any brain could process. If you tried to interpret every detail reaching your eyes and ears, it would be midnight before you got your pants on. In order to survive, you need a fast way to sift the details that matter from the details you can safely ignore. Expectations are the solution that evolved.

The mind is always retrieving expectations from the past to make sense of the details it's taking in. The world makes sense to you when you find patterns in new inputs that basically match the patterns you expected. Once you make sense of something, you move on to the next cluster of detail, and the next. You don't notice all the work your brain is doing to retrieve old patterns and match them to new inputs. You simply notice the "information" you've constructed by recognizing familiar patterns. Stored patterns help us make sense of the world quickly. We could not thrive without them.

The neural pathways you've built from experience make it easy to see what you have already seen, and to hear what you have already heard. Your neurons make it easy to feel what you have already felt. Each person builds a social AutoPilot from their unique history of ups and downs, and relies on it to guide their social interactions in the future. Our goal here is not to lament AutoPilot but to know it.

Our big brains have a relatively small bandwidth for new inputs. In order to survive, we have to zoom in on the most important inputs and ignore the least important. For example, when a gazelle sees a lion, its survival rests on escaping; so it ignores the details of this individual lion and focuses on the details of the ground underneath its feet. By contrast, when a gazelle gets separated from its herd, it survives by ignoring the details of the ground underneath and staying alert for the sights, smells and sounds of its herd-mates. We are always deciding which details to process and which details to ignore. The mammal brain is good at automatically scanning for the inputs most relevant to survival – as it understands survival.

Our brains choose which inputs require our higher capacity and which can be left to automatic. We decide this so fluidly that we don't even notice. For example, imagine you're driving home and another car suddenly drifts into your lane. You had been listening to news on the radio and thinking about your plans for the evening, but now you are on full alert. All of your mental ability is needed to monitor the position of each car and convey that information to your hands and feet. Your reaction succeeded at saving your life. An instant later, the danger has passed and your attention drifts back to the radio. Then, you realize that you missed an important part of the news story you were listening to. The words reached your ears, but your brain didn't process them. That's because emergency driving used up your higher analytical abilities. When driving conditions are normal, you can decode language because you do the driving on AutoPilot.

AutoPilot is often more effective than reality. For example, when you see a typographical error, you make sense of it by relying on your expectations rather than the details actually in front of your eyes. Your brain does this so efficiently that you often don't notice there was a typo.

We are capable of shifting out of automatic when we see the need. Otherwise, we rely on it because it's effective. AutoPilot works because past experience is a pretty good guide to present experience. AutoPilot helps you meet your needs in ways that successfully met your needs in the past. For example, imagine that you get hungry while engaged in a complex task like balancing your checkbook or writing a poem. Your AutoPilot is capable of recognizing that hunger, walking to the refrigerator, selecting a snack, preparing the snack, chewing it, and returning to your desk, while you continue the complex thoughts about your checkbook or your poem. We don't notice our AutoPilot because it's so good.

We can interact with social hierarchies as automatically as getting a snack from the refrigerator. Past experience guides you toward behaviors that meet your needs.

Automatic Knowledge of Social Hierarchy

Over time, you have built expectations about how to raise your status in the niche you happen to live in. It's hard to notice these expectations because you built them automatically and you use them automatically. It's easy to notice automatic social expectations that are different from your own. Consider the etiquette of Japanese business executives boarding a train, for example. By custom, each executive takes the seat in a train compartment appropriate to his rank in the group. Everyone knows how he ranks among his travel companions based on job title and age. Everyone knows the rank of each seat in the train compartment: the window seat facing the direction of travel is number one, the window seat opposite the direction of travel is number two, the aisle seat facing forward is number three, etc. Each individual walks straight to the correct seat without discussion. A party of six instantly arranges itself without explicit analysis.

Similar expectations would apply if you were invited to a Chinese banquet. You would need to know your rank among the guests in order to take the proper seat. Taking the wrong seat can create bad will. If you don't know where you rank, you can ask someone who lives in that cultural niche. They are likely to know automatically.

If you hold a banquet and invite Chinese colleagues, they are likely to ask you where they should sit. You might automatically say, "Sit wherever you'd like." But that may make them uncomfortable; their social AutoPilot tells them it will cause bad will.

The brain extracts patterns from experience that tell you how to get along with the people around you. It learns from the patterns that got you rewards in the past. Learning from experience is different from learning math or a foreign language. It happens unintentionally, as activated neurons build efficient connections and provide smooth sailing for future activation.

Your experiential learning has accumulated since you were born. Every young child notices which actions help it get rewards and which actions risk losing rewards. The older a child gets, the more he relies on his cumulative experience.

Our brains evolved to start relying on past experience between ages two and three. Before that age, the brain makes new connections very easily. This neuroplasticity declines after age three, and that encourages a child to start relying on the knowledge it has instead of seeing the world as a newborn each day. A three-year old starts building on the neural pathways it has instead of soaking up everything equally. In this way, your earliest experiences with other people become the core of your social AutoPilot. Of course, learning continues throughout life, but it layers onto the circuits that are there.

Neuroplasticity peaks once again during puberty because hormones facilitate new neural connections. As a result, the social experiences we have during puberty contribute significantly to our social AutoPilot. Mammals are especially adaptive at puberty because relocating is often necessary to mate. Relocating means adapting to a new ecological niche and a new social group. Humans often married into a new tribe at puberty, which required learning a new language and new customs. Hormones make it easier to store new information about meeting your survival needs in a new environment.

Thus, there are real physiological reasons why teenage experiences are central to our mental models of the social world. We may not remember a lot of individual teen experiences, but our brains extract the patterns. We learn how to tell who is dominant and how to act when we find ourselves in the dominant and the subordinate role. We don't learn this consciously, but experience creates permanent physical changes in our neurons. We store the patterns even when we don't remember the details.

Teen memories can be embarrassing because they include frustrating early encounters with mammalian dominance hierarchies. Unhappy chemicals are triggered, creating neural connections that are still there decades later. Our frustrations feel unique, even though they're routines that helped mammals survive for millions of years.

Popularity Contest: Status in High School

We mammals like the respect of our peers. Teenagers inevitably observe that some peers get more respect than others. Social hierarchies form as teens notice the respect accorded to each other individual around them. The widespread phenomenon of "popularity" in high school is astonishingly similar to the dominance hierarchies of our primate ancestors.

Sociologists who studied popularity in high school found that students give remarkably consistent popularity rankings for each student at their school, including themselves. Researchers interviewed students separately, and repeated the study at several schools.

Overwhelming convergence in students' perceptions of social hierarchies was always the result. These hierarchies may be informal, but they are real. Teenagers focus on popularity because their developing limbic systems are inherited from earlier mammals.

"Our society" is usually blamed for this hierarchical behavior. But teen social status is markedly distinct from the values of our society. Teens value what mammals value: qualities relevant to success in the mating game. Teens respect peers who are attractive as mating partners, have lots of allies, and take risks with confidence. These are precisely the qualities our primate cousins value. When young people choose their personal associations, they are rarely looking for the same qualities their parents are looking for.

As a teenager, you notice that some people dominate. Some people get more attention. When you are the person getting the attention, your happy chemicals flow. Those chemicals automatically connect all neurons that are active at that moment. This prepares you to seek happy chemicals in similar situations, automatically.

When a young person gets disrespected or loses status, unhappy chemicals flow. Those chemicals connect active neurons, which help a person recognize and avoid future circumstances with a similar pattern. Mammals are highly motivated to avoid unhappy chemicals. A young person will vigorously avoid situations that resemble status threats experienced in the past.

In this way, without effort or intention, each individual builds an inner guide to social dominance. Expectations about respect and happiness get built because neurochemicals stimulate connections between neurons. Each person builds a unique set of expectations, but they overlap in important ways because we all build them by interacting with other mammals. We all notice that certain choices get us respect and that it feels good.

Alas, teens learn that it is not easy to get happy chemicals from the brain. They build strategies for triggering more happy chemicals and avoiding unhappy chemicals. Their strategies tend to focus on the present because future happiness is just an abstraction of the cortex. A young brain only focuses on the future when it stimulates happy chemicals today or avoids unhappy chemicals today.

High school popularity is a touchy subject for good reason. In adolescence we realize that our parents cannot give us happy chemicals or protect us from unhappy chemicals. If you want the attention of a special someone, your parents cannot get it for you. You have to do what it takes to get it yourself. Every mammal has to eventually learn to meet its own needs. A species only survives if its children learn to survive once their parents are gone. Each mammal must learn to meet its own social needs as well as its physical needs. A young mammal must learn what it takes to attract mates in order for a species to reproduce itself.

Every primate eventually has to deal with the adult social hierarchy without the shelter of its parents. When you are the one facing a social hierarchy on your own, it's unnerving, even though every primate goes through it.

Our teen years bring the awareness that we are constantly being judged by our peers, and that we have to manage this aspect of life for ourselves. Each brain constructs a model of how to interact with people outside the family. Each mind learns what it can about how to gain status. Frustration is inevitable as we see others getting recognition and learn that we cannot always dominate. This dilemma is universal, but we feel the frustration individually.

Each time a young person is happy, their brain stores the experience as a guide to finding future happiness. Each time they are sad, their brain extracts lessons about what not to do. Without conscious effort, the adolescent brain builds a mental model of social dominance. Experiences relevant to a teenager are the raw material of this model. Where to sit at lunch and what to say in class may not seem relevant to later life, but the brain automatically extracts the patterns.

Measuring Up

Each individual compares themselves to others. You may say it's wrong to make social comparisons. Yet your brain actively scans for the information and your neurochemicals react to what you find. Your unique experience connects your happy chemicals to the details that differentiate one person from another. For example, I do not care what people think about my nails, or about my car; but I do care about the design of my home. I cannot stand to have things in my house that clash with the color scheme. I know the world is full of people whose homes are full of color clashes while they focus on their abs or their public speaking ability. Every brain focuses on the details made relevant by their unique experience.

Contrast is the brain's way of identifying important information quickly. Our senses pick up more detail from the world around us than we could possibly process. Survival rests on our ability to sort details quickly, and we do that by zooming in on contrasts.

When I go to a cafe, I find the loud coffee grinder noise irritating. But curiously, I don't notice my irritation until the noise stops. The sudden quiet triggers relief that makes me aware of my prior tension. Coffee grinders rev up gradually and stop suddenly, so the contrast between the noise and the silence gets my attention more than the noise itself. When we look at the world around us, contrasts get our attention.

You may have heard that a frog cannot see a fly unless the fly is moving. A frog will ignore a fly sitting still right in front of it because motion is necessary to trigger its simple visual mechanism. Our senses are more complex than a frog's, but we do need contrast to extract information from the chaos of raw detail. If you remove a picture that was hanging on a white wall, you will get information that you didn't get from years of looking at that wall. No single spot on the wall can tell you it's dirty, but the contrast between two spots can. We need contrast to make sense of the world we live in.

Contrasts help us make sense of the other people. Their behavior often contrasts with our expectations, and that gives us information about them. We created the information by contrasting their behavior with our expectations.

A newborn baby automatically scans for contrast. When it sees a face, it is drawn to the eyes because of the contrast. Newborns do not know what eyes are for, but contrast guides their attention where it needs to go to develop communication. A newborn will stare at his mother's eyes until his neurons have stored the pattern, and then his attention scans for new contrasts.

A newborn gradually learns to expect others to meet its needs. In later life, each of us learns that others are not necessarily focused on our needs. We all encounter the contrast between our expectations of people and the reality that others are focused on their own needs rather than ours. When people disappoint us in this way, it's hard to see the role of our own expectations.

For example, if I drive down the street with the expectation that other people will get out of my way, their actual behavior might shock me. My expectations automatically suggest that other people's driving is flawed. I "know" the social world by its contrast with my expectations, but I never really notice my expectations.

If you are lucky enough to grow up in a family that gives you a lot of attention, you may be shocked one day to find that the world is not focused on you after all. If your family made every effort to protect and promote you, the world you encounter outside your home will be painful because the rewards will never meet your expectations.

On the other hand, if you grew up with little attention or support at home, life will be painful in another way. You will see other people making demands that you do not make, and often getting rewarded. You will see people benefiting from mammalian alliances that you never learned to create.

There is no easy way to be a mammal. If you expect to rely on your alliances for survival, you will feel threatened when your allies stampede in the wrong direction. But if you don't learn to trust allies, you will be at a disadvantage in a world of group-living mammals.

Your brain compares your life to others. You contrast what you get to what you see others getting, and your neurochemicals respond. You don't intend to be this way, but it's automatic.

The Mechanics of AutoPilot

It's hard to believe that your sophisticated social awareness rests on neurons you connected in your youth. Let us look closer at the real physical changes that occur in the brain as a result of experience. Here are six different types of permanent neural changes.

1. Some neurons atrophy. They literally wither from disuse. The tender age of two is when this happens most extensively. The brain effectively prunes itself, weeding out neurons that never connected to anything. Adults have 40% fewer neurons than newborns. We're born with more neurons than we need, and experience is what determines which ones we keep.

Around age two, you begin to rely on your existing connections rather than seeing the world naively. When electricity speeds effortlessly down one of your existing neural pathways, you have the sense that you "know" what's going on. Relying on these pathways gets you better results than simply building new pathways for every experience. Over time, any neuron that's not linked to your existing network is harder to activate, and more likely to atrophy.

2. Neurons can develop a sheath that's equivalent to insulation around wires. A neuron that's repeatedly fired gradually develops a

wrapping of *myelin,* which causes it to conduct electricity faster. A bundle of *myelinated* neurons transmits information with blazing speed compared to an untried neural pathway – like optical fiber compared to copper wire. Neurons do not conduct electricity the way wires do. They transmit electrical impulses by way of electrochemical changes, somewhat like those in a battery. We refer here to electricity flowing through neurons with awareness that this is an imperfect metaphor.

Our reliance on myelinated neurons, the "white matter" of the brain, is most apparent with physical actions such as a golf swing or a tennis stroke. But we are always using these efficient neural pathways to make sense of the world. Meaning comes easily when you activate myelinated neurons. Without them, you have to struggle to interpret things. Information that lights up your circuits effortlessly feels more true and more real than information you strain to extract from unmyelinated neurons. We are biased toward what we know. As ever, this is easy to see in others.

3. The most familiar type of neural change is the development of the synapse, or gap between one neuron and the next. These subtle changes make it easier for electricity to jump across a gap and activate a neighboring neuron. Once a synapse is developed, a neuron is more likely to fire whenever its neighbor fires. This prepares you to think "Z" when you see "XY."

Experience can develop a chain of synapses that feeds back on itself like a circuit. Electricity surges robustly in a developed circuit, giving us a strong sense of the information it represents. If only one part of the information is present, the whole circuit is likely to fire. If that same information had triggered undeveloped synapses, the electrical impulse might have just petered out instead.

Synapses develop in two different ways: repetition and emotion. Repetition develops a synapse gradually, while emotion develops it instantly. Emotions are chemicals that immediately make a synapse more efficient, so it fires more easily in the future. Repetition slowly improves a synapse's ability to transmit impulses across that infinitesimal chasm between one neuron and the next.

4. Neurons can grow new branches, called *dendrites*. These dendrites literally reach out and touch each other when two neurons are repeatedly triggered at the same time. Imagine a newborn looking at a dog. The baby doesn't know what the dog is because he has no prior experience. But each time he sees it, his optical neurons grow a bit until dendrites are close enough to have a synapse and activate each other. In the future, looking at the dog effortlessly activates this cluster of neurons, and the dog feels familiar.

5. Neurons have receptors on their cell membranes which have been found to change with experience. A cell's ability to receive neurochemical messages depends on the receptors it has. Experience develops these receptors in ways that are not fully understood. Receptors are highly significant in human information processing because neurochemicals can float without wiring. For example, if I have the feeling that "something's not right here," I'm releasing neurochemicals that adjust the meaning I'd usually attach to a circuit. Conversely, I might be releasing warm, trusting chemicals which have a different effect on my response to the activation of that circuit. Each neuron has receptors that process these positive and negative feelings, but those receptors depend on past experience.

6. The cerebellum plays a significant role in AutoPilot. This brain structure was overlooked in the past because it's part of the reptile brain. But we now know that the cerebellum has more nerve cells than the rest of the brain put together. These cells are diverse, fast-reacting, and organized into segments. It seems that the cerebellum learns slowly, but once it has learned something from frequent repetition, it is extremely efficient at co-ordinating complex behaviors. For example, I can back out of my curved and inclined driveway effortlessly because I have done it so often. When my son

tried it for the first time, I suddenly remembered how hard it was for me at first.

Knowledge of the cerebellum is now being used to train athletes. Researchers have learned that you can improve your basketball shot by visualizing it. Your cerebellum produces a better golf swing or soccer kick automatically and than you would produce by consciously "trying." Scientists used to think the cerebellum was dedicated to motor control, but we are learning that this ancient brain structure helps coordinate complex functions including our production of language.

These six types of physical changes taken together prepare your brain to live in the world you live in. A newborn treeshrew wires its brain for life in a tree, and a warthog wires itself for life in a burrow. Some of this wiring is genetically coded, and some is learned from experience. The larger a brain and the longer the childhood, the more a mammal depends on the mental model built by experience. Your neural connections make you who you are. When electricity zips through your existing pathways, you "know" how to survive.

Your survival circuits grow when your happy chemicals are triggered. The happy chemicals tell your brain that something is going on that meets your survival needs. The neurons activated at that moment "consolidate," and you've build a circuit that can help you find happiness in the future.

Your neurons do not record the world the way a camera does. They connect in a way that helps you retrieve information when you need it. For example, a baby sees a dog from different angles but learns that it is one thing. A toddler sees different dogs but learns the abstract concept "dog." Kids do this effortlessly because the characteristics common to all dogs are repeated most often and thus form the strongest neural connections. When a child sees an unfamiliar dog, or only the back side of a dog, electricity surges through those strong connections and the whole circuit lights up. That's how the child "knows" it's a dog. Without trying, his brain extracted the pattern and weeded out irrelevant detail.

You can distinguish a dog from a cat or a fox without knowing how you do it. You never made a conscious effort to build the concept of a dog. You did not "think" about what features constitute a dog because your neurons simply formed the strongest connections from the features repeated most often. And you did it with experience that was unique to you.

You learned to recognize a dog's bark because you experienced that sound in association with the sight. At a young age, you were able to identify the sound without see the dog. And you didn't have to try. The sound reached your ears and triggered neurons that sent electricity into other neurons. Soon, the sound triggered the expectation of a dog.

Now imagine a child hearing someone say the word "dog." His brain eventually connects the sound of the word and all the neurons already linked to his concept of a dog. He does this without consciously setting out to learn the word, or even having a concept of what a "word" is. He ends up with permanent changes in his brain ready to receive the sound of the word and link it to his other "dog" experiences.

This kind of experiential learning is our primary way of knowing the world around us. We have little awareness of this learning because it's effortless. We are more aware of the things we learn with great effort, like school work or people's names. Intentional learning comes from conscious repetition, while experiential learning comes from the accidents of experience.

I became aware of my experiential learning one day while waiting for my husband to pick me up at a train station. I recognized his car, I felt glad to see him, I jumped up and grabbed my things and walked to the curb – and then I realized that his car was a block away. Without realizing it, my eyes had been scanning every car that approached the parking lot. My brain automatically recognized his headlights in the dark from a great distance. I didn't know I could do that, and I surely hadn't tried. I would have thought all headlights look the same. But somehow repetition had taught me to identify the precise pattern for my husband's car model. My brain retrieved that old pattern and matched it with new inputs without my conscious attention. When it found a match, it activated a complex sequence of behaviors automatically. This capacity for unconscious learning builds our knowledge of the social world as well as the physical world.

Emotional Learning

Emotions are chemicals that affect the way neurons work. Imagine a dog barking in a baby's face. The child feels threatened and threat chemicals pave his neurons like asphalt on a dirt road. In the future, electricity will flow down that road more easily. Of course, the child may also have happy experiences with a dog and build a happy chemical connection as well.

We've all had emotional moments that we remember in great detail. Emotions alert a body to the presence of something very relevant to survival, whether positive or negative. Your brain connects everything going on at these important moments so it can promote your survival in the future. The connections will help you avoid similar threats and approach similar rewards.

For example, imagine you see a friend become violently ill after eating berries from a certain plant. You only need to see that once in order to have the berry plant etched into your brain. Seeing your friend in pain triggers emotions that link all the neurons you are firing at that moment. If you encounter a similar plant in the future, your well-developed neural pathway will light up and that will activate your emergency warning system. Decades later, you could be foraging for berries with your grandchildren and be able to warn them of the danger. Before food came with labels, this is how humans survived.

Emotions etch positive experiences as well as negative ones. If you were starving and found a healthy berry plant, you'd remember its location in the future. The thrill of finding it activates a burst of dopamine that makes permanent changes in your synapses.

This learning mechanism has obvious survival value. Young mammals learn to find food simply by observing their mothers foraging for food. Before language evolved, our ancestors learned to feed themselves by repeatedly observing their parents' hunting and gathering. They observed the happy and unhappy reactions of others in the quest for food. They felt pleasure when they found something to eat and they felt pain when they went hungry. In this way, young primates learned survival skills long before there was formal verbal learning. We are always using this learning mechanism alongside our formal training systems.

The mammal brain guides survival learning in a way that is both obvious and widely overlooked. Happy chemicals are released when we experience something we perceive as good for our survival. Unhappy chemicals are released when we experience something we perceive as bad for our survival. This simple system prepares us to do what it takes to survive automatically.

We start storing survival relevant information as soon as we're born. Imagine a newborn baby crying for milk. He screams fiercely without actually knowing what milk is. He is crying because low blood sugar activates his emergency alert system. And it works: milk trickles into his mouth. His blood sugar rises, and happy chemicals replace the unhappy chemicals. The baby's brain connects the milk to that sense of relief and satisfaction. Continued repetition trains the brain to connect the milk to a person who brings it. Without effort or intention, a baby starts building awareness of other people before it has an awareness of itself.

A baby doesn't need sophisticated concepts about survival to start learning. It simply stores experiences that cause pain or pleasure. A young brain soon realizes that other people can cause pain or pleasure. Early experience with other people builds wiring that we bring to later experience. As social experience accumulates, we add branches to the circuits we already have.

Auto Pilot for Social Behavior

When a baby drops his bottle, he hears a sound. At first, he doesn't understand the link between the sound and the bottle. But after a few repetitions, he comes to expect a sound when a bottle drops. Babies often drop things intentionally to see if their expectations are confirmed. We don't need theoretical knowledge of gravity to have a neural representation of it. Experience is all we need.

We learn about people in the same way. A baby sees his caretaker react when he drops his bottle. After a few repetitions, he comes to expect the caretaker's reaction. He may even drop the bottle on purpose to test his prediction.

Soon, these expectations become so automatic that the baby stops noticing them. For the rest of his life, he will expect a sound when he drops something and not notice that expectation unless the sound fails to happen for some reason. It's the same with expectations about people – you tend not to notice your expectations until someone fails to meet them.

Our brains gradually fill up with expectations about how people act. These expectations become as automatic as our expectations about gravity.

Every child builds expectations about the reactions he will get from the world. Experiences with our earliest caretakers build the circuits that provide a foundation for later social experience. In short, your brain expects the world to treat you the way your family treated you. Of course, experience changes things, but not as much as you'd think because your old wiring is part of your new experiences.

Early experiences vary but they have much in common. All of us start out being unable to meet our own needs. Every mammal requires protection until it has learned what it takes to provide for its own survival. Mammals take longer to become self-sufficient than other animals, and a species would die out if its young lost support before they became self-sufficient. The mammal brain evolved attachment to solve this problem.

A newborn mammal produces oxytocin, which motivates it to attach to another. This urge is as strong as the urge to eat and breathe because it is equally important to survival. A baby antelope's survival rests on its ability to stay with its mother even while the herd is stampeding. The mother tracks the baby, but survival prospects improve when the baby's brain actively tracks the mother as well. The baby's brain floods with fear chemicals if he becomes separated from his mother, and with happy oxytocin when they're reunited. This motivates him to stay near his mother long before he's aware of the actual dangers he needs protection from.

A baby mammal cannot understand its own vulnerability. It just responds to its neurochemicals. It does things that stimulate happy chemicals and avoids things that stimulate unhappy chemicals. That promotes survival automatically.

A mammal's attachment to its mother gradually develops into an attachment to the herd. The mammal brain evolved to maintain awareness of the herd at all times. No self-respecting human sees himself as a herd-follower. But our ancestors were more likely to survive if they stuck with the group. Natural selection created a brain that feels good with a group and bad when alone.

Herd behavior promotes survival because predators target the easiest prey. A lion does not attack the antelope at the center of the herd. It attacks a straggler. A mammal can avoid a predator's strike zone by pushing its way to the center of the herd, and that's what the stronger mammals do.

Weaker mammals gain protection from a herd too, thanks to a behavior called isopraxism – the tendency to mimic the behavior of others. (Iso-praxis means "same practice.") For example, when an eagle swoops over a pack of prairie dogs, they all put their heads down. A prairie dog whose head is still sticking up while others are down is the most likely to get snatched by an eagle, and the least likely to pass on his genes. Natural selection rewards the critter who knows when to keep his head down.

Mammals constantly watch their herd mates. The instant one mammal starts to run, every individual in the herd or pack or troop starts to run. The last guy to run when the rest take off is the most likely to become the predator's lunch. Predators do not target the dumbest or slowest critter in the herd – they target the most detached.

A mammal survives by responding quickly when a comrade shows signs of alarm. A lot of false positives may result, but in the end natural selection rewards caution. An antelope who thinks, "I'm not going to run unless I see the lion for myself," is more likely to die young. We can only be descended from mammals who stayed alive long enough to raise children.

Humans pride themselves on their individuality, yet herd behavior is a constant in human affairs. The reason is simple: it works. Groups really do offer protection. When you leave the safety of the herd, your mammal brain reacts strongly in order to warn you that your survival is threatened.

If you look at a painting from any time period, you will see that people are dressed like each other. Extreme differences in clothing occur across time and place, yet within each human group, the variation is relatively small. This is isopraxism at work. Clothing can't protect humans from predators. But sticking out attracts predators in a way that our mammal brain understands and wants to avoid.

Primates are well equipped to mimic their peers, thanks to their mirror neurons. When we watch others act, our mirror neurons fire as if we were acting ourselves. Repetition and emotion build these reactions into our wiring. No effortful practice is necessary; it's all automatic.

In this way, children build neural circuits that mirror the social behavior around them. We build these circuits so early and rely on them so often that we cannot be aware of them. Later experience may build new layers onto our social awareness, but our early experience automatically influences that later experience.

In nature, an ape is almost never found without a troop. Occasionally, an ape gets lost in the forest because he failed to keep an eye out for others. Infrequently, an ape gets ostracized from the group because he offended too many troop mates. But most apes are able to sustain a bond with a group because their brains spend years building neural circuits for getting along with others. A young ape builds this knowledge automatically, without effort or intention.

Humans learn to find safety in social bonds, but we also like individuality. These opposing impulses create internal conflict. An antelope has little inner conflict while stampeding with its herd. It doesn't say, "I want to trust my pals, but I worry about that cliff up ahead." Hesitation would get it killed, so AutoPilot is a lifesaver. A human cortex is large enough to construct alternative scenarios. Humans are troubled by their mammal brain's inclination toward isopraxism. And we are troubled when the herd seems to trample our individuality. But we are also troubled when we're isolated. Again, there's no easy way to be a big cortex attached to a mammal brain.

The human desire for individuality is unique in the animal kingdom. To the human mind, individual recognition is necessary for survival. That's because we are born in a more vulnerable state than other mammals. A newborn human cannot survive unless their individual needs are recognized. Every human brain starts life experiencing extreme dependency on the recognition of others. The urgent need to be heard and understood is our first experience in life, even though we're not consciously aware of it. Let us look closer at this universal human experience.

The Evolutionary Roots of Our AutoPilot

A human infant is the most vulnerable creature on earth. A newborn elephant learns to walk before its first sip of milk, since that's the only way it can reach the nipple. A wildebeest can run from a hyena an hour after it's born. A two-month-old mouse is sexually mature, making it a grandparent at four months of age. Human maturation is extraordinarily slow.

Monkeys develop slowly too, but a newborn monkey can hold onto its mother as she swings through the trees. The helplessness of the human infant is unparalleled in nature.

Humans survive because we get an enormous amount of individual attention as children. Being ignored means death to a human infant. We have no clear memory of our early vulnerability. But our first experience in life – the first awareness stored in our neurons – is the sense of being in distress and powerless to do anything about it. This sense of vulnerability is emotional and repeated, so it develops a neural circuit. We don't notice the circuit because it has always been there. Some babies experience more vulnerability than others, but every human is born fragile and dependent.

Why would natural selection produce such a helpless bit of protoplasm? What possible survival advantage could there be in birthing a child who cannot support its own body weight for a year, and cannot support itself and its offspring for decades?

Research has uncovered a surprising answer: humans are born prematurely. At birth we are uncannily similar to premature chimpanzees. Big brains caused our ancestors to be born preterm, with astounding consequences.

It appears that proto-humans got born ever early as their brains grew too large to fit through the birth canal. Instead of developing fully in utero, a big-brained primate is born when its nervous system is incomplete. Where most creatures are born with a nervous system that's already hooked up, we humans connect ours by way of experience after we're born. That's why we're so different from each other.

Brains grew larger when ancestral mothers got more fat and protein. This outcome fed on itself: bigger brains enabled more social cooperation, which supplied pregnant and nursing mothers with more fat and protein, causing bigger brains and more social cooperation.

But bigger brains meant getting born in a less developed, more vulnerable state. Other mammals can function soon after birth because their brains are already wired to their senses and their limbs. Humans are born with neurons that are not connected to anything. We have more neurons, but fewer connections between them. This left us extremely helpless, but it also led to amazing survival advantages.

First, it enabled us to wire ourselves for the ecological niche we happen to be born into instead of coming pre-adapted to one niche. Animals tend to die outside the ecosystem they evolved in. Their behavior is not very flexible because their genes code for more specific neural connections at birth. Humans are born with the ability to make connections rather than with the connections themselves. Thus, we have the potential to survive in a wider range of environments. We wire ourselves by interacting with the world we find ourselves in – the physical world and the social world. We build the wiring for behaviors that promote survival in the place we're in.

Our prematurity brought a second big advantage: it forced us to communicate. A newborn human is so helpless that it cannot survive without communicating its needs. Many babies died in the past. But some babies were better at signaling their needs, and some mothers were better at interpreting the signals. Babies who got their needs met lived to pass on their genes and their mother's genes. We were thus naturally selected for the ability to communicate.

Human communication begins long before we have words. Babies signal their mothers in many different ways. Research makes it clear that babies give feedback specific enough to get their needs met. A mother responds to a baby's signals, and soon a baby responds to its mother's signals.

Thus, a baby quickly learns to expect something from others. One of the first neural connections we make in life – the foundation on which later thoughts get layered, is the impulse to relieve distress by getting the attention of others.

Mother-infant interactions vary widely, which is one reason our AutoPilot varies so widely. But beneath this uniqueness is something eerily common: a sense of urgency about being noticed. Every living human was once a helpless infant unable to meet its own needs. Every brain survived by having its specific needs acknowledged, understood, and taken care of. The urge to be recognized as an individual is thus the common heritage of big-headed premature primates.

Every group of humans is made of individuals for whom a lack of recognition is akin to a survival threat. Of course no one thinks this consciously, but we can often see it in others.

Automatic Learning about Survival

Having extra neurons doesn't automatically promote survival. It does just the opposite. Neurons consume so much energy and oxygen that they make it harder to survive. Neurons consume more oxygen than muscles that are running. A big brain forces a creature to work harder just to stay alive.

Extra neurons only promote survival if the benefits are more than the costs. Those neurons must be connected in ways that provide survival knowledge. Such connections take a long time to build, and that explains why mammals have long childhoods. The length of a mammal's childhood correlates closely with the size of its cortex. The more neurons a creature has, the longer it takes to develop them into something worthwhile.

A mouse's childhood is only three weeks long, but that's infinitely longer than the zero childhood of a lizard. A wolf is a juvenile for twenty times as long as a mouse, and a baboon doubles the childhood of a wolf. A chimpanzee takes six years to become independent, fitting neatly between monkeys and humans in both brain size and juvenile dependency.

Maturing slowly is a risky approach to reproductive success, but if it evolved it must have advantages. The advantage of having fewer children and investing in each one is that each one is more likely to survive.

Mammals protect each child with great vigilance. But there's more to survival than protection. Children must develop the skills it takes to survive without their parents are gone in order for a species to live on. Mammals prepare their children for self-sufficiency while protecting them. They do this in a manner that is likely to shock humans: they don't feed their kids – except for breast milk. If a young mammal wants solids to eat, he has to get it himself. So he does. (Some carnivores are exceptions because hunting skills take longer to develop than foraging.)

A little monkey get no nourishment except mother's milk until he develops the skill of grasping edibles. Monkey brains are perfectly evolved for developing this skill. When a young monkey sits in his mother's lap, he watches her feed herself. He is close to her mouth and hands, so he easily sees what she is doing. Crumbs fall on her chest right near his mouth and he is curious. He has the impulse to grasp the crumbs and put them in his mouth. But his fingers are not coordinated, so he has to invest time and effort before he gets the reward.

This all happens automatically. No one designed a curriculum to optimize his hand-eye coordination. A contingent reward is all it takes. He only gets the food if he performs the action. Breast milk sustains him long enough to learn. He is motivated by curiosity and imitation more than hunger because he doesn't understand the reward of food before his first bite. But if he takes too long to learn, breast milk is not enough nutrition and neurochemical hunger kicks in as an extra motivator. Better he go hungry now than after Mom is gone.

Junior progresses from eating Mom's crumbs to eating Mom's leftovers. A mother drops leaves while foraging, and her child picks them up and eats them. The food gives him a good feeling, so he starts picking leaves off trees as his mother picks. Over time, through repetition, his brain comes to recognize the precise leaves and trees that Mom chooses.

When Mom cracks open a nut and picks out the meat, Junior goes for the crumbs in the shell. Then he starts imitating Mom's nut-cracking behaviors.

Cracking open a nut is a difficult skill that takes a long time to master. Young primates can spend years failing before they succeed. I once watched a little monkey struggle with a nut for fifteen minutes. It upset me so much that I went and talked to a zookeeper. She dismissed my concerns, telling me he was well-nourished and just playing. My urge to "help" is not the way of mother monkeys. If it were, their offspring might not develop survival skills and we might not be here today.

Young primates learn about other individuals as they learn about food. For example, a young ape may get bitten and scratched by a bigger ape when it reaches for a piece of food. He learns that grabbing food can have unpleasant consequences. He learns how to manage these consequences at his Mother's knee. He observes Mom seizing food from some individuals and yielding food to others. After years of trial and error, a primate develops a neural network that tells it when to take food and when to restrain the urge to take food. Conscious study of the social hierarchy is not necessary. The brain simply consolidates the neural pathways that were most triggered by repetition and emotion.

A human child likewise builds pathways that reflect the rewards and pains of its daily experience. Children are learning survival skills long before they have conscious awareness of their long-term needs. If survival learning depended on a child's sense of personal responsibility, survival prospects would be bleak. Instead, our mammalian neurochemicals guide us toward survival behaviors.

Each neurochemical triggers distinct experiences, which builds distinct neural pathways.

Experience with oxytocin wires us up to know when it is safe to trust others.

Experience with dopamine wires us up predict valuable rewards.

Experience with serotonin builds circuits to enjoy mastery of our surroundings.

And endorphins wire us up to triumph over physical pain.

This neurochemical guidance helps us boot up the systems that are unfinished when we're born.

These systems get a lot of attention when they fail. Neurochemical dysfunctions distract us from appreciating just how much goes right when human beings function at all. Most of the time our neurochemistry works and we barely notice it. From the flimsiest beginnings, we develop into competent survivors. Instead of berating our failure to live up to some hypothetical ideal, it's important to recognize the complexity of the human contraption. Disdain for our species is often expressed without recognizing how well our hybrid brain succeeds at its survival function. Our brains do not produce happiness at every moment because that is not the job they evolved to do.

Early experience varies so widely that we end up with different expectations about what will make us happy. We arrive at schools and workplaces with individualized expectations about how people interact. These expectations can leave us feeling that something is not quite right with other people. But we need to navigate that world-of-other-people in order to meet our needs. Learning about the behavior of others is central to our ability to promote our legacy and stimulate our happy chemicals.

You Mean I've Been Using AutoPilot All These Years?

Imagine seeing a co-worker who's just back from vacation. He looks different but you can't put your finger on why. Did he lose weight? Change his hair? Plastic surgery? You feel foolish. Your brain contrasts the image it sees with its stored image of the coworker. You know there's a contrast but you can't pinpoint it.

Your brain is not stupid – it's efficient. Its image of your co-worker had only as much detail as necessary to interact with him. Your well-worn neural pathway was perfectly adequate as long as the world stayed the same. You didn't notice your pathway when it worked; you only noticed when it failed. Your AutoPilot developed to meet your needs, not to be a comprehensive encyclopedia.

The limits of AutoPilot are revealed when you try to give someone directions to your home. It should be easy since you make your way home every day. But we rarely find our way home by reading written signs. You might pass a sign every day without reading it because you are relying on experiential cues instead. Perhaps you have learned to pull over into the exit lane once you pass a red building. You do this automatically, without knowing that's your strategy. When you have to give someone else directions, you're at a loss and you don't know why.

AutoPilot is so efficient that something feels wrong with the world when you have to function without it for any reason. I experienced this when I cooked my first dinner in a new home. I was thrilled by the new house, but soon became very frustrated. Cooking is usually a series of automatic actions. In my old house, I could boil water without thinking about it. But in the new house each motion took thought – where is the pot? where is the faucet? how do you turn it on? where is the stove? My AutoPilot didn't work, so my higher powers got used up on the simple things. That made it harder to keep the big picture of the meal in mind. My unhappy chemicals surged and I got angry at the new kitchen. I didn't know the real source of the problem because I had never been aware of my cooking AutoPilot. But in a short time I forgot to hate the house because a new AutoPilot built up in my brain. I was back to my usual routine of cooking at the speed of light. Of course, I didn't notice my new AutoPilot as I reached for the pot and turned on the water. But the next time I moved into a new house, I understood the adjustment problem and didn't blame the house.

When you're in a new environment, your old AutoPilot doesn't work. Something feels wrong and you don't know why. It's easy to blame the new environment. The same problem arises if you move to a new social environment. Your old AutoPilot fails, but you never knew you had it so you can't identify the problem.

It's easy to blame the world around you instead. Many people start hating the world the way I hated my beautiful new kitchen. Advice-mongers tell us we should not do things on automatic. This advice is unrealistic. We spend a lifetime building neural pathways because we need them to function efficiently.

Automatic "isms"

In college I knew a girl whose attention was focused on racism and sexism. She often condemned the wrongs of the world, and was good at getting others to listen. One day I asked her opinion about some readings for a class we were both in. I was genuinely seeking her views. She told me it was obviously racism and sexism. I didn't see her point so I asked for more specifics. She suddenly got angry at me. I had a feeling she hadn't done the reading, so I backed off. We didn't talk much after that, and I blamed myself.

This girl became a prominent student leader so I often heard about her. One day I ran into her and expressed interest in a prominent campaign she'd been leading. I sincerely wanted to know more about it. She got angry at my innocent questions. At first, I blamed myself again. But as I read more about her in the student news, I realized that she had learned to raise her status by making blanket condemnations. If you questioned her opinions, you threatened her status, and she defended it the way an alpha defends his position against all challengers.

Years later, I worked alongside a man who frequently accused people of destroying the Earth. He surrounded himself with allies who agreed with him. He was very successful in his career, and amassed rewards that he shared with his allies. I saw people court his attention by accusing people of destroying the Earth. And it worked – their status rose and so did his.

When I heard their accusations, my mind would search for evidence. If I didn't see the evidence, I asked questions. "You don't get it," his allies would bark at me in a dominant tone. Over time, their status rose and mine did not, so I had little interaction with them. But this time I did not blame myself. I understood that mammals hunt in groups because it improves the rewards. I was glad I had enough to survive without having to join their pack. I get to decipher evidence for myself instead of submitting to their definition of "getting it."

The Persistence of Automatic Social Habits

I once belonged to a ladies' tennis ladder. Each lady was ranked by ability. To establish our rankings, we were obligated to challenge another club member twice a year. You'd take her rank if you won, and you'd stay where you were if you lost. This made sense because tennis is more fun when you play with people of similar ability. Even when a group is more social than competitive, some objective way of ranking skills helps to keep it fun.

I found it difficult to call another lady and challenge her to a tennis match. It should have been easy because the club spelled out the etiquette for making a challenge. But my experience with organized sports was limited. I was just not used to issuing challenges. It turns out that many of the ladies felt the same way. Few of us honored our semi-annual commitment. The Board of Directors declared that we would be dropped to the bottom of the ladder if we didn't make our challenges. But we still didn't do it.

The fact is, we were the Board of Directors. We refuseniks had to rotate through the positions on the Board to keep the club going. We knew what we should do, but we didn't do it.

This story has another wrinkle. The tennis club had an "A Ladder" and a "B Ladder." Most of the A ladies did their challenging duty, while most of the lawless ones, like myself, were B players. The A players seemed to have more experience with athletic customs and institutions, and they enjoyed playing at a more competitive level. It would not be correct to say that the A ladies cared more about status. We B ladies cared about status in other areas of life. Each of us seeks happiness with the neural pathways we happen to have.

A system emerged that gave everyone what they needed. We B ladies did our own thing and anyone who wanted to play more seriously was free to challenge her way up to the A Ladder. The A ladies enjoyed the competitive play that the rules produced. The B ladies enjoyed the casual play that a casual attitude toward the rules produced. This system allowed a large number of people to sustain an alliance whose existence benefited all of them. We had tournaments and awarded separate prizes to each ladder: a cheap wine glass with the club logo.

The system would have been ruined for everyone if a B lady insisted on playing in the A ladder without winning her challenges. It's not easy to create a mammalian alliance that allows many people to seek happiness in their own diverse ways.

We are always seeking happiness because any burst of neurochemical happiness lasts for such a short time. When we find a strategy that stimulates our happy chemicals, we are disposed to repeat it over and over.

When we repeat a behavior often, any side effects it has are repeated too. The mammal brain doesn't think about the long-term side effects of its habits because it focuses on the here and now. The human cortex, by contrast, can imagine future consequences of today's actions. But the cortex has a curiously hard time over-riding the mammal brain. A behavior that triggers a burst of happiness today can feel more relevant to survival than abstract projections of cumulative negative side-effects.

We are strongly motivated to repeat a behavior once we've linked it to our happy chemicals, regardless of the side-effects. That is why the pursuit of status and happiness seems to hurt survival prospects more than it helps. The following chapter explores this curious feature of the human brain.

Chapter 6

Self-destructive Status Seeking

...A dog wastes a lot of saliva before it gives up on the steak...

I learned a lot about self-destructive status seeking from a hypnotist who helps people quit smoking. "Imagine you're a fourteen year-old boy wanting to talk to a girl at a party," he told me. "You're afraid it will go badly, and you decide to try a cigarette to steady your nerves. Then you talk to her, and she likes you. Your brain builds a connection between the cigarette and the joy of success. Logically you know that smoking didn't cause the success, but the next time you face a challenge the thought of smoking pops into your mind. Over the years, you build up the connection. Now imagine that you suddenly decide to quit smoking. The insecurity of the fourteen year-old surges up the moment you resist the urge for a cigarette. Smoking is the way your brain learned to manage those feelings. If you don't build a new way to channel them, you will feel like you're going to die every time you pass up a cigarette."

The smoker's brain "learned" that smoking promotes survival. He may not consciously believe that, but his mammal brain connects smoking with getting the girl. Anything relevant to reproductive success gets the brain's attention. To that young man's brain, smoking works.

If you go out and conquer the world after your smoke, your drink, your shopping, or any other habit, you build a neural connection between the habit and success. To your brain, the habit works.

When a smoker tries not to smoke, it feels like a threat to his survival. Without his reliable source of happy chemicals, he is left with the unhappy chemicals that trigger a sense of threat. The threat feels bigger without the usual happy chemicals flowing.

Smoking does not raise your status in the modern world, and fortunately many people avoid smoking these days. But we all turn on our happy chemicals with circuits we built from past experience. Once something triggers your happy chemicals, your brain marks it as something valuable for your survival. The chemicals build real physical pathways in your brain. Whatever made you happy in the past is likely to have appeal in the future, even if it's something misguided or inconsequential when viewed from another perspective. The more you activate that happy circuit, the more you build connections that automatically activate it in the face of future survival challenges. This is why coping strategies can have negative side effects that undermine your survival.

The negative side effects mount up when you rely on a strategy often and automatically. You may notice the unfortunate consequences, and feel bad about them. The bad feeling triggers the desire for something that makes you feel good. This can automatically trigger the very habit that is making you feel bad. Addiction is a neural pathway that triggers the expectation of a reward. That expectation feels good immediately, even if the future side-effects feel bad. Your brain wants happy chemicals, and seeks them in the ways it has already learned. The electricity in your brain seeks the path of least resistance.

So you're inclined to repeat a "survival strategy" you have already learned, even if it hurts your survival.

You wouldn't expect natural selection to produce such a flawed system. How could a brain that evolved for survival develop habits that impair survival? This chapter shows that the mammal brain has a few blind spots in the way it perceives survival. You can get happy chemicals from your mammal brain while overlooking significant threats. We will explore three specific blind spots.

The first blind spot is your mammal brain's tendency to put the survival interests of your DNA above the survival interests of your body. A race-car driver is a simple example. Like a peacock with a big tail, his risky behavior can raise his status with females and with other males. Mating opportunities are likely to result. His body may die young, but he will have an abundance of chances to pass on his genes before that. He is not trying to have children, but the mammal brain evolved at a time when status, mating, and reproduction were inseparable. So if car racing raises your status, your mammal brain rewards it with happy chemicals, and that motivates more car racing. The riskiness of this behavior is easy to ignore while prospects for your legacy are skyrocketing.

Sometimes, what's good for your legacy is not good for your body. When that happens, your mammal brain tends to favor your legacy. That's why the smoker who gets the girl isn't so worried about his lungs and the dieter who gets the guy isn't worried about her nutrition. When romance triggers happy chemicals, your mammal brain "learns" from the experience in ways that need not obey the laws of logic. Such "junk learning" is blind spot number two.

Junk learning is routine for the mammal brain because it learns from experience. Sometimes the lessons of experience are just-plain wrong. For example, if you win the lottery the first time you buy a ticket, your brain will learn that buying a lottery ticket brings success. The happy chemicals released when you win pave the neural pathways active at that moment, making it easier to turn happiness on in that way in the future. You may understand statistics quite well. But your happy chemicals circuits are just as real as statistics. When you want to feel good, thinking about statistics doesn't turn on your happy chemicals. Buying lottery tickets is where your mind goes, even though it's junk learning.

The third blind spot is the mammal brain's limited ability to anticipate the future. Animals try to anticipate danger to protect themselves, but their ability to predict is limited. Ignoring the future has survival value in its own way; a mammal that delayed action until all potential future risks were eliminated would never do anything. Instead, the mammal brain scans for immediate danger and then goes for it.

Sometimes mammals fail. More animals die of injuries than of old age. Animals can't eliminate risk from their lives, so they concentrate on reproducing as soon as possible. The bigger a mammal's cortex, the more it can analyze potential risks. But no matter how skillful the analysis, success is impossible unless the brain initiates action at some point. This ability to move from deliberating to action resides in the mammal brain. It reduces things down to the urge to move toward something good and the urge to withdraw from something bad.

Humans have a brain region for anticipating future consequences that animals do not have. Our pre-frontal cortex supports sophisticated foresight. But researchers were surprised to find that the emotional brain makes our final decisions. Our higher intelligence simply reports its findings to the mammal brain, which blends these abstractions with our mammalian notion of our interests. This is a good thing, because our pre-frontal cortex can always find evidence of potential harm. If we did nothing until our cortex found a risk-free alternative, we would be at standstill and that would be even riskier. We inherited the ability to damn the torpedoes and speed ahead.

These three blind spots in our mammalian inheritance make self-destructive status seeking possible. Our brains are disposed to repeat status-seeking strategies even when they do us harm. Sometimes the self-destructiveness is obvious, like getting behind the wheel of a car when you're drunk. But often the damage is subtle. For example, a person may get into the habit of raising their status by being oppositional. They may hurt themselves with their oppositionalism, but keep repeating the strategy anyway. At the end of this chapter, we will explore a few subtly self-destructive strategies, such as one-upmanship, rescuing, doomsaying, and busyness.

We rarely think of ourselves as status seekers. We think we are just doing our best to survive. But once our survival needs are met, we tend to seek something more. The something-more feels necessary for your survival because it is necessary for more happy chemicals. People are tempted to risk what they already have to seek that something-more. When you are taking these risks, you feel sure that what you seek is vital and necessary. But when you see other people risk what they have to get more, you see there are blind spots. Risking what you have for the sake of status is something we don't see ourselves doing, but we easily see it in others.

Every brain has learned happiness-seeking strategies from past experience. We don't notice our own strategies, but other people's strategies often get our attention. I spent a few summer weekends in the Hamptons in the 1970s, and the suntan strategy got my attention. Everyone seemed to be "working on their tan" with a strange intensity. In a social setting like the Hamptons, people worry about their status. The mind wants to do something about it, but we often have little control over social hierarchies. Tanning is something you can control, so many people focused on that. If you weren't as popular as you'd like, there was something you could do about it: get tanner.

Some people tanned themselves to the point of self-destruction. Others became popular in the nick of time, or they just accepted being unpopular. And some people were driven to experiment with alternative status strategies, such as being thinner or richer or wilder, or even nicer. Every strategy, even being nice, can become self-destructive if taken too far.

It's easy to deride other people's self-destructive strategies. But when you feel dominated, your unhappy chemicals flow and you have a strong urge to do something about it. The world is always letting you know that you're not in charge. Everyone feels dominated at times, and each mind looks for ways to improve things. Anything that helps you feel better about your status restores your tranquility and soothes your sense of threat. Even a moment of status enhancement is enough to stimulate your happy chemicals, so your brain seeks that out. Your strategy leaves you feeling better for a moment, but soon you are likely to feel frustrated about your status again, and try to do something about it again.

No one thinks of smoking as a status-seeking strategy. But anything that makes you feel higher when you are feeling lower is a status-seeking strategy. It could be intoxicants, or material wealth, or beauty, or aggression, or self-righteousness, or even self-deprivation. Anything that helps you feel more secure in a precarious world is desired by your mammal brain. When a strategy works, happy chemicals etch it into your memory. When you feel dominant, the neurochemicals you release pave the pathways activated by that experience. This wires you to repeat the behavior that stimulated the neurochemicals.

Our status-seeking strategies are as unique as our individual lives. Each of us learns from our early triumphs. Maybe you won applause at school. Maybe you persuaded a sibling to give you his cookie. If it made you happy, your brain made connections, because happy chemicals are the mammal brain's guide to survival.

Gaining the respect of others feels good. The happy chemicals wire a brain to repeat whatever experience was associated with the gain. That experience may not make logical sense. It may have negative consequences. But to your mammal brain, happy chemicals mean survival. Experience may lead one person to seek happiness by running up their credit cards and another by committing credit-card fraud. One person may risk the relationship they have to seek a higher-status relationship and another may risk their life savings for the chance to add a bit to their savings. Even if you know that a behavior hurts you, your mammal brain may long to repeat it simply because respect feels good and losing respect feels bad.

Self-destructive status seeking is a paradox. People try to advance their interests in ways that hurt their interests. People pursue happiness in ways that ultimately make them less happy. The urge to repeat self-destructive behaviors seems to defy nature. Many people presume that "the culture" or "our society" causes the problem. "Our times" is another familiar rationale. But self-destructive status seeking is not unique to our time and place. Other cultures and other time periods have plenty of self-destructive status seeking if you look for it.

In pre-modern China, girls' feet were bound to raise their status. Families would start inflicting painful bindings on their daughters as soon as they reached subsistence income levels. Bound feet meant desirability on the marriage market. Men preferred brides who were effectively crippled because it showed the world that they didn't need their wife's labor. Bound feet also raised parents' status by showing the world that the parents didn't need their daughter's labor.

Bound feet are a status symbol because they say "I have so much to spare that I can risk handicapping myself." Biologists observe "handicapping" in animal competition for mates. The most famous example is the peacock's tail. It is self-destructive because it dangerously reduces a male's mobility. But the tail raises his status with the ladies enough to pass on his genes before a predator gets him.

Handicapping is still with us. Women wear high heels that reduce their mobility but enhance their reproductive success. Extreme thinness is another form of handicapping. It raises your status while making you less physically robust. Starving destroys your quality of life, but can earn you the respect of others. Modern forms of self-destructive status seeking are variations on a very old theme.

How can a brain that evolved for reproductive success reach the conclusion that hobbling or starving one's self are good ways to get ahead? This brain we've inherited tends to overlook the side effects of a behavior that seems to promote reproductive success. Your mammal brain decides what's good for you in a way that seems irrational until you take an evolutionary perspective on your well-being.

Blind Spot #1: The Quest for Immortality

All creatures die, so all brains ultimately fail in their effort to sustain life. But the brain keeps striving to prolong life despite the inevitability of its failure. Creating children is one of the mammal brain's strategies for promoting life. Animals do this automatically, but humans use their extra neurons to create abstract legacies instead of, or in addition to, having children. We build pyramids, create art, help the needy, and send children to good colleges, all in an attempt to create something that will outlive us.

Your mammal brain is always dividing your energy between efforts to survive in the present and efforts to create a legacy for the future. Animals do this without cogitation. For example, a reindeer grows antlers that are too large for his own good. His antlers attract females and in turn he creates a legacy, even though the big antlers make it harder for him to survive.

We often hear stories about a mother lifting a car to rescue her child. Superhuman strength seems to come from nowhere when it's needed to protect one's legacy. When these mothers are interviewed afterward, they typically say they didn't think about it. The strength does not come from the part of the brain that thinks verbally and analytically. The mammal brain releases a surge of neurochemicals that give you strength when your legacy is at stake.

Your mammal brain cares more about your legacy than your body. When it sees opportunities to advance your legacy, it seizes the moment, even at the expense of your physical well-being. Just how your brain defines your legacy depends on your individual stock of life experience. It might be a flock of grandchildren, but it can be many other things too. A childless woman might pour her energy into starting a school. A man who already has two wives and many children might channel his energy into building a prestigious organization. A young artist might starve and go dateless to pursue glory in artistic recognition. An elderly couple might pour all their energy into efforts to raise the status of one spoiled grandchild. We mammals want to leave something behind, even if we have to hurt ourselves to do it.

Since a mammal will die eventually no matter how careful it is, it makes sense for the brain to divert some survival energy to things that will outlive the body. Animals can only do this in one way: reproduction. But the human brain can find infinite ways of creating something that will live on. The neurochemical drives that motivate a mammal to create and nurture offspring can motivate any pursuit that you believe will perpetuate yourself after you die. It could be a bottle cap collection. It could be the perfect crime. Anything you decide will make people remember you will make your neurochemicals flow, even to the point of putting your present welfare at risk.

Mammals did not evolve to care about bottle cap collections. But they did evolve to care about status. You may not see status in a bottle cap collection, but for the person whose collection brings recognition from others the happy chemicals triggered are as real as the ones in a person who donates a new wing to a hospital. Anything that raises your perception of your status gets your neurochemicals flowing.

Status advances a mammal's legacy. It helps get attention to your creations and get better mating partners for you and your children and your grandchildren. Your neurochemical system stays tuned to what helps and hurts your legacy, however you happen to define it. Happy chemicals flow when prospects for your legacy advance, motivating you to do more for your legacy to get more happy chemicals.

The mammal brain weighs the risks of action against the risk of inaction. In the animal world, inaction means annihilation of your DNA. You don't consciously worry about that, nor does a salmon swimming upstream to spawn consciously worry about it. But the brain always weighs the danger of disappearing without a trace, even as it weighs immediate threats to your safety.

The mammal brain doesn't use probability analysis to decide between asserting itself or playing it safe. It uses neurochemicals. Serotonin flows when you dominate and dopamine flows when you dominate more than expected. The dopamine tells you "Wahoo! That works!" You remember the "Wahoo!" because the chemicals create neural connections. The more happy chemicals you learn to expect, the more any risk seems worthwhile. Risk may trigger fear chemicals , but those extra neurochemicals tend to beef up the neural circuit. This makes it easy to embark on the risky road to higher status.

Past successes do not make you happy. They made neural circuits for future successes, but you have to keep activating those circuits to get more happy chemicals. So if you own a plastics factory and have a nice family, that doesn't keep your mammal brain happy. If you are an award-winning artist with a scrapbook full of press clippings, that doesn't make your mammal brain happy. If you won a medal for rescuing hundreds of refugees from a shipwreck, it doesn't keep you happy. The happy chemicals stopped flowing shortly after those things happened. Then your mammal brain started scanning for new opportunities to get a surge of happy chemicals. You are driven to promote your legacy again and again, even at the risk of your health, wealth, and social bonds, because that's what makes the mammal brain happy.

If you think about being insignificant, unhappy chemicals flow. Animals don't think in words about being insignificant, just as they don't think about having large families. But they never stop trying to advance their legacy and stimulate their happy chemicals. They don't say "I've had enough reproductive success so I'm opting out of the rat race." They just keep producing more rats. Male chimps hold onto their positions in the dominance hierarchy as long as their waning strength can intimidate new challengers. Female chimps keep reproducing until they reach an advanced age. (Research shows that male chimps prefer older females to younger ones, and for good reason – the children of older mothers have higher survival rates because they have more parenting experience.)

Your brain constantly faces opportunities to take risks in pursuit of your personal legacy. If you go for it and succeed, you enjoy large shots of dopamine at the finish line. You enjoy nice shots of serotonin when others applaud your brilliance. You enjoy oxytocin as you bond with allies. If you don't take risks, you may be safer in some ways, but you won't have this flow of happy chemicals. This is why people are disposed toward behaviors they've already linked to success, even if the links have no obvious logic.

Blind Spot #2: Junk Learning

The brain relies on past learning, but some of what we learn is just plain wrong. Personal experience feels real and true, even when it teaches you a bad lesson. For example, imagine winning at a slot machine. Lights flash, money pours, people look on with envy, and happy chemicals surge. Your brain constructs the idea that happiness comes from gambling. Such junk learning stays with you because those emotional chemicals cements neural pathways.

Of course you're smarter than that. But if you won at a Las Vegas craps table when you were young, and a pile of chips was pushed toward you in front of a glamorous crowd, your brain would have "learned" on a deep level that gambling feels good. You might lose at craps in the future, but your neural link between gambling and happiness would still be there. A new link might build between gambling and unhappiness as you keep losing. But the unhappiness of losing at craps sends you searching for a way to cheer up....and playing more craps is the idea your brain comes up with. Your brain looks for way to triumph, and it draws on what it knows to do that.

Probably you don't play craps. But you had some other triumph when you were young that fused a connection, and that prompts you to repeat a particular strategy over and over. Learning from experience makes sense because in nature the past is a pretty good guide to the future. If a certain tree had fruit last year, there's a pretty good chance it will have fruit this year. Remembering this year's fruit trees is a pretty good way to ensure next year's survival.

Formal education guides us with intentional learning, but our brains fill up with unintentional, or experiential learning as well. Some of our experiential learning is a good guide to life, and some of it isn't. If we could easily weed out the bad lessons, life would be simple. But we cannot because the mammal brain equates experiential learning with survival, and clings to it for dear life.

A fascinating example of the endurance of junk learning is the case of a girl whose brain linked laughter with death. I heard this story from the psychologist she consulted for panic attacks. The girl had been in a devastating car accident as a teenager. She woke from a coma to hear that some of her friends had died. She did not remember the accident, but in treatment she remembered partying in the car that night. Laughter was the last sound she heard at the moment of impact. The psychologist explained that her brain connected the sound of laughter with the pain of the accident. When she heard laughter, her mind activated the trauma that she had otherwise closed off. Her mind "learned" that laughter signals an immediate survival threat, and it had trouble unlearning this threat indicator.

Junk learning is easy to understand when you know how the reptile brain works. Reptiles are not great at learning, except when it comes to pain. Pain is the information the reptile brain evolved to learn from. Imagine you're a lizard lying in the sun and you suddenly get snatched by an eagle. You feel pain as the eagle's claws clench your body. The pain triggers neurochemicals that connect every synapse that's active at the moment. That wires you to recognize the warning signs of an eagle attack – if you struggle to freedom and live.

One warning sign of an eagle attack is sudden darkness overhead, because an eagle blocks the sun as it swoops down. The lizard associates sudden darkness with pain because that is what it experienced at the moment it was grabbed. A lizard never "knows" what an eagle is. It simply links darkness overhead to its "run for your life" response. The sounds and smells of an eagle are also part of the pain circuit because the associated neurons were active at the moment of pain. The reptile brain efficiently learns everything it can about pain in order to triumph over survival threats.

Lizards run from threats without comprehending the source of the danger. As a result, a lizard's life is full of false positives. Its emergency escape behavior gets triggered by things that are not really dangerous. Lizards run from shadows. They run from me when I step outside, even though I would never want to step on one. But lizards have survived for millions of years with their sketchy mental model of the world. The reptile brain successfully promotes survival by honoring its experiential learning.

The girl in the car accident "learned" that laughter is a warning sign of pain. Her reptile brain did not understand a car accident conceptually – the same way that a lizard does not understand an eagle conceptually. It simply triggers her emergency alert system at the familiar warning sound. She obviously knows that laughter does not cause car accidents, but her neural link was strong because it was paved by a huge quantity of emotional chemicals. Our brains learn from experience even though experience can be a poor guide to how the world works.

A mammal learns from happy chemicals as well as unhappy chemicals. The mammal brain honors its own happy experiences. It is not inclined to ignore or unlearn them. Neurochemicals tell a brain that something is relevant to survival. The brain trusts its own operating system. How could it function otherwise?

It's easy to see how experiential learning helped our ancestors survive. Imagine you are wandering the desert feeling thirsty and you stumble on an oasis. Happy chemicals flood your brain. The chemicals etch the moment in your memory, with details of the sights and sounds. You will be able to find water the next time you are in this part of the desert. You may not consciously "know" where the oasis is, but when your senses report sights and sounds that match your oasis experience, electricity will surge through the circuits you built, and that will get your attention. You will survive by being open to your experiential learning.

Our ancestors found their way back to fruit trees and hunting and fishing grounds that were in season. They thrived by following the non-verbal prompting of past experience. The mammal brain did not evolve to ignore its own experiential learning. Once it learns something from real experience, it believes itself.

Today, we place a high value on challenging and rejecting old learning. If your grandparent told you not to eat the berries from a certain plant, you might go out of your way to sample them. But that doesn't prove you're immune to junk learning, especially in an era in which you can call 911 if it turns out your grandparent was right. We challenge our elders and that raises our status, but we pick up junk learning from our peers. We are still susceptible to junk learning because we have the same old neural equipment.

Natural selection rewarded individuals who honored their own experiential learning. Imagine a cave man who reached for a poison berry as soon as he got hungry. He would probably die young without leaving heirs. We are not likely to be descended from him. We are descended from ancestors who honored their stored learning, and resisted the poison berry even when they were hungry. Challenging old learning can be useful, but you can't survive by rejecting all accumulated experience. Determining which experiential learning is a good predictor of the future and which is junk learning is no easy matter to resolve. That's why the mammal brain relies on neurochemicals. The more pain or pleasure an experience triggered, the stronger the neural connections that recognize it.

Experiential learning is our guide to the social world as well as the physical world. When you are young, you learn that some behaviors bring social rewards while others lead to pain. Your brain absorbs the information by connecting neurons. Sometimes, alas, it's junk learning. For example, if your parents bought you an ice cream to stop you from crying, you may have learned that crying gets rewards, or that food is the way to calm yourself. If you were neglected and given a toy to "keep you happy," you may learn to expect happiness from toys. Some children get special treatment when they are cruel to others and learn to expect special treatment when they are cruel. Some children lie or steal and it gets them what they want. We're not aware of our accidental learning, but it's there the next time we look for a way to get rewards or avoid pain.

Pains and rewards experienced during adolescence build a lot of connections because of the brain's extra plasticity in puberty. A teenager may be rewarded by their peers when they do something dangerous. They may get rewards from teachers or part-time employers by way of cheating. Such experiences are stored by the mammal brain as facts about how the world works. This learning can result in self-destructive behavior in the future.

Imagine you are a teenager talking to a special someone. Joy surges if they seem interested in you too, and that etches the moment in your brain. You will rely on these details to figure out what worked in the future. If the special someone loses interest in you, pain chemicals are triggered and that etches more information. You will draw on this "knowledge" to avoid pain in the future.

Social pain is distinct from physical pain, but social rejection triggers the same threat-warning chemicals as physical pain. That's because social rejection is truly a survival threat in the animal world. Your mammal brain treats social threats as survival threats, and strives to learn from them.

As we learn from social experience, it's hard to distinguish the useful life lessons from the junk. Imagine a teenager getting applause for performing a song he wrote. Happy chemicals floods his brain, and he learns that creative expression is rewarded. That could be a useful life lesson, motivating him to work hard in expectation of rewards. Or it could be junk learning, motivating him to give up all other activities to write songs, even after numerous attempts are ignored. It depends on what else is stored in that particular brain.

Some of our accidental learning will be useful, and some will be harmful. The social world is maddeningly unpredictable. Sometimes you win the goodwill of others, and sometimes your best efforts fail. We humans try to sort it out with our pattern-seeking cortex. We analyze our stored experience in search of neat patterns. If we can figure out how the world works, we can predict rewards and threats. But our predictions cannot be perfect because our information cannot be complete. Our knowledge of the world reflects the accidents of individual experience.

Imagine that your status is soaring in a new job. Lots of rewards and promotions come your way. Now imagine landing in a great new job where everything you do is wrong. Suddenly you're at risk of being fired. What happened? Your survival rests on figuring out the patterns in your new social world. But you bring a lifetime of experience to the task. Should you discard what you learned from the past in favor of incomplete new observations?

The mammal brain values old learning. This is why it leads people to keep smoking or drinking or gambling or overeating or overspending or overworking. You see the negative feedback; but when you're out there trying to survive, the thought of discarding your proven strategy seems more dangerous than repeating the strategy.

The mammal brain is better at learning than at unlearning. A dog that learned to salivate at the sound of a bell will keep salivating for a long time when no steak appears. It wastes a lot of saliva and endures a lot of frustration before it gives up on the steak. Pavlov's dog was manipulated in a laboratory. In nature, a dog would have reason to keep expecting steak where a steak had been before. Persevering through disappointments would mean survival, not addiction.

Animals learn about the environmental niche they're born into and hold onto that learning for a lifetime. If their environment changes, they usually die. The mammal brain evolved to stick to the survival learning it has. Habits are hard to break once a mammal brain links a habit to survival. Humans can override their accumulated learning better than animals can because we have more cortex to focus on alternatives. But acting on an alternative is much harder than just imagining it. When you try to reject your own survival learning, your mammal brain perceives it as a survival threat and sounds the alarm.

Blind Spot #3: Risk Tolerance

A mammal might get eaten by a crocodile when it drinks from a watering hole. But it needs water to survive, so it tolerates the risk.

The mammal brain is good at monitoring risk, but it's also skilled at ignoring risk when necessary. A baboon sees the risk of crossing a river, but when his whole troop crosses he knows the risk of being left alone is even greater. So he ignores the risk and plunges in.

Mammals evolved to live with risk. Monkeys see the risk of snakes and leopards, but they don't try to solve the problem permanently and proactively. They stay alert for immediate warning signs, but sometimes a predator kills one of their troop mates. Monkeys don't "do something about it." They just tolerate the risk.

Mammals manage social risks the same way. Monkeys avoid conflict with more dominant troop mates instead of trying to change them. A monkey simply restrains his impulses until the dominant's back is turned. A monkey will challenge a more dominant troop mate when he feels sure of winning. He seizes safe chances to raise his status and otherwise tolerates the risk of the dominant's aggression.

A monkey's ability to predict the outcome of a conflict is not perfect. Sometimes he loses a challenge and debilitating injuries result. Yet the monkey still trusts his own judgement. If he didn't, he would never try and he'd always be at the bottom of the hierarchy. Instead, he lives with the risk of making flawed predictions.

We humans use our sophisticated cortex to prevent risk. We like to think we can avoid all risk permanently once we have good enough data. But life is not always forecastable, and if we waited for certainty we might wait forever. My son's Little League coach summed it up brilliantly when the kids saw him holding statistics on the opposing team. "Will we win?" they asked. He put down the sheet and said, "You can never be sure; that's why we play these games."

When you feel bad about your status, doing something feels better than doing nothing. The "something" you choose depends on the neural pathways you have linked to your happy chemicals. The results may not be perfect, but our brains evolved to balance the risk of action against the risk of inaction. It would be nice to have infallible forecasts so that all of our actions brought success. But the world does not fit neat patterns, and if we refused to act until all risks were eliminated, we might never act. Our mammal brains help us get past "analysis paralysis" and live in the uncertainty that is life.

Uncertainty has always been part of a life. A mammal can never be sure if a water hole is safe because crocodiles have effective camouflage. A mammal never knows the real size of his rival because mammals puff up their fur to look bigger. Mammals don't wait for an all-clear signal before they take action to meet their needs. Humans have so much analytical ability that we often defer action until all the data are in. But empirical certainty is almost impossible, so we need our mammal brain to forge ahead regardless.

The mammal brain's tendency to ignore all but immediate danger prompts a feast-or-famine approach to life. This is easy to see in traditional societies, where there are actual feasts and literal famines.

Traditional feasts were a form of status seeking that anthropologists call a "big man system." The "big man" raised his status by throwing huge dinners for everyone in the tribe or village, often multi-day affairs. He would butcher all his livestock and wipe out his food reserves in order to underwrite such festivals. The big man took a big risk to make a big impression.

For some guests, the meat offered at public festivals was an important part of an otherwise spare diet. They gladly gave their respect to the big man in exchange for food. Fathers would offer their daughters to the big man and his sons. The big man's clan thus expanded, helping him produce a bigger surplus and throw bigger feasts. In a few generations, egalitarian tribes ended up with aristocracies. No oppression or aggression was necessary – just ambitious givers and willing receivers.

But life is unpredictable, and a family that pours its reserves into a big bid for status can end up in ruin. With all its pigs slaughtered and its grain reserves spent, a family could fall to the bottom of the status hierarchy. Such a fall might destroy the big man, but the group would survive. Another status seeker would soon take the risk of holding a feast.

The pursuit of status can only drive people to ruin if they volunteer for the risk. Yet people keep volunteering. Either they are enjoying immediate rewards, or they believe big rewards are just around the corner. People seek status despite potential risks because the world is always full of potential risks.

When a smoker lights up a cigarette, he gets the courage he needs to advance his interests in a world full of risk. Of course, cigarettes add to that risk in the long run. But the immediate risk of low status may get more of the mammal brain's attention. Feeling good about your status in the short run can seem more important than a future risk that may or may not happen. To the smoker's brain, the habit promotes his welfare.

Most of us avoid smoking, but it's not necessarily because of the health statistics. Smoking lowers your status in many sub-cultures. No one wants to kiss a smoker. This status threat prevents smoking more effectively than health arguments that appeal to your intellect. The status threat links smoking to your unhappy chemicals rather than your happy chemicals.

Most people end up with some kind of self-defeating habit linked to their happy chemicals. We're often confused by our habits because the damage is so obvious while the appeal is so obscure. We don't see how our mammal brain links that appeal to our legacy. Our habits are learned from happy accidents experience, not rational planning. Once those happy chemicals make permanent changes in your brain, a behavior seems desirable even if your cortex sees that it's bad for you.

Let's say that your bad habit is cutting corners – that is, breaking the rules (and perhaps the law) when you think you can get away with it. You feel dominant when you get away with something. Maybe you're a clean-living person in other ways. Maybe you volunteer at a soup kitchen or rescue puppies. But when you see an opportunity to cut corners, you do it, and it works. So you do it again. Soon, you are committing larger and larger violations. Eventually, you are hit with large consequences. You may wonder how you got into this mess. Once your mammal brain decided that breaking the law is good for you, the risks were easier to ignore. Like smoking or splurging or any other self-destructive habit, the side effects are easy to overlook when your mammal brain thinks it's good for your legacy.

Any habit that makes you feel good about your status builds connections to your happy chemicals. The happy chemicals make the habit appealing. But the appeal is often mystifying because the mammal brain doesn't explain it in words. Few people imagine themselves tolerating risk for the sake of status, even though it's easy to see everyone else doing that.

Bad habits are easier to resist if you never "learn" them in the first place. Once you build that neural link to your happy chemicals, resisting the bad habit feels like a survival threat to your mammal brain.

Though self-destructive habits are common, we successfully avoid risk in many areas of our lives. Indeed, our brains are so conscious of risk that we need an important motive to take action. Motivation comes from neurochemicals. They guide the constant choice between seizing an opportunity and playing it safe.

This constant need to choose can feel frustrating. It would be nice to have a guaranteed formula for feeling safe and in charge. Guaranteed formulas get a lot of attention. Such formulas don't work because the brain did not evolve to feel good about your survival at every moment. But advocating a guaranteed path can raise a person's status, so we hear a lot about them. They start to seem real.

We all strive to transcend self-destructive habits while living with the inevitable insecurities of life. It helps to have more links to your happy chemicals. You are likely to continue a self-destructive status-seeking habit if you have no other way to feel good about your status. The following chapter shows how to strengthen the links to your happy chemicals. But first, let's look at some dominance-seeking habits that do subtle harm rather than obvious harm.

Subtly Destructive Status-Seeking Strategies

When a person spends themselves into bankruptcy, the damage is obvious. If a person has a penchant for fist-fights, their dominance-seeking strategy hurts themselves and others. But many dominance-seeking habits have no obvious side effects. They raise our status without hurting us in ways we can see. We're highly motivated to repeat such rewarding behaviors. If there are subtle damaging side effects, repeating compounds them. The damage can mount up, but we don't see how it's linked to our success strategy.

Over-working is a good example. Work raises your status and provides satisfying opportunities for dominance. When you're not at work, you may lose those good feelings. You may even have bad feelings about your status when your attention is not focused on work. So your brain stays focused on work to feel good. The narrow focus has unpleasant side effects, but when life disappoints you explain it in other ways. You try to feel better in the way your brain knows, which is work. The side effects accumulate, convincing you of the flaws of the world, and increasing the attractions of over-work.

We mammals feel frustrated when we interact with individuals we perceive as more dominant. Such interactions are inevitable, so we are often looking for ways to relieve that frustration. Anything that works feels rewarding, so your brain wants to repeat it. Here are a few of the infinite variety of human dominance-seeking strategies, and some of the consequences that are routinely overlooked.

Controlling

People enjoy being in charge. Some people take on the alpha role in every situation. It seems to work. When you control situations, you appear to get what you want and others seem to defer. There are costs to this strategy, of course. People who don't want to submit to your controlling may avoid you. You may become surrounded by people willing to submit, and you might not even realize this has happened. You will develop a limited view of how the world works, and it could get you into trouble.

Doomsaying

If you focus your mind on danger signals, you will find them. Some people raise their status by looking for danger and alerting others. Dire forecasts are believed because every mind knows on some level that something will kill it some day. Predicting danger can earn a person respect, but they pay a high price for this status. They must remain focused on the worst in life. A crisis mongerer dare not see the good in things because that would undermine the status they've achieved by forecasting doom. Focusing on threats erodes the happiness you earned by raising your status. But you fear losing that status if you relinquish the apocalyptic outlook. It's a lose-lose proposition.

Rescuing

People feel good about their status when they rescue others. It can become a habit, where you need someone to rescue in order to feel good. Any rescue will do, so negative side effects are ignored. A rescuer may enable others to perpetuate self-destructive behaviors. Sometimes rescuers are hated by those they seek to rescue. When a rescuer's efforts are frustrated, they seek another victim to rescue. It feels like their only choice, and they reinforce that view by surrounding themselves with other rescuers.

Oppositionalism

It is natural to be frustrated with those above you in the status hierarchy. Some people respond by automatically opposing anyone they perceive as dominant. Oppositionalists embrace anything that undermines their perceived dominator. This narrows their options and wastes their energy. They oppose automatically without an alternative notion of what is in their true best interests. Instead of seeing the self-destructive results of their choices, oppositionalists are proud of their strategy and disposed to keep repeating it.

One-upmanship

Some people can't stand to be in the number two position, no matter how small the interaction. They pour energy into goals they don't really value just to avoid being in the one-down position. The one-upper does not see a pattern in this behavior. They believe others are putting them down, leaving them no choice but to resist this domination by dominating others. Everyone is entitled to invest their energy in winning as long as they play by the rules. But if one-upmanship fails to create the positive feelings a person seeks, it's a self-destructive use of their energy.

Criminality

Some people raise their status by violating others. Violence and theft create a feeling of dominance, and people may get away with it in the short run. Violators tell themselves they are only doing what others would do if they had the skill. Criminals overlook what they are likely to lose as a result of their actions. They ignore alternative ways of raising their status. They presume the world is trying to dominate them, and overlook the cruelty they are inflicting on others. They often surround themselves with others who engage in the same criminal dominance strategy, and thus share these blind spots.

Busyness

Activity distracts you from the feeling of being dominated. Thus, any activity can leave you feeling better about your status. But the moment you are not immersed in activity, the sense of frustration with your status may return. Your brain seeks happiness by distracting your attention at every moment from the unpleasant feeling. But busyness is draining, so it can trigger more frustration than you started with. You may think the external world imposed the frustration on you and overlook your own role in creating it. Thus you don't see your power to undo it. All it would take is to acknowledge that you care about your status. When you accept that you are a mammal and care about your status, you will see that every mammal gets frustrated about their status because every mammal risks being dominated by others. Knowing this frees you from the constant need to distract yourself away from your status frustration.

Displaced Venting

When people feel dominated, they want to fight back. Often it's not safe to resist the person actually dominating you, so your mind looks for a safe place to vent. People get into the habit of venting against safe targets. The venting feels so good that you easily forget the original source of your frustration. Whether your feelings of oppression originated with someone now dead or someone still actively hurting you, you can't make them stop. But you get relief when you find a safe way to dominate. The familiar cliche about kicking the dog after your boss kicks you must be updated because most people would not kick a dog these days. People find other targets that cannot retaliate, such as service employees. Venting at "management" and public figures in the news are a popular ways of distracting yourself from the inevitable status frustrations of life. But such venting is self destructive if it distracts you from dealing with someone who is directly abusing you. Many people tolerate abuse at home, and then build social alliances around venting at safe targets.

Irresponsibility

A person can dominate by being irresponsible because it forces others to be responsible for them. Being irresponsible can give you the upper hand over others, even while it hurts your real interests. If you feel dominated, anything that gives you the upper hand feels good. The good feeling thus wires you for habitual irresponsibility. You wire your brain to focus on getting others to rescue you instead of investing your effort in satisfying your own needs.

Self-destructive status-seeking strategies are hard to change on your own. People get so frustrated about their inability to change their own behavior that they long for change to come from somewhere else. The feeling that "something must be done" arises when you can't get yourself to do something.

If everyone else stopped caring about status, it would be easier for you to feel good about your status. It's tempting to feel that "something should be done" about other people's status-seeking.

But our fellow mammals will continue to care about social dominance, despite their claims to the contrary. Our unhappy chemicals will continue to get triggered, sending us seeking happy chemicals in whichever way we know how. Other people cannot free you of the burden of managing your mammalian reactions to the world. You must make a separate peace with your own mammal brain. The following chapter describes a way to stimulate your own happy chemicals without a self-destructive cycle.

Chapter 7

You May Already Be A Winner

...Eventually the brain learns to expect satisfaction instead of expecting to be deprived...

An old sweepstakes ad made famous the claim that "you may already be a winner." The ad got people's attention because the thought of winning turns on our happy chemicals. Dopamine floods your system when you encounter more rewards than expected. Serotonin flows when you contemplate the security your winnings will bring. Oxytocin flows when you imagine these winnings strengthening the trust bonds in your life. If you were already a winner, these good feelings would just appear without your having to do anything.

Could you already be a winner without knowing it? It seems impossible except in the world of phony sweepstakes ads. But this chapter shows that you are already more of a winner than you realize. Your brain focuses more on your losses than your wins, so your triumphs tend to get overlooked. However, you can train your brain to focus on how well you are already doing, and thus enjoy the neurochemical rewards.

Feeling like you're already a winner may not ring true. Your brain replays past slights and disappointments easily because those circuits are well-developed. Circuits that represent your triumphs may not be developed. If you were already a winner you would hardly notice. So the feeling that you're *not* a winner can be just as false as the feeling that you are one.

Nice people may object that it's wrong to focus on winning and losing. But when others win, nice people notice and their unhappy chemicals flow. They could enjoy happy chemicals instead by focusing on their wins rather than their losses. Forgoing these happy chemicals achieves no higher purpose because you cannot give to others the happy chemicals you don't produce in yourself. Each brain must make its own, so you can enjoy happy chemicals without depriving others.

Alas, mammal brains produce a lot of unhappy chemicals. We evolved to monitor potential threats in order to survive. Unhappy chemicals notify your brain of potential threats. When you feel dominated by others, unhappy chemicals etch information that you use to avoid potential threats in the future.

We are skilled at processing information about losing because attention has developed those circuits. We could develop our circuits for winning simply by focusing our attention there. You can train yourself to appreciate your wins the way you can develop an appreciation of art or music.

Of course, you can't just go around presuming you're the winner. You have to live in a world of rules that determine wins and losses. The people around you want to win just as much as you do. If you acted on every momentary urge for dominance, you'd end up in trouble just as surely as if you acted on every mammalian urge for food or sex.

But ignoring your desire for status brings trouble just as surely as ignoring your desire for food and sex. You could starve yourself for happy chemicals. You could end up believing you are always dominated, stimulating unhappy chemicals with great efficiency. Your brain will interpret the unhappy chemicals as danger signals, and search for evidence of danger. It will not be looking for evidence of success.

Success lies in the middle ground between ignoring your mammalian urge for dominance and seeking dominance automatically regardless of the consequences. Finding the middle means managing your natural appetite for status the way you manage your natural appetite for food and sex. We start managing these appetites the moment we're born. Most of the time, we succeed at avoiding the extremes of unbridled excess and unhealthy self-deprivation. We don't notice this success because it takes constant struggle. Struggle doesn't feel like success. We'd rather have an easy way to manage our mammal brain. That doesn't exist, unfortunately. Life is not easy with a hybrid brain bent on promoting its legacy. The best we can do is celebrate our successes.

This chapter shows that the feeling of winning can be learned, and that the feeling itself helps satisfy the urge for status. The feeling of winning helps prevent self-destructive excess. You can experience the pleasant sensation of winning without investing all your energy into the constant pursuit of winning. You can experience more happy chemicals from the wins you already have. Focusing your attention on them is all it takes.

Your mammal brain does not automatically focus on celebrating your accomplishments. If an animal escapes a predator, it doesn't celebrate much because it would succumb to the next predator while distracted. If an animal dominates a rival, it doesn't celebrate for long because it would soon be supplanted by the next rival. When we triumph, we quickly shift our attention back to business.

If you learned to enjoy each triumph a little longer, you would not rush into the next status-seeking risk.

Actively recalling past triumphs can trigger your happy chemicals. Your experience of triumph expands when you focus on it. It's not easy to evoke positive memories in a way that feels real, but when you do, your status disappointments feel less frustrating.

"I want real triumphs," you may say. Celebrating old micro-triumphs may seem misguided to you. The problem is, no matter how many real triumphs you have, they will not satisfy your mammal brain for long. It quickly embarks on the next quest. You may be better off without that next quest, but your mammalian neurochemicals create the impression that it's necessary for your survival. At these times, the ability to feel your past triumphs will free you from the need for more.

Too much celebrating may sound risky. We have all seen people "celebrate" in self-destructive ways. But a person would not need self-destructive habits if they could activate the feeling of celebrating without them.

Anyone can feel triumphant, no matter how small or remote their past triumphs. You can stimulate your happy chemicals with mental images of what you have already accomplished.

Appreciating your accomplishments triggers more happy chemicals in the long run than actually accomplishing more. You can make peace with your mammal brain by cultivating awareness of your triumphs.

Many people think it's not nice to feel triumphant. But that leaves them feeling stuck in the subordinate position, and they bitterly resent it. A better alternative is to imagine triumph without conflict. This is expressed brilliantly in the song *Because We Believe*, the theme song of the 2004 Olympics in Italy. The lyrics revolve around the Latin word *vincere*, which is the root of the words "to win" and "to shine" in Italian (as well as "to gain"). When Andrea Bocelli sang "we were born to shine," it triggered the Latin sense of winning without the implied conflict. This song could be the mammal brain's theme song, since it satisfies the urge for dominance with none of the excesses that lead to trouble.

Here are some of the lyrics. They alternate between English and Italian – Bocelli wrote the song with David Foster and Foster's daughter (a mammal promoting his offspring). I have translated the Italian and italicized all the uses of *vincere.*

> "Like stars across the sky,
> We were born to shine.
> E per *avvincere* (And to shine)
> Dovrai *vincere.* (You must win.)
> E allora, *vincerai.*" (And so you will win.)

These lyrics highlight the appeal of the Olympics. You see athletes getting recognition for their achievements and your mirror neurons feel their pride. They shine, whether they win or not. You can imagine that feeling, even though you didn't train for the Olympics and you are not getting the attention. Imagining the feeling triggers your happy chemistry, providing a valuable opportunity to develop that good feeling.

The Neural Pathway Not Taken

Anyone can start having neurochemical happiness right now by replaying a past triumph in their head – even a tiny one from years ago. This may seem delusional, yet you probably still feel the sting of past status disappointments. Even tiny ones from years ago. Your brain is skilled at feeling dominated, and it will keep doing that unless you train it to do something else.

It may seem like cheating to stimulate one's happy chemicals without actually winning. But you may already dominate more than you realize. We have all been around domineering alphas who are constantly on guard for others dominating them. They don't appreciate the dominance they already have because they are so focused on protecting their status. Becoming aware of your own dominance frees you from investing in more dominance than you really need. Recognizing your own dominance creates a sense of security that offsets those automatic threat signals.

Some threats are real, of course, and we should pay attention to them. Ignoring signs of threat is not a safe way to live. But we can develop our happy circuits and still be safe. Indeed, we become safer when we stop dwelling on the same old threats because we are more open to new evidence of real threats.

A mammal is safer when it avoids unnecessary risk. Some risk is necessary to satisfy our needs, but once our needs are satisfied we are better off avoiding risk. The ability to know when you're satisfied thus frees you to enjoy what you have instead of risking to get more.

Yet, it's curiously hard to know when you are satisfied.

Satisfaction

The mammal brain is always striving to satisfy its needs, but it is surprisingly bad at knowing when it has succeeded. When you eat, for example, your mammal brain doesn't know that your hunger is satisfied until twenty minutes after your nutritional needs are met. You may already be satisfied without knowing it.

The mammal brain evolved to seek food, sex and status until these appetites are satisfied. Satisfaction is an internal experience, not a property of the food or the sex or the status. The more you have developed neural pathways for experiencing satisfaction, the easier it is to feel satisfied. Satisfaction is a skill that results from a well-developed neural infrastructure, just like any other skill. The more skilled a person is at feeling satisfied, the less they need to keep feeding themselves with more food, or more sex partners, or more status.

Anyone can learn to feel more satisfied with the status they already have. Feeling satisfied doesn't mean giving up, or rejecting status entirely. Denial doesn't work because our mammalian appetites are real; they don't go away just because you ignore them. Feeling satisfied means extracting more enjoyment out of the status you have. When you feel satisfied, you don't need to look for more status right away.

Dieters learn to feel satisfied with less food. Dieters do not practice abstinence the way alcoholics do. Abstaining from food is a bad way to diet because starving increases the risk of succumbing to your mammalian impulses. The same applies to status. Starving yourself for status leaves you tempted by self-destructive status-seeking strategies. Your urge for food is best managed by filling up on nourishing foods, and your urge for status is best managed by filling up on nourishing status.

Each person has to define healthy status for themselves. Dieters learn to find healthy foods that satisfy them, and healthy status can be discovered in the same way.

You don't have to wait for the world to change in order to feel good. All it takes is focusing on the healthy status that you already have.

Feeling satisfied will not make you an alpha. But being an alpha would not satisfy your mammal brain. Alphas are too busy protecting their position to enjoy it. You are free to live that way if you want, but you have an alternative. Learning to enjoy what you have gives your mammal brain the feeling of security that the mammal brain associates with being dominant.

Anyone can get more enjoyment from the status they already have. No one is stopping you from doing that right now. It's free. It's painless. And no one can do it for you.

If you feel dominated by others, you may hate the idea of being satisfied with the status you have. "It's my turn to dominate," you may think. But once you learn to trigger your own happy chemicals, you may discover that you are not as dominated as you'd imagined. Your unhappy chemicals may have fed the perception of being dominated. Your perceptions may change as you build circuits that focus on your wins.

You may think it's selfish or arrogant to feel good about your status. But if you think about it, it's easy to see that even more selfishness and arrogance are provoked when one feels bad about their status. Feeling satisfied rather than deprived can help you without hurting others. Of course, there are selfish, arrogant people who dominate with cruelty, and self-destructive consequences result from such over-indulgence in status seeking. The best way to avoid such excess is to learn to enjoy the status one already has. Everyone can.

Your Appestat

The brain evolved a mechanism that recognizes when hunger is satisfied. The mechanism has been called the *appestat* because it's a thermostat for your appetite.

When you have eaten enough to meet your needs, your digestive system sends a message to your brain. Research suggests that the brain does not receive this satisfaction signal until twenty minutes after you've eaten enough. It seems like a glitch in the system, and over-eating is the obvious consequence. But overweight mammals do not exist in nature because they are soon eaten by predators. Natural selection would eliminate a faulty appestat. Our appestat is not faulty. Its time lag has a survival value that's important to appreciate. Understanding the quirks of our appestat can help us understand the parallel temptation to over-indulge in status.

The mammal brain evolved in a world where sugars and fats were scarce. Our distant ancestors ate a lot of coarse foods, and even those were often scarce. When they occasionally stumbled onto a delicious abundance, it made sense to stuff themselves. A little cushion helps you survive in a life where your next meal can be threatened. But after you stuff yourself for twenty minutes, your digestive system can handle no more and it signals your brain to stop. It's fascinating to watch a monkey or lion stuffing down food as fast as it can when opportunity knocks. But they also know when to stop.

There's no temptation to keep eating food that's bland and chewy. Our primitive ancestors spent a lot of time foraging and chewing just to get enough nutrition. Eating was work. You would stop eating when your hunger pangs subsided because the food was not rewarding enough to motivate extra foraging and chewing. Undereating was more of a risk than overeating. The primitive appestat seems designed to trick you into eating a little extra, so you don't become malnourished before the next available food source.

When richer food became available, this primitive appestat wasn't enough to manage behavior. Richer foods arrived ten thousand years ago, when humans cultivated grain. Our ancestors would have a storehouse full of grain at harvest time, but if they stuffed themselves it wouldn't last until the next harvest. In order to survive, they learned to feel satisfied before they felt stuffed. They could manage their appetite because the grain they did without today would be there to satisfy their needs tomorrow.

Apes do not store food – they look for food when they feel hunger. This strategy is obviously risky, and humans thrived by focusing on the future. Farmers planted seeds before they got hungry. Mothers baked bread before their children were hungry. Today, we build careers instead of looking for ways to earn money when we're hungry. We satisfy our needs by anticipating the future.

Just as we learn to anticipate future hunger, we learn to anticipate future satisfaction of hunger. You learn that if you stop eating now, you will feel full in a few minutes.

In the past, most people ate from a common platter. Food was scarce for most of human history, and social bonds discouraged you from taking more than your share. Each individual developed a sense of what they could take without straining their social bonds. Our living situations are more individual today, and we learn to make individual eating decisions as well. Instead of relying on social constraints to know when we've had enough, we develop an awareness of our own internal state.

It works the same way with our other mammalian appetites: status and sex. Our primitive mechanisms can tempt us to over-indulge in behaviors with self-destructive consequences. In the past, social pressure helped restrain us from overdoing it. Today, social pressures have weakened, and we have to rely on our own internal awareness to lead us to good decisions. Internal awareness can tell us when continued seeking is not worth the risk. But we have to build the neural circuitry for internal awareness to do the job.

We build our circuits from past experience, but the past is not always a good predictor of the future. You can drive drunk ten times without crashing, and your brain might "learn" that drunk driving is safe. If you feel good about your status when you drink, your brain might "learn" that drinking promotes survival. It's hard to unlearn this. But instead of relying on the circuits you built from accidents of experience, but you choose new experiences that build new circuits.

Feeling satisfied comes easier when you make it a habit. Here's a simple example. When I get an ice cream with my husband, he insists on sitting down with it. I would rather walk around while eating, and the sitting frustrates me. But my husband has a small waistline, so I decided to try it his way.

He is doing what experts call "conscious eating." He feels satisfied with less food because he's learned to increase the pleasure he extracts from whatever he eats. Anyone can do this. All it takes is conscious attention.

Why do I find this frustrating? I love ice cream, so why wouldn't I automatically dwell on the pleasure of it?

The reason is that my brain is always scanning for new opportunities to promote my survival. The deliciousness of the ice cream is not new after the first few licks. After that, my brain processes it on automatic like other familiar things. While I'm eating my ice cream, my mind automatically seeks information on my next object of desire. When I force my brain to focus on the ice cream I frustrate its search for new information. The mind is curiously resistant to dwelling on satisfaction.

Since we're always seeking satisfaction, you would think we'd notice it when we achieve it. But satisfaction can be hard to notice. It can be a faint positive feeling amidst many other neurochemicals sloshing around the brain. Paying attention to this feeling allows it to grow by developing the neural connections. Next time it will be easier to feel. Eventually, the brain learns to expect satisfaction. Instead of expecting to be deprived and looking for evidence of that, it will look for evidence that it is satisfied. Expectations shape the information we feed to our mammal brain. When we expect to feel satisfied, we get more happy chemicals from less ice cream or less alcohol or less status.

My husband built his conscious-eating habit by accident. He was forced to sit with ice cream when he was young because his parents were worried about wasting money if he dropped his scoop. He was often pressured to sit still and to worry about money. Like everyone, his early experience built some helpful circuits and some unhelpful ones. And like everyone, he was challenged to build on the helpful ones and leave the junk circuits to atrophy. When I notice a good habit in him, I focus on it and my mirror neurons take it in. Mirroring the satisfaction of others is a good way to strengthen the habit.

The feeling of satisfaction can be stimulated in myriad small ways. The more you create the feeling yourself, the less you need to wait for the world to express its satisfaction with you.

People often get the idea that there's something wrong with feeling satisfied on your own, without the world's approval. When a person is called "self-satisfied," it's meant as an insult. You may notice yourself disliking people who are satisfied with themselves. You may try to avoid appearing "self-satisfied" by routinely embracing the one-down position and avoiding the one-up position. But in doing that, you risk wiring yourself up to be a wiener.

You May Already Be a Wiener

A wiener identifies with anyone who loses and resents anyone who wins. Zero-sum thinking is at the core of being a wiener. When you think one person succeeds by making others fail, success seems bad.

Even if you say you don't care about winning, your unhappy chemicals surge when you find yourself in the one-down spot. Yet you often wind up there because you think there's something wrong with winning.

You will be stuck in resentment unless you build a mental model of success that has positive rather than negative connotations for you. A useful way to think of success is embodied in the French word *debroullier* [day-broo-ee-yay]. It means "to get yourself out of a mess." The French applaud the *debrouillard* [day-broo-ee-yard] – someone good at extricating themselves from messes.

The root meaning of the word is "to untangle a knot." When you untangle a knot, you triumph without mistreating others.

I once had knots in a necklace and worked on them in my lap while sitting on a bus. It took me a long time to succeed, and I felt a thrill through my whole body when I did. Then looked up from my task and realized that a number of bus passengers had been watching me. They were smiling, as if they felt the thrill of success as well.

I chose a French word to describe this feeling because a foreign word is a good foundation on which to build a new concept. It does not mean that France has less self-destructive status seeking. The French struggle with their urge for dominance just like other mammals. In fact, a *debrouillard* in France is often what we would call an "operator" – someone who gets out of messes with bribes or other lapses of integrity.

If you were already a wiener, you might not even try to untangle knots. And if you succeeded at untangling them, you might squelch the thrill. If you were already a wiener, you would not even notice if your star were rising. No matter what status you had, you might allow yourself to be dominated for no good reason. Even monarchs and presidents and captains of industry are often dominated by someone in their life, as biographies plainly show.

The mammal brain needs to triumph to feel good. There are infinite ways to triumph, so everyone can find a way. But each mammal brain relies on the circuits it has, and most of them were learned from watching others. If your brain is surrounded by people who feel dominated and defeated, your brain is likely to build those circuits. If you are surrounded by people who only feel triumphant when they take self-destructive risks, those circuit will easily develop. You are always free to build new circuits, simply by focusing on the good feeling of untangling knots and managing your way out of messes. If you don't, your old circuits could make you a wiener.

You can celebrate your ability to get out of messes instead of berating yourself for getting into messes. A *debrouillard* automatically enjoys their triumphs because this circuit replaces the old idea that success is somehow not-nice.

Children often learn to feel bad about themselves. Many adults perpetuate that habit unwittingly. Where I live, for example, children are taught to feel bad about being American. They are taught to associate any bad in the world with America, and any good in the world with other cultures, or with opposing America. The people who teach this may have good intentions, yet they persistently burden American children with the presumption that their culture is bad. They would never expect children from other cultures to think badly of themselves. The harm done to children "educated" in this way is yet to be explored.

Abstinence

I often hear people celebrate those with low status and disdain those with high status. I hear people automatically sneer at status without interest in the individual facts. Abstaining from status in this way can be as harmful as overindulging in it, just like abstaining from food and sex. Yet many people make a habit of condemning the natural urge for status.

A whole social group can adopt the habit of rejecting status. Group members reflexively put themselves down and berate people who don't put themselves down. Such a group might be dominated by a self-serving alpha who pays lip service to "equality" while commanding submission. Members of such a group feel frustrated by the rigid domination, but their shared frustration builds strong social bonds that they can't let go of.

Running with a herd that "rejects" status inflicts terrible strain on your mammal brain. You risk being shunned by your herd if you express your natural urge for status. But if you keep rejecting your natural urge for recognition, you reject a core piece of yourself. Running with a status-hating herd does not free you from mammalian frustration with social dominance.

Your mammal brain needs to see your star rising to release happy chemicals. You do not need to light up the galaxy; you only need to believe in your own momentum. You can say it doesn't matter, but that is likely to leave you with unhappy chemicals.

People with high formal status feel bad about their status as people with low or middling status. A high-status person might have the habit of seeking status regardless of the consequences. They might fear losing everything they have the moment they stop their automatic status seeking. Their well-being would benefit most from learning to feel satisfied with whatever status they happen to have.

Feeling good about your status is hard whether you feel like you're at the top, the middle or the bottom. Your fellow mammals will never stop challenging your place in the dominance hierarchy. No amount of status will protect you from feeling this threat. Your only security comes from the feeling of satisfaction you create internally.

You can create circuits that amplify your sense of satisfaction, even if your present circuits amplify your sense of deprivation. But new circuits are not easy to build. Re-wiring your neurochemistry is as hard as quitting smoking and learning a foreign language at the same time. It's like learning a foreign language because you're hacking a new trail through your jungle of neurons, so even routine things suddenly require great effort. It's like quitting smoking in the sense that you have a well-travelled path through your jungle of neurons but you are struggling not to use it.

Learning to feel satisfied is not easy, but it has fewer negative side effects than other ways of managing your neurochemicals.

Those who insist on rejecting all status opt for starving their mammal brain instead of teaching it to feel satisfied. Abstinence from food leaves you weak and easily tempted by junk food, and abstinence from status leaves you weak and easily tempted by junk status.

Bingeing on Junk Status

When a person is hungry, junk food is very tempting. When a mammal brain is hungry for status, it is tempted to binge on junk status.

Dieters learn that starving is not the best way to lose weight because it often leads to bingeing. A person who says they don't care about status is starving their mammal brain, and that leads to binging on junk status. Any status looks good to a person who feels dominated and status-starved. Self-destructive actions that indulge your craving seem appealing.

Junk status, like junk food, satisfies the craving but doesn't supply real nourishment. The difference between junk status and real nourishment must be decided by each brain for itself, since happy chemical circuits vary with unique life experience. Each brain must determine the nourishment it needs to avoid being tempted.

Dieters learn to prevent bingeing by eating moderate portions of nourishing foods. The mammal brain likewise needs to be nourished with healthy status before it is tempted by junk status.

People who say they don't care about status often end up seeking status in some other way. People who feel dominated find their own ways to dominate. They may find themselves bingeing on status-seeking strategies that have unhealthy side effects. The best way to avoid junk status is to become aware of one's desire for status, the way a dieter becomes aware of true hunger. Honoring your true hunger works better than starving and bingeing. Honoring your true need for status helps you avoid feeling deprived and bingeing on junk status in response.

It's easy to notice other people bingeing on junk status. A memorable example for me is the day I heard the words "What idiot designed this parking lot?" I was stuck in gridlock after picking up my son at soccer practice. It was annoying to be trapped in a car, wasting time and gas. Someone next to me was managing that annoyance by putting down the designer of the parking lot. When life is frustrating, it's easy to assume that you could easily fix the problem if only you ran the world.

I did not want to teach my son that habit. More important, we knew the "idiots" who had designed the parking lot. We lived on steep hills, with little flat space for playing fields. My son's practices were often held in other towns, requiring terrible commutes. We were thrilled when the volunteer leaders of our town's athletic organizations figured out a way to carve enough space from a hillside for a new soccer field. The cramped site left little room for parking, but the improvement was satisfying.

The critic whose voice drifted into our car did not focus on the accomplishment. Gridlock is unpleasant, of course. The mammal brain feels threatened when it's trapped. When it sees no escape, unhappy chemicals surge.

Life often lands us in gridlock of one sort or another. We find ourselves in unpleasant subordinate positions every day. Our mammal brain dislikes this feeling, and if we don't find a way to feel satisfied with our status we will be tempted by any status that's immediately available. Hating the "idiots in power" is a common status-seeking strategy in my corner of the world. Parents who think this way build the thought habit in their children. A new generation gets wired to automatically put down those in positions of responsibility when feeling frustrated

The junk-status habit is easily provoked by a visit to the Department of Motor Vehicles. When you're stuck in a line, it feels like submission to your mammal brain. Feeling hostile toward the DMV helps the mammal brain raise itself from the subordinate position to the dominant position. That makes you feel better, and the brain learns from whatever makes it feel better. It's tempting to binge on finding fault with the clerks and the rules of this institution.

When you focus on faults, it's hard to see accomplishments. I see the DMV as an accomplishment because so many of my students paid bribes for drivers licenses and traffic violations in their countries of origin. These students often asked me how we prevent this. And I had to tell them we take it for granted. In some countries, drivers take it for granted that they will have to bribe police who stop them for traffic violations. And then drivers feel free to violate traffic rules on the presumption that bribes are inevitable anyway.

When a DMV works without bribery, it's a cause for celebration. But most people don't see how they benefit from the

DMV's bureaucratic procedures. Auto thefts and accidents are prevented when the rules are enforced. Bureaucracies enforce the rules and thus make the benefits possible. Most people complain about the enforcement while taking the benefits for granted. The next time you go to the DMV, you can try looking at it as an opportunity to feel satisfaction instead of scorn.

I was tempted by junk status when I brought my car to the dealership for servicing. I caught myself blaming my mechanical problem on the manufacturer. I had no evidence, but it felt better than facing a repair bill. Then I realized that cars wear out like everything else. I am not being dominated by the manufacturer when I wear out a part on my car. Paying a repair bill is not submitting. So I did not try to dominate the service desk by aggressively insisting it was their fault. I did not want to wire my brain for a world where aggression wins. I wired myself for a world in which evidence wins. I celebrated the fact that spare parts are available when I needed them. My urge to binge on junk status passed. I didn't feel dominated so I didn't need to dominate in response.

But the lure of junk status tempted me again when I was in a car rental line at an airport. I was frustrated because I had already done the paperwork online. Why should I wait to do it again? Then I thought about what a miracle it is that something as expensive as a new car is entrusted to strangers with so brief a transaction. It's a marvel that the staff is so pleasant to customers who are often looking for flaws to critique. It's a triumph that labor and capital are managed in such a way that a clean car is waiting at a competitive price when I need it. I felt satisfaction with the process while I waited in line.

We are often surrounded by large complex systems. It's easy to feel dominated when you interact with something bigger, and the mammal brain looks for ways to avoid submitting. It's helpful to see large complex systems as mammalian alliances struggling to satisfy the needs of the whole herd. If you see a system as an alliance rather than a dominator, you are likely to have a better experience. But it will not raise your status. You will have to find other ways to meet your status needs, or you will be tempted to binge on junk status when you encounter a person behind a counter in a large rule-bound system.

Our urge for dominance will not disappear. It is part of our core operating system. An appetite for status is part of being a healthy mammal. Feeling good about your status frees you from junk status binges that don't really improve your life.

One Man's Status Is Another Man's Junk Status

Sometimes I feel like I'm surrounded by people bingeing on junk status. But if I find fault with everyone, I am really just bingeing on junk status myself. So when I'm tempted to think everyone else is misguided, I try to remember that everyone else is a mammal who cares about their status.

This was especially hard for me at a particular PTA meeting. I was listening to mothers griping about their children's homework. Half of the mothers complained that their kids had too much homework, and the rest complained of too little. One mother moaned that her child was too stressed for homework when he finished his daily music, sports and language lessons. Another moaned that her child needed more homework to prevent falling behind a cousin whose school covered more math. Each mother was focused on her own interests and expecting the school to submit to them. I thought it was all junk status as each mother tried to dominate the curriculum.

I expected conflict between the more-homework mothers and the less-homework mothers. But I was wrong. Within minutes, these mammalian mammas had built an alliance to blame the school. They agreed that teachers should tailor homework to each family's individual needs.

I did not agree. As a teacher, I had tried yielding to individual appeals and gotten bad results. I had agreed to give students make-up exams only to have them not show up for the make-up. In my experience, students put schoolwork last when standards are negotiable. They quickly fill their time with other things.

The herd of PTA mothers outnumbered me. Since their view was held by so many, I decided to understand it instead of dismissing it as junk status. And I realized it was the mammal brain at work. In the modern world, reproductive success depends on your child's status. Our children are not likely to get eaten by predators, so all of that protective energy gets focused on other ways of protecting our children. These mammalian mammas saw the teacher as the predator – not consciously in words, but in their automatic neurochemistry.

People often feel dominated when educational standards are imposed on them. But real learning suffers when educational standards submit to the domination of each student and their mammalian mamma. My students would treat my office as if it were the Complaint Department at Macy's if I allowed it. Their experience of customer service built the expectation that you can return an outfit the day after a party and get a refund, no questions asked. Students used to come to my office the day after a test saying "I'm not satisfied with my grade," as if they expected me to provide "excellent customer service" in the form of extra points. Instead of taking responsibility for their studying choices, I think they were mirroring parents like the ones at my PTA meeting. Dominating the teacher instead of mastering the material can become a habit.

Parents today put their eggs into fewer baskets, so each perceived threat to a child's prospects feels like a big threat to reproductive success. Your intellect knows that a child is better off actually learning rather than "winning" against the educational system. But happy chemicals flow when a mamma mammal dominates a teacher and protects a child's interests as they see it in the moment.

People say they want high standards, but their actions are shaped by mammalian neurochemicals.

Students can find ways to "win" at the education game without actually learning. This temptation is widespread because the mammal brain is always looking for ways to win. When a person learns to satisfy that urge in other ways, they can avoid satisfying it in ways that undermine their true interests.

Mammalian Legacy vs. Human Legacy

In the past, many people had a large troop of grandchildren. But today our planet is crowded, and having fewer children raises the survival prospects of each one. Some people will have no grandchildren at all, but their mammal brain can't stop caring about its legacy. Without grandchildren to focus on, the mammal brain is anxious. Its future seems bleak. To feel good about the future, the mammal brain needs an alternative legacy to focus on.

Every brain wants to see its own impact on those who will come after them. One person strives to get hits on their blog and another to set a record at their local bowling alley. The mammalian urge to reproduce as much as possible can be satisfied in many ways. But our happy chemicals still depend on building a sense of long-term survival. Without that, your mammal brain looks at the future and sees nothing but annihilation.

Whatever legacy you focus on, everything that seems to threaten it will frustrate you. You will see other mammals getting in the way of your legacy and feel alarm. The unhappy chemicals drive you to seek happy chemicals by raising your status. This is what the mammal brain does.

You cannot always dominate. You cannot eliminate every obstacle to your legacy and secure it with ironclad certainty. If you want more happy chemicals, you have to believe in your legacy despite the apparent obstacles. You can learn to feel satisfied with your legacy.

Ignaz Semmelweis May Already Be a Winner

Great contributors to humanity sometimes die without getting recognition. Ignaz Semmelweis did more for the world than most people ever do, yet he went insane before his contribution got respect. His story shows that social status is too unpredictable to rely on during the span of one human lifetime. The happiness of building a legacy must come from small daily triumphs instead.

Ignaz Semmelweis is the nineteenth-century Hungarian doctor who accidentally discovered germs. He proved that doctors can save lives by washing their hands with disinfectant. Dr. Semmelweis was disdained and ignored during his life, and his legacy is now only dimly recalled. Like so many people, he enriched the lives of everyone who came after him, but he didn't know it. If he knew he was already a winner, his troubles could have been easier to bear.

Semmelweis managed a maternity hospital in Vienna when a natural experiment fell into his lap. His hospital had two wards: one with a very high death rate for post-partum mothers, and another with a very low rate. The low death rate occurred in the free clinic, which was attended only by midwives. The tragedies were occurring in the ward attended medical doctors. Semmelweis was agonized by these deaths, but he couldn't figure out the cause.

Then a doctor friend of his died mysteriously of the same symptoms as the mothers who'd contracted "childbed fever." The dead doctor had been cut by a student's scalpel while teaching an autopsy class. Suddenly, Semmelweis got it. The doctors were often performing autopsies during their spare time between deliveries. Invisible particles from the cadavers must have been on their hands when they were called to the delivery room, he reasoned. He required his staff to wash with disinfectant before leaving the autopsy room, and maternal deaths plunged to zero.

That would seem like a happy ending. It would seem like convincing proof. But the human animal is complicated. Semmelweis got a bad reaction when he tried to spread the word in the European medical establishment. His idea that "invisible particles" cause disease was ridiculed as "unscientific." Semmelweis watched more women die in agony and more newborns become orphans while he struggled to convey his message.

Poor Dr. Ignaz hit up against closed doors for the rest of his life. His behavior became erratic and his family sent him to an asylum, where he died shortly after being admitted. He seems to have sustained injuries in a conflict with a caretaker, causing infection by the invisible particles he spent his life battling. Semmelweis has been critiqued by posterity for his poor communication skills, but it's hard to imagine acting differently in his situation.

Semmelweis did outstanding work, but he could not take pleasure in his legacy. It's hard to feel satisfied when your efforts are disdained or ignored. The mammal brain cares about the respect of others, and it's easy to become embittered when the desire for recognition is frustrated. Unhappy chemicals are triggered by a loss of status in your herd or pack or troop.

What if Semmelweis had known he was already a winner? What if he'd known there would eventually be statues of him in medical schools, and his birthplace would become a museum? Perhaps he could have protected himself from his own unhappy chemicals.

You do not always get recognition for your good deeds in your lifetime. It's easy to respond by torturing yourself with unhappy chemicals. But you don't have to. It's your brain, so you always have the option of feeling satisfied with your efforts regardless of the reaction of the world.

I went to the Semmelweis Museum when I was in Budapest. I saw the good doctor's lab and his instruments, and my mirror neurons responded to his devotion to his work. But it was a bittersweet experience because the museum was empty except for my husband, myself and the ticket-taker.

"Do you want to be right or do you want to be happy?" This question is constantly posed by TV's Dr. Phil. The guests quickly answer that they want to be happy, but I suspect that they want to be right as soon as they leave his stage. Ignaz Semmelweis wanted to be right more than he wanted to be happy. Being right means sticking to the facts as you see them. That creates impossible conflict because each brain sees the truth through the lens of its unique life experience. If you want the safety of the herd, you will be with people who think you are wrong. We will not know who is actually right while we are alive.

You can be right and happy if you can tolerate others thinking you are wrong. Whether the future proves that you were right or not, you need not put others in charge of your happy chemicals. You can manage them yourself.

Happiness Is a Warm Neuron

Before I understood the mammal brain, I thought my ups and downs depended on the state of the world around me. I didn't know about my mammalian neurochemicals, or the neural pathways I've built from accidents of experience. Once I figured this out, I knew I could activate my happy chemical pathways without depending on the state of the world.

Accepting my existing pathways is not something noble and glorious but something pragmatic and mundane. Here's a small example. I have always found pleasure in interior design. I can't sit in a room without looking for ways to improve it. My mind starts envisioning a new design project as soon as I near the end of the last one.

When I was young, this pleasure was limited by my time and money. In a more perfect world, I imagined, all my designs could be realized.

But when I had more time and money, I realized that another big remodeling project would not really make me happy. Strangely, my mind kept imagining new projects anyway. I needed a way to say "no" before I was up to my ears in plaster dust, so I decided to figure out why my mind was going there. That's how I discovered the link between decorating and my happy chemicals.

When I was twelve, my mother inherited two thousand dollars from her father and spent it redecorating. It doesn't sound like a lot of money. But it would be about ten thousand dollars today, and it was a lot to us. It was especially meaningful to my mother because it came from the father who had abused and abandoned her. I think she was determined to enjoy it, and she uncharacteristically spent it all in one place.

My mother took me along on the shopping trips, and showed me lots of color swatches. She asked my opinion.

That's all I remember, but my mammal brain clearly marked it as important information about happiness. The reasons are obvious.

First, I witnessed the pleasure my mother took in the project. She was not happy often, so this was the happiness my mirror neurons got to mirror. Many people enjoy sports for the same reason – they experienced a parent enjoying sports. When I was barely a teenager, I etched that first decorating circuit and started re-decorating my bedroom. Soon, starting decorating projects became a safe, acceptable way to escape from unpleasant goings-on around me.

The second key to happiness is the respect my mother showed for my opinion while we were decorating. Before that, she was generally hostile to my opinions. So when she brought me along and showed me the color swatches, my brain seized on that small shred of respect. Obviously, it's not about the decorating.

I know there is nothing inherently virtuous about decorating itself. But the random chance of experience made it important to me. My neural connections are real. To turn on my happy chemicals, I must use the neural connections I have.

I discovered that these connections get stimulated when I pick out the colors for any project I'm working on. If I am making a digital presentation, I dwell on the design and the colors. I have no illusions of changing the world with my color selections. I know I am just using the circuits I have to make other projects more enjoyable. And that actually develops circuits that make other projects more enjoyable. New circuits don't develop quickly at my age, so I keep finding excuses to design and color things.

Lingering over the pleasure of color might seem like a silly strategy with all the suffering in the world. Some might say it's frivolous. With all the opportunities in the world, some might say it's trivial. But life often frustrates our hopes, and we have only our existing neural circuits to fall back on. The happy circuits we have can help us avoid the temptation of self-destructive status seeking.

I thought about being an interior designer when I was in high school. No one in my family had ever gone to college, and the whole idea of going to a "sleep-away college" was looked on with suspicion. Talking about being a designer helped get me out of the house. But once I was in college, I was persuaded that "changing the world" was the only respectable career goal. It took me decades to realize that re-decorating and changing the world are just two different strategies for raising your status and triggering your happy chemicals.

You May Already Be A Finalist

I have been judging high school science fairs in recent years. It's a thrill for me to be in a huge convention center full of young people pursuing independent empirical research, and old people volunteering to give them positive feedback. Everyone at this fair is a winner to me.

The majority of students who enter will "lose," even though modern science fairs award a huge number of prizes. But an enormous number of students value participating enough to do it voluntarily – these projects are not school assignments. Every entrant is called a "finalist" at the fair I attend, because each student won a regional science fair before being admitted to the international fair.

When I tell friends about this wonderful activity, I am sometimes shocked to hear them attack it. They seem to be uncomfortable with an activity that confers status on some children and not others. I think my friends dream of a science fair without "winners and losers," where no science is "excluded." I tried to explain that the barriers to entry are low because good research need not be expensive, and many organizations eagerly support students willing to do the methodical, sustained data collection on which scientific progress depends. But my friends were not interested.

There's a difference between good science and bad science. If every science fair project got equal recognition, the fair would be an empty ritual and it would not build real science skill.

The competitive process in today's science fairs offers an unparalleled learning opportunity. Each student is visited by five to ten judges in separate time slots. A young researcher gets invaluable one-on-one attention from sympathetic professionals. It's rare for students to have such an opportunity to share their thought process with experts who really understand it. For the judges, it's great to hear the thought process of a person who hasn't already been shaped by the conventions of their discipline. It's a treat for all parties. Everyone is already winning.

There's so much good here that it would be tragic to allow idealized visions of a perfect world to obscure it.

Chapter 8

A More Perfect World

...You're the center of the world in your own brain, but life keeps invalidating this model. It's tempting to conclude something is wrong with the world...

Biologists now avoid terms like "primitive species" and "lower mammals" because that suggests an animal is somehow lacking. Each animals is perfect as it is, say biologists, because each is a successful adaptation to its environment.

If we can accept other species as they are, we can accept ourselves. Like other mammals, we strive to promote our own legacy. But unlike other mammals, we seek peace and sustainability. Animals, by contrast, deplete natural resources and act on their aggressive impulses without hating themselves for it. Humans aspire to survive without aggression and resource depletion. While we are pursuing these goals, we need not hate ourselves for our basic instincts.

People are often frustrated, and much of this unhappiness is caused by our disappointed longing for status. We find it hard to accept our mammalian appetite for status, however, so we look for other explanations. We look for evidence of survival threats, because that's what unhappy chemicals tell the brain to do. If you refuse to believe you care about status, your brain must find other survival threats to explain the unhappy chemicals. Many people settle on the idea that something is wrong with the world. Once you blame the world, your mind easily absorbs inputs that support the belief.

"Who can be happy in such a world?" people often say. They presume the world must change before they can be happy. Alas, the world rarely changes in the ways people believe it must.

This chapter presents an alternate view. Happiness will pass you by if you wait for the world to change. You can be happy in the world as it is if you understand and accept your own mammal brain.

This chapter shows clearly why:

- the state of the world is not the cause of your neurochemical ups and downs;
- the mammalian urge for dominance causes the frustration that every human struggles with;
- the world often fails to reward our efforts the way we predict, but most human accomplishment has sprung from efforts whose rewards were disappointing at the time.

It may seem like constant happiness prevails in other places and other times. Something has gone terribly wrong here and now, you may think, as you wait for constant happiness to be restored when things are set right. We can build perfect worlds in our minds, and they feel so real that nothing seems to stand in their way except "the idiots in power." A mammal can always see how their desires are blocked by other mammals in the hierarchy. It seems obvious.

But the world has never fit idealized visions of how things should be. If such perfection were necessary for happiness, then no one in   human history was ever happy. The world cannot stimulate your happy chemicals for you. You have to do it yourself, while surrounded by other dominance-seeking mammals.

You might say it's wrong to be happy while others suffer. You can refuse to be happy until there are no problems in the world. That's your choice to make. But your unhappiness is not a contribution since you can't donate your unused happy chemicals to a good cause.

If you think happiness lies in changing the world, you make that come true. Your efforts to change the world raise your status, and that makes you happy without noticing that status is involved.

But your burst of neurochemical happiness is soon metabolized, and your mammal brain soon gets frustrated with the world again. It would be nice if the world stimulated your happy chemicals constantly. But that will not happen because the mammal brain did not evolve to release happy chemicals all the time. These chemicals exist to signal important information about your survival prospects. A signal that is on all the time has no signaling power. Our happy chemicals must turn on and off to do their job.

It's hard to manage your mammal brain if you refuse to see how it's focused on status. Understanding your true motives gives you a more accurate mental model of the world. When you ignore your true motives, your brain grasps at other ways to assemble the pieces. The human brain is good at finding patterns in the details around us. You can spend your whole life blaming one pattern or another for your neurochemical ups and downs while dismissing the one that fits best.

When you accept your own urge for status, your ups and downs make sense. You will still feel threats to your status because your mammal brain evolved to scan for potential obstacles to its legacy. But the world seems less menacing when you know that your mind is actively seeking the menaces.

Life is uncertain and your brain knows that you are never completely secure. A perfect world with no insecurity would be nice, but instead of waiting for this fantasy you are better off creating security in your mammal brain. You can appease it by taking continual steps toward your legacy. These steps rarely bring all the rewards we expect, so we're often disappointed. But continual small steps satisfy the mammal brain enough to prevent self-destructive status seeking.

The State of the World Is Not the Problem

"We haven't had a good president since Kennedy," I once heard a TV commentator declare. The speaker had been thirteen years old when Kennedy died. Youthful admiration for the president was clearly the baseline against which he judged and condemned later presidents. To me it seemed obvious that his adolescent baseline was the problem, not the presidents. Skeptical adults don't find leaders as inspiring as innocent thirteen-year-olds. But the pundit was sure something was wrong with the world, not with his expectations. He blithely condemned four decades of presidents and hundreds of millions of voters rather than come to grips with the bias in his own expectations. Condemning the world gives you an air of authority that gets you on television. Refuting your childhood fancies does not.

When we are young, it seems like life will be perfect as soon as we escape the control of the alphas who oppress us. But life never looks so perfect once we have to pull our own weight. Your mind sees the contrast between your expectations about life and your life as it is. Disappointment triggers unhappy chemicals, and your mind struggles to explain them. If you don't see how your own expectations are the cause, you will embrace external explanations.

The present always looks bad if you contrast it with the perfect world you imagine. Yet perfect-world expectations are hard to avoid. We learn in school that "man is born free but is everywhere in chains." Absorbing Rousseau's view prepares us to blame the world for chaining us when we don't feel as free as we'd learned to expect. Of course, you don't always feel free as you go about the business of surviving as a group-living mammal. So your mind tries to free you by finding the chains. You believe in the chains, so you find the evidence.

Every generation learns Rousseau's philosophy as they start making sense of the world. Not surprisingly, every generation ends up believing that the world is grossly flawed. Each generation is seduced by the idea that happiness is the default state of life that we've been wrongfully deprived of. This stokes adolescent hope for the future, but it denigrates all that is good in the present.

Being "born free" means different things depending on your perspective. Imagine a wild animal peering at a zoo animal. The zoo animal is free to lie about in the sun while the wild animal is chained by the burden of finding food and escaping from predators. Few of us would choose to be the zoo animal despite this contrast. Most people would elect to be the free animal. But the choice to be the free brings the responsibility of meeting your own needs, and the frustrations that come with it.

Two centuries after Rousseau, man is freer than ever, but many people still feel chained. Our lives are quite safe compared to life in other times and places, but we don't realize it because our brains are just as alert for threats. They keep doing the job they evolved for. They brain correctly recognizes the precariousness of life, and that triggers the sense that something is wrong with the world.

The brain did not evolve to dwell on what is right with the world. In the Preface of this book, I described the humbling moment when I noticed my own negative bias. I was lecturing on the "zero-defect" strategy of Japanese factories, and condemning American factories for their sloppy 99.9% standard of quality. I was teaching my students that a 0.1% defect rate would bring collapse and ruin. I'm ashamed to think of it, and I want to say "everyone" was teaching that in 1995.

It's true that 99.9% adds up to a lot of defects – one per thousand. But I'd lost sight of the positive. American managers were shooting for a 0.0001% defect rate by implementing "Total Quality Management" programs. Today, most organizations have achieved big improvements in the quality of their goods and services. They constantly solicit feedback and investigate flaws. We are happy to let them know when things go wrong. As a result, quality has improved substantially. But we never celebrated the improvements because we are so focused on the flaws. We don't notice when things go right because we expect thing to be perfect all the time. Pointing out flaws can raise a person's status more than celebrating things that go right.

As a teacher, I contributed to this negativity. I trained my students to expect an apocalypse if things went right only 99.9% of the time instead of 99.9999%. By my count that was eight apocalypses ago: the loss of manufacturing in the mid-90s, the Y2K computer risk, the dot com bust, jihadi terrorism, epidemic diseases, global warming, the sub-prime financial collapse, and unemployment. By the time you read this, a few more apocalypses will have emerged.

These problems are real, and we do well to pay attention to them. We succeed at solving problems because we focus on them. And as soon as a problem is solved we shift our attention to the next most urgent problem. But we don't take note of the triumph. We may even think it's dangerous to lower our guard enough to enjoy it.

Our awareness of threats makes us long for a more perfect world. But our minds have to locate that world in a different time or place because any world we see up close is soon riddled with flaws.

Why did I suddenly notice my own negativity at that particular moment in 1995? I thought about this as I studied the mammal brain. I looked at the historical context, and was embarrassed at what I discovered. In 1995, Japan had been in a recession for five years and I was still singing the praises of Japanese management as if nothing had happened. Japan's "bubble economy" had collapsed in 1990, but in my mind Japan was still the perfect world I longed for. In the US, by contrast, a recession had begun in 1993, and I saw that as a sign of systemic decay. Everyone I knew thought that way.

But in 1995, the US economy showed signs of lifting out of the recession. I struggled to make sense of the good news since it conflicted with my expectations. And that's how I became intimate with my own expectations. I was living in a world where criticizing "our society" was so automatic that we were almost incapable of seeing anything else. It was distressing to realize that I could ignore huge chunks of reality. But I was heartened by my new ability to see the good in the world.

My openness to positive information strained my relations with the doomsaying herd. In 1996, the US economy boomed instead of collapsing, and the doomsayers rushed off in search of a new calamity. The Internet was taking off then, and doomsayers issued dire warnings of a coming "digital divide." Their fears of "digital haves and have-nots" were soon met with a flood of computers in the classroom. That didn't please the alarmists. They shrieked that teachers' lacked the skills to use the new equipment. Soon teacher training increased, and the outrage herd found new pastures to graze in.

The good in anything can be obscured if your mind only searches for the bad. I remember the thrill I felt when I sent my first e-mail to Europe. I couldn't get over the fact that it was free. I couldn't believe that websites provided information for free. The US government gave the Internet to the world for free. I was brimming with appreciation. I was through with hearing only alarm bells.

Outrage is a status-seeking strategy. It can raise a person's dominance faster than being appreciative can. Sometimes outrage has value, but it can become automatic. Good things can be taken for granted in the rush to find flaws.

People who condemn today's world rarely understand the harshness of life in the past. A simple example is the fact that virtually no one had flush toilets or electricity just a century ago. Three-quarters of the world has them today. In one century, life was transformed for most people. This timeline traces the progress in these basic comforts.

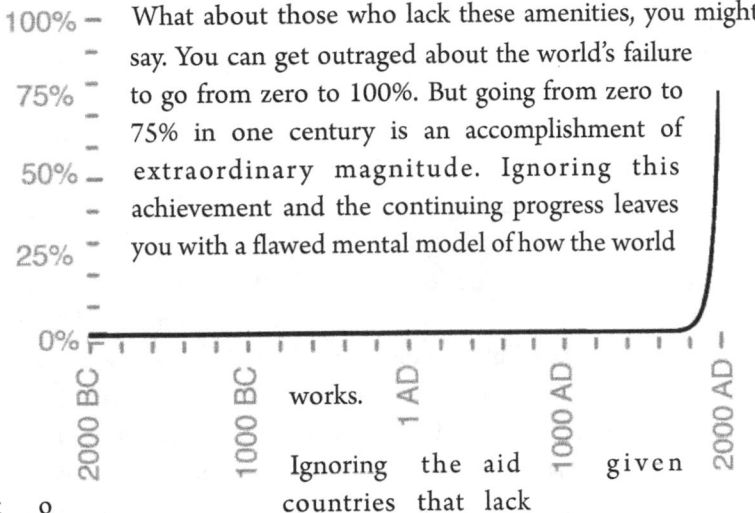

100% — What about those who lack these amenities, you might say. You can get outraged about the world's failure

75% — to go from zero to 100%. But going from zero to 75% in one century is an accomplishment of

50% — extraordinary magnitude. Ignoring this achievement and the continuing progress leaves

25% — you with a flawed mental model of how the world

0% — 2000 BC — 1000 BC — works. 1 AD — 1000 AD — given 2000 AD

Ignoring the aid to countries that lack infrastructure (not to mention the additional aid provided when earlier funds leaked into private pockets) leaves you with a distorted perception of the world. Enormous good can be overlooked while we are focused on imperfections.

People worked intensely over the past century to create the infrastructure we take for granted today. You can refuse to feel satisfaction as long as a single person lacks these comforts. But your dissatisfaction might have other causes. It may give you a sense of moral superiority which helps you feel good about your status.

Electricity and flush toilets don't make us happy, you may say. But if you were born before flush toilets and electricity, you would have gone to the vermin-infested outhouse in the dark. Cesspools and kerosene lamps would have filled your world with foul odors, toxins and disease. Animals would have tracked dirt between your outhouse and your cooking area, creating a vector for intestinal worms that would steal the nutrition from the food inside your body. It's easy to dismiss the value of infrastructure if you've only done without it on camping trips.

Electricity and indoor plumbing were bitterly criticized when first introduced. Early models of these technologies had bugs, of course. The first toilets and electric generators malfunctioned dangerously and bankrupted their investors. But developers of infrastructure overcame the negativity. They surmounted huge obstacles and provided us with the comfort and safety we take for granted just one century later. At my age, I know how short a century is.

The difficulties of the past don't feel real because we haven't experienced them with our senses. Freedom from pit toilets and river water doesn't feel like a cause for celebration because we were born free of them. Sexual freedom is easier to celebrate because it's easier to remember not having it. If you were born in another time or place, you would not have been free to choose your sex partner. People today rage about small infringements on sexual freedom without noticing the extreme restrictions of the past.

For much of human history, males were obligated to brides their parents had chosen for status reasons. Females were often mated without their consent, frequently to much older men with status.

In the past, men were typically denied mates until an advanced age because girls were controlled by families who held out for high-status mates. Men went to prostitutes instead, and so accelerated the spread of disease.

In the past, women had to obey their husbands regardless of the circumstances. A woman beaten by her husband was rarely protected, and a woman abandoned by her husband had no means to support her children. Infidelity was severely punished – the loss of one's children or death was always a possibility. Just being friendly with a man could cause a woman to be shamed and shunned, even by other women.

Sexual exploitation of children was widespread. Children who dared to complain typically got retaliation or blame rather than support. No statistics were kept.

Romantic notions about love in other times and places persist despite the facts. When Paul Gauguin left his wife and five children in Europe to consort with young girls in Tahiti, he reinforced the myth that free love is the norm far from home. But it was not free for the young girls he was with. Their parents coerced these unions in a quest for status. Pre-industrial societies severely restricted mating opportunities – the evidence is abundant if you are willing to see it.

The suffering of the past is hard to see because our minds are preoccupied with the suffering of the present. The brain is inclined toward *chronocentrism* – the habit of using the present time as the lens for seeing the past and future. People believe today's suffering is worse than the past because direct experience triggers more unhappy chemicals than suffering you only know from a book or a screen. But the brain is not aware of this bias. Our chronocentrism makes it easy to believe today's problems are more pressing than those of the past.

If life is so good today, why aren't people happy? Because the mammal brain never stops looking for survival threats. If you don't face hunger, predators, or sexual rivals right now, your mind finds more distant and subtle threats to focus on. If the worst thing that happens to you is not getting a party invitation or a hoped-for promotion, then that's the threat your brain feels. It does not celebrate the fact that you have a reliable food supply, basic hygiene, sexual freedom, and no one is violently attacking you.

Status Anxiety:
The Unhappiness that Dare Not Speak Its Name

You may be absolutely convinced that you don't care about status. But when you see other people getting all the glory, it triggers your unhappy chemicals. When you see others getting the recognition that is not coming your way, it feels like something is wrong. You may prefer not to think about status, but it's hard to ignore the world's failure to recognize your true worth.

Your brain compares the recognition it gets with the recognition it expects. When reality falls short, unhappy chemicals flow. This is status anxiety.

Your expectations are central to your satisfaction. You built these expectations from past experience. Here are some common examples of the expectations people build.

• A child may be treated like an alpha in his own home, for any number of reasons. The child's brain may learn to expect others to submit to him. But once he leaves the niche he adapted to, he finds that the world does not bend to his wishes. Frustration and disappointment are the likely result. He might respond in different ways, depending on his other experiences. One child might grow into a ruthless dominator, while another works hard to become a leader in the best sense of the word.

• A child may be aggressively dominated by someone in his life. His brain learns that a bigger person can act on the impulse to dominate instead of restraining it. One child may go on to mirror this aggression when he can get away with it. Another may grow up to be extremely restrained, protecting himself from potential aggressors. It all depends on the other experiences his brain encounters.

• A child's parent may have status anxiety. The adult's frustration with their insignificance activates the child's mirror neurons. The young mind builds circuits that prepare for this way of interacting with the world. The child's attention will focus on evidence that he is short-changed rather than evidence of his own effectiveness. The child could easily grow into an adult who makes no effort because he expects his efforts to go unrewarded. But he could also grow into an adult who makes constant effort because he feels inadequately rewarded. It depends on his other experiences.

• A child may be neglected and learn that nothing he does will get recognized. Something is wrong with that child's world, but their brain has no way to make sense of it. In the future, the child may excel at meeting his own survival needs. Conversely, he might learn that all effort is futile and fail to act on his own behalf.

• A child may find strength in alliances that bond around a common enemy. As he grows he may substitute different enemies but continue to depend on such alliances. Of course, he might learn to find other sources of strength instead.

Early experience is significant, but it does not shape a person in ways that can be predicted statistically. Early experience with social dominance prepares us to interpret later experiences. No matter what your life circumstances, you can find myriad reasons to feel bad about your status in relation to others.

Unhappy chemicals evolved for a purpose. They let a mammal know of a threat that must be addressed. They motivate survival initiatives despite risks.

Once a mammal's immediate survival needs are met, the survival of its DNA preoccupies its attention. Status is central to reproduction, so as soon as a mammal is safe and well fed, it is likely to focus on its status. It must get busy because it risks dying before it has heirs. To the mammal brain, death and status setbacks are the same thing because they both prevent reproductive success. The same unhappy chemicals communicate both of them, which is why status threats feel so bad.

Death is the ultimate status threat. At some point in the future, you will be gone and the world will get along without you. That is a very troubling thought. A brain emits unhappy chemicals when it contemplates its own demise. These unhappy chemicals color our thoughts about the future. I realized this at a lecture on long-term petroleum reserves. The speaker pointed to a chart with projections for a hundred years from now. Everyone in the room had to confront the fact that they wouldn't be around at that point. It's enough to give you a very bad feeling about petroleum reserves, or any other long-term projection.

In the future, the world will spin perfectly well without you. This thought is so uncomfortable that the mind can be strangely comforted by the idea that things are going to hell anyway so you won't really be missing anything. Of course, no one consciously wishes for the world to decay as they decay. Only an extremely dominating alpha-type like Louis XIV would come right out and say *"Apres moi, le deluge."* (After me, the flood.) But every brain has its own modest way of finding fault with a future from which they will ultimately be excluded.

No adult consciously thinks "the world should revolve around me." But a brain sees itself as the center of the world. That's the only way it can organize information efficiently. Life experience quickly frustrates this sense of your place in the world. You're the center of the world in your own brain, but life experience keeps invalidating this model. It's tempting to conclude there's something wrong with the world.

Confronting one's own insignificance in the world can be quite a blow. Humans have traditionally eased their mortality fears by focusing on the legacy they will leave behind. We invest in children and take heart in the thought of those children carrying on. We invest in all kinds of legacies that will outlive us, and it helps ease our fear of the future. But potential threats to our legacy keep popping into our minds. The brain keeps doing its job, looking for potential survival threats so it can prevent them.

No matter what your status, you can think of ways to make your legacy more secure by raising your status a bit more. As long as we have energy left in us, we keep anticipating threats and trying to do something about them.

So there is not likely to be an end to people's tendency to be frustrated about their status. The best we can do is to avoid the aggression that accompanies the pursuit of dominance in the animal world. When you consider the natural inclinations of the mammal brain, we humans have prevented violence quite successfully. Most people don't realize this because even low levels of violence alarm us, for good reason. We don't celebrate the fact that we can walk among strangers every day without the violence that was routine in the past. I appreciate the enormity of this accomplishment because my family had a legacy of violence.

Sicilians don't like to acknowledge the culture of violence that occurs behind closed doors. Often they blame it on history, since Sicily was invaded by one civilization after another over the past three millennia. During the Roman Empire, most Sicilians were slaves, producing the grain that Romans lived on. As recently as 1912, Booker T. Washington reported that children were enslaved in Sicilian sulphur mines under conditions more brutal than any he'd heard of.[1] But regardless of what happened in the past, each person who's born has the power to manage their neurochemicals in a way that avoids violence.

Violence is a status-seeking strategy because it brings immediate dominance. In school I was taught that violence is caused by "our society." But I learned for myself the enormity of violence before and outside of "our society." Spin the globe and put your finger down anywhere, and you will find a place whose history includes one wave of violence after another. Between wars and invasions there would be in-group violence, including domestic violence. The evidence is available if you want it, though it may be more comforting to presume a perfect world in other times and other places.

---

1 *The Man Farthest Down*, p. 203-15

Research on surviving tribal societies reveals ancient traditions imbued with violence. Raiding, revenge killings, and violent rituals of all sorts are almost continual. Research on the Yanomami of the Amazonian rainforest shows that violence claims the lives of about a third of all males.[2] Male chimpanzees die from aggression in approximately the same proportion.[3] More evidence of violence among those we imagine as peaceful can be found in *Sick Societies: Challenging the Myth of Primitive Harmony,* and *Demonic Males* (female violence is omitted from this one). In *Jungle Child,* a contemporary culture of violence in a Stone-Age tribe in New Guinea is described by a girl who grew up there.

Despite the abundance of conflicting evidence, the illusion of a peaceful past endures. It's not hard to understand why. A social scientist can raise his status by generating evidence of a peaceful past. By contrast, a scholar who finds evidence of violence in early man is often ridiculed and shunned. A good example of this is recounted in *Constant Battles,* a fascinating account of the bias in archeology. The author, Steven LeBlanc, explains that he stumbled on evidence of ancient battles wherever he dug. He was not looking for battlefields, but his digs were always turning up masses of arrows and human bones broken by arrows. His colleagues dismissed his findings with the flat assertion that war did not exist during the early time period he was excavating. They filtered the evidence to match their presumptions, and Leblanc's status suffered.

Why would so many people share the view that "our society" causes violence and close their eyes to other violence? There's a certain comfort in the idea that some natural state of perfection can be restored. Perhaps people think they are helping to prevent violence by

---

2 Chagnon also reports that Yanomamo war veterans have 2.5 times more wives and three times as many children as other males.
Napoleon Chagnon "Life Histories, Blood Revenge, and Warfare in a Tribal Population." *Science* 239 [February 20] pp.985-992. As quoted in Wrangham, page 70.

3 Richard Wrangham p.70, based on data from Goodall, *The Chimpanzees of Gombe*

promoting the illusion of a peaceful past. But the opposite result is likely. Ignoring the legacy of human violence obscures the effort it takes to raise children who eschew violence. Today, most homes are not violent and most places are not at war most of the time. Mass pillaging and raping is rare, even in wars. Such behavior was the norm for our distant ancestors. We must recognize the enormity of this accomplishment so we can continue investing the effort it requires.

Apes are inclined to attack any stranger that approaches. Today, you can travel to any city far from home and rub shoulders with thousands of strangers in safety. We have done something right. We must value this achievement and the constant effort it takes to perpetuate it. Every new generation has the potential for violence unless they learn alternate modes of feeling good about their status. Understanding our legacy of violence is not a means of excusing it but a means of preventing it.

The habit of equating violence with "our society" rests on our tolerance for open discussion of unpleasant subjects. In some societies, domestic violence is widespread but it is taboo to mention it. The custom of reporting, quantifying, and investigating child abuse and spousal abuse is not universal. Statisticians do not know what goes on behind closed doors when the people behind those doors are pressured to keep their mouths shut.

In many societies, violence was and is accepted as a routine part of life. Even violence against children has been tolerated until recent times. In places where violence against children is the norm, each generation grows up expecting the world to be violent. In such places, people do not lament the evils of their society in public. It's too dangerous. To know about the violence in those societies you need access to personal stories. I have been honored with such stories by many students and teachers from other countries. Of course this is anecdotal evidence, but I cannot ignore the abundant reports of domestic violence, neighborhood violence and even classroom violence that has reached my ears.

When I lived in the academic world, other cultures and other species were presumed to be peaceful. If a student questions this view, teachers tend to say "they don't get it." If a student embraces the view that "our society" causes all the suffering of humans and animals, teachers are likely to smile on their work. Students understand this reward structure. They can mirror the views of their teachers or subject themselves to extra scrutiny. Their mammal brains seek rewards and avoid harm.

Condemning "our society" is a good way to raise your status. Opposing high-status individuals is a good way to build alliances that can help raise your status. New alphas eventually replace old alphas in every group of mammals. The transition happens without violence in most human groups today. That is a tremendous accomplishment. New alphas build alliances with words rather than physical force. People support new alphas when they think it will raise their status. Would-be alphas encourage us to be unhappy with our status under the old alpha. We feel the unhappiness and fail to celebrate the immense feat of having non-violent leadership transitions.

Reports of aggression are repeated endlessly in the news, but physical violence has actually become rather rare in most people's daily experience. If we grow up around adults who manage their urge for dominance without aggression, we are likely to learn that as well. Humans can manage their mammalian urge for dominance, but it's hard to do unless you learn it while you are young.

Living without violence does not automatically make you happy. Your mammal brain will still feel frustrated and disappointed when others dominate you in subtle ways. Your mind will seek its own ways to dominate. But you will be able to manage your unhappy chemicals without aggression against others. This is a huge achievement. We don't appreciate our own success because we are so busy trying to manage our frustrations without aggression.

To your mammal brain, a better world is one in which you are dominant and stay dominant. Obviously we will all be disappointed in this quest, so our mammal brains will always have reason to find fault with the world. Being out-ranked or out-classed or out-done triggers real unhappy chemicals. But if this frustration is the worst thing in your life, some part of you can know that things are not really so bad. In the animal world, being one-upped threatens the survival of your DNA. But a human cortex can recognize their unhappy chemicals as a survival alarm from an ancient operating system.

Rewards Come from Effort, But Not Predictably

Frustration has evolutionary value. Today I watched lemurs feeding at the zoo, and was shocked to see one lemur stand aside while the others ate. The keeper told me he was the bottom of the totem pole, and the others wouldn't let him eat until they were satisfied. The critter was actually overweight because the keepers made sure he had chances to feed. But they couldn't prevent the dominance behaviors that went on when the food first came out.

The lowest-ranking lemur would starve to death if he were happy with this situation. Instead, unhappy chemicals keep reminding him "this is not good for you," so he stays alert for opportunities to feed.

Disappointment is part of every life. Your mammal brain starts seeking new opportunities as soon as it satisfies one desire, so you constantly have new opportunities to be disappointed. No society can guarantee the fulfillment of your expectations because we keep developing new expectations.

Yet we need expectations to motivate effort. We need effort to get rewards. It would be nice if rewards came in a predictable way so we never have to waste effort and experience disappointment. Our cortex is always looking for the patterns that predict rewards. But alas, the world keeps failing to fit those patterns and give us the rewards we expect.

We could hold out for guaranteed rewards before we invested any effort. That would protect us from disappointment, but we'd end up with few rewards. Thus, the ability to manage disappointment is our greatest strength in an unpredictable world.

Most great human achievements yielded disappointing rewards. The things you value today were created by people who did not get the rewards they expected. If you look at the lives of great innovators and contributors, you find:

- people who worked hard and got little recognition
- people who got hostility or ridicule in response to their innovations
- people who did something big and got only a small reward
- people who got a brief big reward and then were forgotten, their achievement taken for granted
- people who were celebrated after they died
- people who worked hard and had an impact, but it was not noticed beyond their immediate social circle
- people who were both celebrated and attacked for their achievements, so their enjoyment was always accompanied by a fear of attack.

All of these people persevered despite the disappointing rewards. Your quality of life today rests on their efforts. Human civilization is the accumulation of useful work done by people who were rarely celebrated and often disdained while they are alive. It is hard to understand this because we honor famous people when we study history. We presume they lived lives of honor and glory, but that's not often the case.

It's easy to imagine that other people are getting all the honor and glory. You can easily conclude that you are being neglected or deprived. Looking for evidence to support this belief can preoccupy your attention, distracting you from more constructive pursuits.

It helps to know that rewards are unpredictable. Other people are not enjoying continual honor and glory, even when it seems that way. You are not missing out on anything. Other people are just mammals scanning for the next opportunity to raise their status, and the next potential threat to their status. Everyone experiences frustration about their status, because everyone has a mammal brain.

When I'm frustrated with my rewards, I think about Prince Albert, the husband of Queen Victoria. You may find it hard to imagine a prince having status problems. And you may find it hard to believe that your present quality of life owes so much to him. His story is a fascinating lesson in persevering through disappointment.

When Prince Albert married Queen Victoria, the British Parliament refused to give him a title. This was a problem because European diplomatic functions seated people according to their title. Albert was not officially entitled to sit next to his own wife because he was only the second-born son of a minor Germanic duke. To make matters worse, diplomatic protocol required calling guests to dinner in rank order with a loud announcement of each guest's title. This made a public spectacle of Albert's lowly status. His own children outranked him, because they got their status from Mum. Exceptions were made at functions held by the Queen and her allies, but Albert always lived with the risk of this humiliation.

There are worse things in life, of course. But Albert suffered those much-worse things too. When he was five years old, his mother was banished by his father and Albert never saw her again. Albert's father was an especially decadent duke, and Albert's older brother took after Papa. Albert was dragged along when they caroused their way through Europe's capitals, and it humiliated him. Venereal disease ravaged their minds and bodies, as it did for so many of their day.

Albert had little freedom of choice over his own life. Perhaps the worst injury from a modern perspective was his lack of freedom over his own heart. Albert was expected to marry his cousin Victoria from the moment he was born, and if that weren't indignity enough, he was commanded to make her fall in love with him. Having this life path imposed on him deprived him of career choice as well as romantic choice.

When he succeeded in winning Victoria's hand, he was badly received by the British aristocracy. He hoped they would see him as a king, but they tended to see him as a bull hired to mate with an especially prized cow. Albert was extremely well-educated and cultured, both in arts and in sciences, which was not at all typical of British royals. This erudition became more fodder for those who mocked him. A man who didn't drink, gamble or womanize was regarded as a fool in that world.

Thus, Albert's "advantages" in life did not bring him respect or happiness. The only respect he could get was that which he earned through his direct interactions with others. So he focused his attention on that. Instead of despairing about the flaws of the world, he worked endlessly to contribute in every way possible. Today, most people do not appreciate his legacy, even though we all benefit from it.

Albert organized the first world technology fair, the "Crystal Palace" Exhibition of 1851. That event sparked the world's fairs and the cross-borders technology sharing that we take for granted today.

Albert advanced democracy by keeping the monarchy out of politics. Victoria was inclined to meddle in government for her own enjoyment. He prevailed on her to maintain scrupulous neutrality and avoid even the appearance of royal preferences among political parties and candidates. Thanks to this foreigner, the legislature became the real seat of power, and the monarchy became a cultural institution with little role in government.

Albert's most misunderstood contribution was his insistence on marital fidelity in his staff. Today, the word "Victorian" is synonymous with priggishness. But if you had a father who came home after work instead of visiting his mistress, you can thank Prince Albert. He challenged the double standard in marriage, and prevailed. In his day, wandering husbands spread venereal diseases to innocent wives and children. Albert stood up to the "everybody does it" mentality, and fired staff who violated their marriage vows. Not surprisingly, this earned him jeers and rebukes rather than appreciation. And perhaps most frustrating of all, his first born son, the future king Edward, publicly flouted his principles, thus undermining his efforts to add respectability to the tarnished British monarchy. Edward was more popular than Albert with the public, however. Gluttony and womanizing have a certain appeal to the mammal brain.

Albert was widely sneered at during his lifetime. But instead of giving up, he worked constantly to build things of value. Indeed, he was a workaholic who drove himself into an early grave at age 42.

Some of his efforts were rewarded during his lifetime. His integrity and effectiveness were commended by those who valued such qualities. But sometimes he got seated at a "bad table." The rewards of the world are unpredictable, so he just kept making efforts despite the uncertainty of the rewards. He put his energy into meaningful projects instead of junk status.

Our lives today are enriched by the efforts of earlier individuals who may or may not have been honored while they were alive. We are all free to resist the lure of junk status and invest our energy in worthwhile efforts, though the rewards are uncertain in our lifetime.

Our expectations may be disappointed and we may end up feeling frustrated. These frustrations are caused not by "the system" but by our lust for life. No system can save us from the core frustration of being alive and mammal. And that's good news because we can stop waiting for a perfect world to make us happy and start making ourselves happy.

In every civilization and time period, humans have imagined the perfect world that would result from ousting their present group of alphas. This urge has slowly improved the human condition. New alphas never make things perfect, of course, but things are not as bad as they look. Status frustration is what makes the world look bad. When your status rises, things look good...for a short time. Then the feeling is metabolized and your brain seeks more.

The constant desire for progress means we're often disappointed. Our worthwhile efforts fail to change the world; and our efforts to win the respect of others get less respect than we hope for. The idea that something is wrong with the world always tempts us.

But you can always say to yourself "I'm a mammal. I'm frustrated because my brain evolved to care deeply about my legacy." No one likes the idea that they care about status. Everyone can see other people's status seeking, and the self-destructiveness that can result. But our own pursuits seem righteous. Our aspirations bring frustration, but we can manage frustration without aggression or despair. And that is a triumph to celebrate.

Keep in touch

Please write and tell me how you explain the inner mammal to the people in your life. Loretta@InnerMammalInstitute.org

Please review this book on your favorite website.

And please enjoy my newsletter and the many free resources at The Inner Mammal Institute: InnerMammalInstitute.org.

Epilogue

A Mammal at the Movies

...Mr. Darcy's large brain sets its sights on the girl who hates him for being rich. In fiction, girls who hate rich guys always seem to land one in the end, despite the abundance of available poor guys...

The mammal brain's interest in status is easy to see on the big screen. Your mammal brain can run free while you're watching a movie because you're not burdened with the real-life need to act. Your mirror neurons respond to the characters' actions so you understand more than just their words. Their actions are often focused on status even if their words suggest otherwise. This chapter describes fifteen great mammalian moments in the movies – moments when a character's mammalian neurochemistry exerts its curious pull toward status seeking. So start buttering the popcorn and invite friends to watch the mammal brain in action in these movies.

Mean Girls (2004)

The Gods Must Be Crazy (1980)

Doctor Zhivago (1965)

What Makes Sammy Run? (1959)

Caterina in the Big City [Caterina Va in Citta] (2005)

Pride and Prejudice (2005)

The Last Emperor (1987)

The Prisoner of Second Avenue (1975)

The Good Earth (1937)

Young Victoria (2009)

Goodfellas (1990)

The Bicycle Thief (1948)

Ninotchka / Silk Stockings (1939 / 1957)

Mrs. Brown (1997)

Creation: How Darwin Saw the World & Changed It Forever (2009)

The movies explored here are not about greed or evil. They're about people you would like to know as they struggle with their automatic appetite for status. (I made an exception for a Mafia movie because it revolves around my old neighborhood.)

Every minute of every movie is a mammalian moment, in truth. But the scenes described below show people confronting the social dominance concerns that creep into their lives. We will not focus on cruel dominators and reproductive maniacs, or craven status seekers getting their comeuppance. We will focus on honorable people trying to get happy chemicals from their brains in whatever way works. We will see how the mammal brain rewards whatever promotes reproductive success in the state of nature.

Movies often revolve around status triumphs. Watching these triumphs helps develop neural connections that respond to our real-life successes. Movies help people stimulate that triumphant feeling without taking self-destructive risks.

Of course, movies are not real human stories; they are the screenwriters' and investors' idea of what audiences will buy. But screenwriters, investors and audiences are all mammals. Movies are made by mammals and for mammals. They sell by appealing to the mammal brain, despite their many biases.

All of the movies covered here are available from Netflix.com. Spoiler alert: plot twists and endings are revealed as necessary to explain the mammalian moments. This will not "spoil" the movie, however, because watching with an eye for the mammal brain's familiar footprints is more fun.

Outstanding nature documentaries are also available on Netflix. The recent *Life* series has remarkable up-close photography of primate and mammalian social interactions. Attenborough's *The Life of Mammals* and *Planet Earth* are also noteworthy, especially the primate segments.

Human evolution is the subject of many excellent documentaries, including these Netflix offerings: *Ape to Man, Walking with Cavemen,* and *Walking with Prehistoric Beasts* (episode 4 on australopithecines, our "missing link" ancestor).

Mean Girls

Tina Fey adapted the popular sociology book, *Queen Bees and Wannabes*, into a comedy about teen status conflicts. We see the meanness of a high school alpha female (the "Queen Bee") to her "best friend." The friend has to accept this treatment if she wants to keep her place as the second-ranking girl in the school. In primate troops the alpha usually has a beta, and this sidekick role is immortalized in the movies. Sociology illuminates this mammalian pattern. The "Wannabe" has invested a lot in status, but they haven't yet attained the top reward. If they give up they lose all that investment, so it behooves them to hang on and put up with whatever the alpha dishes out. Lower-ranking individuals can easily remove themselves from the game because they have less to lose.

The herd behavior of high school is brilliantly depicted in *Means Girls*. One scene shows the alpha female returning to her locker to find that her clothing had been vandalized while she was in PE. Holes were cut into her T-shirt in two strategic places. She calmly puts the shirt on (over an under-layer) and strolls to her next class. She personifies the confidence of a dominant individual as everyone stares at the prominent holes. The next day, in a mesmerizing mammalian moment, we see the halls at school filled with girls wearing holes cut in the same strategic places.

Imitating the alpha is a mammalian way to raise your status. The isopraxis of mammals is obvious when we see other people doing it. But when we are the ones blending in with a herd for our own protection, we often find other ways to explain our choices.

Linsey Lohan plays the heroine of *Mean Girls*. Her character, Cady, is the daughter of a field biologist, and thus disposed to see the parallels between the behavior of wildlife and the behavior of the herd she is trying to break into. We get to hear Ms. Lohan pontificate on mammalian behavior when Cady goes to the mall with friends. The mall has a fountain reminiscent of the watering holes Cady saw in

Africa with her mother. While students strut and preen around the fountain, Cady has a revery in which they morph into baboons and elephants splashing around a drinking pool. Cady perceives that high school is a mammalian social dominance hierarchy motivated by reproductive success. The opportunity to hear Ms. Lohan expound this view is priceless.

The movie presumes to be a critique of social hierarchies. Yet it unwittingly proves the rule that mammals care about status. Cady sets out to oppose the Queen Bee and her retinue rather than just going her own way. She eventually sees the error in that path, but then she suddenly becomes an alpha herself. In the guise of a Mathletes champion, she substitutes one status indicator for another.

Cady is elected Homecoming Queen despite her professed disdain for status. Fiction often revolves around the fantasy of rejecting status but acquiring it anyway. Cady goes to Mathletes instead of the prom, but she drops by in jeans just to refuse the crown. This unlikely scenario ends in her giving a triumphal speech about how everyone is special. Fat girls cry when they hear her words. Ugly girls glow when Cady says they're beautiful. They suddenly feel beautiful because the popular girl says they are beautiful. The movie aptly shows how much people voluntarily focus their attention on high-status individuals.

Opposing status is tempting, but it's useful to realize that status hierarchies are not always forced on us. People often choose to engage with social dominance hierarchies. They enjoy the dream of status, and they look to high-status individuals for leadership. We don't see this in ourselves because our mammal brain does not speak to us in words. So we may feel like victims of a hierarchy even while we are active participants.

Mean Girls ends with some authentic assertions of individuality. The beta girl finally carves her own path instead of just submitting to the alpha girl. And in real life, the actress who played the Wannabe (Amanda Seyfried) went on to be the Queen Bee, starring in *Mamma Mia!* and other movies.

The Gods Must Be Crazy

A South African woman is bored with her office routine and takes a job teaching at a bush school. In the bush village, she makes the acquaintance of a good-looking field biologist. The scientist falls all over himself trying to capture the schoolteacher's attention. He is effectively the last man on earth, since the bush school is run by a priest. Yet the biologist's courtship signals are so bumbling that he only succeeds at annoying her.

Competition for the schoolteacher's hand soon appears in the form of a safari operator. He wines and dines her like an evil capitalist from central casting. If the biologist doesn't up his game soon, the competition will be over. Male mammals often win female attention by providing protection for the female's children, and the biologist embraces this strategy. He rescues the damsel and all of her students when they're kidnapped by a band of guerillas. Suddenly, he looks good to her, even though he hasn't really changed.

The rescue effort is aided by a Kalahari bushman who happened to be walking by. The movie takes its title from the bushman's story. He's a hunter-gatherer from a tribe sometimes known as the !Kung or San. He's on his way to the end of the earth to dispose of a Coke bottle that brought conflict to his tribe. The Coke bottle fell from a helicopter in the opening scene, and we saw his tribe find many uses for this unfamiliar "tool." But having only one posed an unprecedented problem. The gods must be crazy to have sent only one, they complain.

A heroic tribe member volunteers to save his people by walking to the edge of the earth and throwing the thing off. These opening scenes are presented with subtitled !Kung speech, and a narrator who hails the indigenous people for their pristine freedom from the taint of private property. As the bushman saunters off on his mission, we see breathtaking shots of African wildlife. Herds of gazelles, zebras and giraffes prance majestically across the savannah as the bushman moves toward his encounter with the biologist, the safari, and the guerillas.

The bushman's hunting skills help the scientist triumph over the guerrillas and rescue the woman and children. When the school teacher falls for the biologist, it's a charming mammalian moment. We see that he's still a bumbler, but he has proven his ability as a protector. She did not want him when he was only gorgeous, kind, and a successful professional. Female mammals confer status onto mates capable of protecting children.

The schoolteacher went to the bush to find happiness in good works and nature, but finds it instead in the arms of a tall blond guy. A movie that starts with narration about the discontents of civilization ends up with the predictable contentment of romantic love. The reason things unfold this way so often in movies and in life is that reproductive success is a huge trigger of mammalian happy chemicals. Sex is only a small part of the agenda. Everything that promotes surviving children triggers mammalian happy chemicals. Movies are popular because they trigger happy chemicals without all the fuss and bother of reproduction.

The sequel, *The Gods Must Be Crazy 2*, combines all these elements in a fresh way, and is a joy to watch.

Doctor Zhivago

Doctor Zhivago finds true love while the Russian Revolution shatters the world around him. We want to see him enjoy his island of security amidst the ruin because he has done so many good deeds. But he throws it all away when another alpha male enters his territory.

Zhivago's rival barges into the lovers' hideaway in the snowy tundra. The rival declares that advancing troops pose immediate danger, and he offers to help them escape. He invites them into his special train compartment to cross Siberia into the relative safety of China.

Zhivago's mammal brain responds badly to this invitation. He wants to save his lover, but he would rather die than be stuck in that train compartment in the subordinate position, dependent on the rival for survival. A silverback gorilla would react the same way. Mature male gorillas never tolerate proximity to another mature male gorilla. They will risk their lives in a bid for the dominant position if they can't withdraw.

In a tragic mammalian moment, Zhivago tricks his lover into boarding the train without him. Why would a hero just give his girl to the rival and stay alone on the brutal steppes? To the human mind it makes no sense, but to the mammal brain it's clear that Zhivago's hatred of submission is stronger than his love for the woman. Once Zhivago makes this choice, he's a broken man. Though he miraculously survives the massacres and deadly deprivations of the early communist years, his zest for life is gone. Zhivago is portrayed as a person of enormous intelligence, sensitivity and courage. Yet that momentary urge to avoid the one-down position was stronger than every other fiber of his being.

Zhivago's lover was carrying his child when they parted. That child is the frame of the story. We see history from the perspective of this orphan who knows nothing of her own ancestry. She'd gotten separated from her mother in the Soviet Far East. She never knew her father, and being descended from an aristocrat would have been dangerous anyway for a child in the Soviet Union. When she's told who her father was, it means nothing to her. We feel a sense of hopelessness over Zhivago's lost legacy. Then, the camera lingers on her holding hands with a boy. It reminds us that the cycle will continue. Her mammal brain will seek happiness in reproductive success, whatever the calamities of her moment of history. Zhivago's DNA will survive.

What Makes Sammy Run?

Sammy is a social-climbing clod. He kowtows to high-status individuals who can help him and snubs those who can't. We are told Sammy's story through the eyes of his best friend. The jealous friend solicits our disdain for Sammy's ruthless ambition. But the friend's protestations ring hollow. He does nothing to realize his own "higher values." All he does with his life is criticize Sammy's life.

The movie is based on a novel that became a hit Broadway musical before the movie. The author, Budd Schulberg, aims to mock the Jewish ghetto boy who clawed his way to the top of the movie biz. Sammy is a jerk, so it's easy to cluck your tongue at his actions. But if the best friend is so offended by Sammy's self-seeking, he is free to go out and live what he considers a better life. Instead, he dwells in his resentment of Sammy's choices.

The friend is too proud to admit that he cares about his status. His capacity to tolerate risk is too limited to pursue his own status. Feeling superior to the high-status Sammy is the guy's short-cut status strategy.

This quirk of human nature is perfectly capsulized in a brief mammalian moment. The friend rages for the umpteenth time, "Sammy, what makes you run?," and Sammy responds: "what makes people run after me?" The point is not that Sammy is good, which of course he's not. The point is that good people seek him out because they care about status. Mammals care deeply about social dominance, even when they pretend to despise it. Frustration prevails, but there's no one to blame but natural selection. It's tempting, during moments of frustration, to blame anyone you perceive as outranking you. But this leaves your attention focused on them and what they have instead of on the pleasure of your own accomplishments.

We are all free to reject status and to invest our energy into worthy and productive ends. But that's not easy to do, so people often invest their energy into critiquing other people's choices.

Caterina in the Big City (Caterina Va in Citta)

This movie is the least known on the list, but it has my favorite mammalian moment. Imagine you're the new kid in school, watching two rival cliques sparring against each other. Imagine it's a fancy private school in Rome, and the cliques reflect the politics of the students' parents. Now imagine both cliques are courting you, and your father courts your friends in an effort to raise *his* status.

Caterina is so embarrassed by her father that she erupts into a brawl with both clique leaders. The three girls' parents get called into the principal's office, so Caterina's Dad gets to rub shoulders with the two alpha-male Dads. One is a right-wing Cabinet minister and the other a left-wing media star.

As they all leave the principal's office, the alpha Dads greet each other with the same gestures that high-ranking chimpanzees use to cement alliances. They back-slap and head-bob with such exuberance that one can't help thinking of a nature documentary. Caterina's Papa makes social overtures to the other two Dads, but they flatly ignore him. Papa looks on with grief as they as they chat cozily, and Caterina takes it all in. It's an iconic mammalian moment.

Caterina's Dad expresses his bitterness to her. He points out the irony of these political enemies enjoying each other so much because of their shared alpha status. "They are both the same kind," he tells Caterina. "The kind who know how the world works." He warns her that you can't get anywhere in Italy without being part of a clique.

It was hard for me to watch this because my mother also shared her bitterness about status with me. Caterina's father has good insight into mammalian social dominance. But his constant raging about other people's status seeking is self-destructive. His life falls apart because he loses control of his bitterness. Caterina's challenge is to make peace with the mammal world despite the lack of peace in those around her. Of course, that is everyone's challenge.

Caterina looks to her other parent for guidance. Mamma begins a love affair with a neighbor as Papa melts down in a frenzy over slights and disappointments. The mother is a very submissive character, and the attention of a shy neighbor gives her what she doesn't get from her self-centered husband. Soon, Caterina adopts this strategy. She gets a twinkly eyed look for the boy next door and by focusing on him she retreats from the conflict between her peers and her parents.

Romantic love is a popular refuge from status anxiety. You can't always get the respect of the world, but you can get respect from one person. This feels good for a while. But the mammal brain did not evolve to sit around and enjoy it. It evolved to keep seeking more ways to advance its legacy. As a result, our lives have complex plot lines.

Pride and Prejudice

Elizabeth Bennett hates the pressure to "marry well." She especially hates the alpha male next door. She blames British high society for her frustrations, without realizing that every female primate faces the same dilemma. Should a gal choose the alpha as the father of her child, or should she lean toward the guy she finds strong and clever regardless of his position in the eyes of her troop?

Female chimpanzees are often attracted to outsiders who have no status in their troop. A lady sometimes prefers a gentleman for reasons unrelated to the public esteem he commands. Yet there are distinct advantages to mating with the alpha, and most female chimps end up preferring him too. A baby can only have one father, alas, so these choices have consequences.

Mating decisions are fraught with uncertainty because you cannot really judge the quality of a partner until long after your mating decision. Whether you're male or female, human or chimp, this conundrum is real no matter how carefully you choose. Mammals have always struggled to maximize their mating choices; it did not begin with "our society."

Every society develops ways of sorting out this mess. Every female decodes the signs of male potential according to her particular life experience. If all ladies used Jane Austen as their guide we would not be here today, because she was so picky that she never mated. Romantic fantasies are nice, but if every lady over-analyzed the matter as Ms. Austen did, a species would not reproduce itself.

Of course, modern women are not consciously shopping for father material most of the time. They are shopping for "attraction." But the mammalian drive to keep your DNA alive is at the core of neurochemical attraction.

Our mammalian inheritance perplexes modern males as much as modern females. Low-ranking males may find themselves shut out by pushy high-ranking males and status-conscious females. And even alpha males have mating problems. Consider Mr. Darcy, the hero of the book behind this movie. He is rich, good-looking, and socially prominent. So many ladies want an alpha male's attention that he could not protect all the babies that would result. He must choose between the quantity strategy (having lots of babies and hoping some of them turn out well without his involvement) and the quality strategy (concentrating his attention on the best mother, however that can be determined). Mammals with small brains opt for the quantity strategy. Mammals with larger cortexes tend to create fewer children and invest more time in each.

Mr. Darcy's large brain ends up setting its sights on Elizabeth Bennett, the girl who hates him for being rich. He displays his protective skills to her over and over until she falls for him, despite the blemish of his wealth. In fiction, girls who hate rich guys always seem to land a rich guy in the end, despite the abundance of available poor guys. This construct seems unrealistic to me, and Ms. Austen's real-life failure at romance reinforces my suspicion. Even a female baboon knows better than to antagonize an alpha male and expect him to respond by becoming ever-more devoted.

Yet rich-boy meets poor-girl remains a staple of fiction. The theme is recast in a modern setting in the TV sitcom, *Ugly Betty*. Betty is out of step with the herd, but every season another rich, handsome guy falls for her. We like the idea of attraction that's not based on social status. But what really gets our attention is attraction that raises someone's status. We want to think status doesn't matter, but what we really want is for status to come anyway as a reward for virtue.

Elizabeth Bennett and Mr. Darcy share an abhorrence of the status-driven mating game, and they think they're unique in this! Of course, almost everyone hates the status-driven mating game. Yet it continues because mating choices have huge consequences. A primate does not risk letting another primate get close until they have reason to expect unthreatening behavior. But unique life experience makes primates hard to predict, so we take all available information into account – including status.

The Last Emperor

The emperor of China is the most alpha human there is if you judge alphas by the size of their troop. This movie follows the life of the last "son of heaven," Pu-yi, who was born as China's imperial system fell. We watch the last emperor tumble down the status hierarchy from boy deity to elderly graduate of a communist reeducation camp. Bertolucci filmed it on location in the Forbidden City, so it's a visual delight.

Displaced emperors find few suitable jobs openings, so Pu-yi is glad when an Emperor slot opens up in Manchuria. The Japanese install him to help keep control of the territory they invaded. But in a touching mammalian moment Pu-yi realizes that he is a powerless puppet rather than a real alpha.

In nature, weaklings like Pu-yi don't dominate the social hierarchy. But as mammals grew larger brains, they increasingly cooperated in pursuit of shared goals. Cooperating with a dominant is one way for a mammal to raise its status. Pu-yi is a cooperator. We have compassion for his weakness because we see him being ripped from his mother at age two and raised by the scheming palace staff. The staffers clung to him to raise their own status. So Pu-yi learned to raise his status by cooperating with dominators.

In his old age Pu-yi finally stands up to aggressors. During the Cultural Revolution, he witnesses Red Guards attack the elderly communist official who had dominated him in prison years earlier. Pu-yi recalls the moments of humanity the official displayed during his long imprisonment. Pu-yi tries to protect the official from the Red Guards, while all the other witnesses submit to them. He takes great risk in doing this, but he's near death anyway and perhaps this will enhance his legacy.

During China's Cultural Revolution, Red Guards dominated their elders and gained status in the social hierarchy. Every generation of primates strives to do this in some way. Young male primates have no reproductive opportunity until they displace their elders, or at least impress elders with their strength. Older male monkeys bite and scratch younger troop-mates who try to mate with available females. This goes on until the rising youth are strong enough to retaliate, either at home or in a new troop. Humans have an ancient motivation to rise in the social hierarchy, but we dress our motives in lofty language. We explain conflict with theories that overlook the underlying mammalian drive to rise in the status hierarchy.

The Prisoner of Second Avenue

Neurochemistry plays a lead role in this Neil Simon gem about unemployment. Jack Lemmon plays an executive who falls apart after losing his job of two decades. His devoted wife, played by Ann Bancroft, does everything she can to help, but nothing works. They try therapy for his depression, and 1975-style therapy is fascinating to watch. It doesn't help, and the frenzy of Midtown Manhattan makes everything worse in classic Neil-Simon fashion.

What finally works is inappropriate rage. Jack Lemmon thinks he's been pick-pocketed, and fights back. This is not the cliched rage-at-the-system plot, because it's obvious that his aggression is misplaced. He jumped to the conclusion that his wallet was stolen when a stranger pressed against him on the street. The stranger is a very young Sylvester Stallone. Jack Lemmon chases Stallone around Central Park and Fifth Avenue, through the neighborhood inhabited by Jackie Kennedy, Bobbie Short, and the Metropolitan Museum. Finally, the depressed man tackles the presumed thief in front of aloof Manhattan passers-by, and grabs a wallet.

Jack Lemmon realizes the wallet isn't his when he gets home and shows his wife. But he suddenly notices that he feels good. The physical exertion and the vigorous pursuit of his self-interest jump-started his depressed neural circuits. His wife doesn't understand. She concentrates on the wrong he has done. In a compelling mammalian moment, he tries to put into words the sudden feeling of well-being he's experiencing. He suddenly feels adequate to face the challenges of life, from making amends with the owner of the wallet to finding a new job.

This is not just some playwright's fantasy but a real physiological phenomenon. Novelist Nick Hornby describes the same experience in his memoir, *Fever Pitch*. Hornby was in a deep depression for seven years, which coincided precisely with the losing streak of his favorite soccer team. When they finally won, his depression suddenly lifted. He was glad for that, but he was ashamed to think he'd hitched his emotions to such a banal guiding star. A more satisfying explanation is that his explosion of joy in a stadium full of like-minded people sparked his positive neural circuits enough to get them going again.

This movie shows how neurochemical reactions to events can be more significant than the events themselves. Our neurochemistry is rarely as easy to control as we expect. Our unhappy chemicals do not always yield to the verbal logic we impose on them. Sometimes, a mammalian problem requires a mammalian solution.

The Good Earth

This movie is a useful antidote to the belief that "life is hard these days." No one wants to watch a movie about people slowly starving to death, but the joy people feel when they triumph over scarcity is well-portrayed here. The movie is based on the book that won Pearl S. Buck the 1938 Nobel Prize for Literature and a 1932 Pulitzer Prize. The story is set in rural China, but the characters react to their status ups and downs in ways that humans from any time or place will recognize.

The husband and wife react differently, and that is the core of the drama. The wife seems unable to enjoy abundance when she has it. She grew up with cruelty, and once she has money the only thing she wants is to flaunt it in front of her former tormentors. She never built neural pathways for enjoying herself. She's a brilliant survivor, but she doesn't know it because her attention is always on the next crisis. Mammals have survived for millions of this years with this skill.

The husband is a lover of life as well as a survivor. When he gets rich, someone says it's time he take a second wife. His reaction to that suggestion is a captivating mammalian moment. He scoffs loudly, but he is clearly rolling it around in his mind. Soon, Wife #2 is installed in his home. A mammal turns its attention toward the survival of its DNA as soon as its immediate survival needs are met. We express this in different ways, but the same basic drive to leave a legacy generates the energy.

Wife #2 wrecks this prosperous home in classically primate ways. The women antagonize each other in a manner that is characteristic of female apes. Ugly male rivalries surface too, because Dad bought himself a woman without buying one for his two grown sons. One son retaliates in the time-honored manner of young primates. The junior wife is pleased to receive the attentions of the younger, stronger male. The alpha male reacts badly to this challenge.

When this family was starving, the actors played them with big smiles and erect spines. Once they become rich, the director presents them as petty and fatuous. The merchant father is practically twirling his mustache most of the time. Vilifying the rich and idealizing the poor is a simple way to make sense of the world, both on screen and in one's own mind. In the real world, rich and poor have the same mammal brain. That brain looks for ways to advance status, causing frustration and disappointment at the top, the middle, and the bottom. If poverty truly brought happiness, everyone burdened by silk robes would just rip them off and be happy.

Young Victoria

You don't expect a queen to have status problems, and you surely don't expect yourself to sympathize with them. But in this movie, we see how Queen Victoria was utterly dominated, even while the Crown of England was being handed to her.

Victoria did not have the alpha upbringing you might expect. Her ties to the British monarchy were weak. Her father was the fourth son of King George III, and died as soon as she was born. Her mother, a German, clung to status hopes by keeping her a virtual prisoner in Kensington Palace (later the home of Princess Diana). Little Vicky was slated to rule when every other legitimate heir to the throne died. Mum was determined to rule Victoria when Victoria ruled England.

The reigning king subverts Mum by clinging to life until Victoria's eighteenth birthday. When he dies, England's top leaders rush from his deathbed to Victoria's home in the middle of the night to recognize her as their monarch, according to custom. Mum refuses to wake her up, invoking parental authority. If Queen Victoria submitted to her mother at that moment, she would have had trouble reclaiming her power. But in a stirring mammalian moment, she straightens her spine, puts her shoulders back, and commands her mother to stay back as she goes in to accept the fealty of the Archbishop of Canterbury and the Prime Minister.

Alas, Victoria's life is full of people struggling to dominate her. Many status-seekers aspire to control the British Empire by controlling this petite, inexperienced teenaged girl. Hereditary titles don't exist in nature. Wild animals only rule if they are able to dominate their group-mates. Mammal enhance their dominance by building alliances. Many mammals sought alliances with Victoria.

Like every group-living mammal, Victoria had trouble figuring out who to trust. Whether you're a queen or just the monkey in the street, there's no easy way to predict which potential allies you can trust and which individuals will only hurt your survival prospects.

In the end, Victoria put her trust in Albert. He was also surrounded by manipulators, and their shared need to manage challenges to their dominance strengthened their bond.

As we've seen, Albert had unique status problems. British law did not accord him a title. The males at the top of Britain's status hierarchy were not keen to just give away the top slot. Albert's power to impregnate the Queen was the only power he had. So he did.

Albert settled into Buckingham Palace to find the kind of sexual intrigues that ruined his childhood. He catches a palace staffer *in flagrante,* and Victoria shrugs it off with an "everyone-does-it." Albert boils over and decides it's time to resist her and the whole palace bureaucracy. He fires the staffer, and in so doing sparks change in the cultural acceptance of male infidelity. It's hard for us to understand Albert's contribution now that the word "Victorian" has become a pejorative. By taking a stand, Albert helped to stop the epidemic of venereal disease in the only way possible at that time. Of course infidelity continued. But keeping mistresses was no longer an accepted routine because it could cost you your job.

People who mock Victorian values today do not know how they have benefited. In the past, any extra money a father had was likely to get diverted to a mistress. Today, a straying father risks losing half of everything. Women and children can thank Albert instead of sneering at him. We will always be mammals, but cultural institutions evolve to manage the consequences.

You can get more of the story from the two-disc BBC teleplay *Victoria and Albert* (2001), also available from Netflix.

Goodfellas

Mafiosi, like baboons, can move fluidly between cooperation and lethal rivalry. Primatologists like to focus on the cooperation part. They celebrate the caring and sharing of apes and skim over the brutality that regularly erupts. Movies often do that too. They focus on the camaraderie of criminals, representing them as a bunch of fellas uniting in common goals.

Goodfellas is more honest about the criminal urge to dominate. The movie is based on the life of Henry Hill as he told it to a journalist in the book *Wiseguy*. Hill had no formal status in the Mafia's social hierarchy - he was only half Italian. But he was very outspoken about the dominance-seeking behaviors they engage in.

The movie has special significance for me because it opens with the caption "East New York, 1955." That's the Brooklyn neighborhood I was born in, and the year my father moved us to the suburbs. My father was quite a submissive person, and this movie helps me understand. He grew up on the same streets as Henry Hill, watching Mafiosi dominating and getting "respect." My father never talked about it, but it's clear he did not embrace Henry Hill's strategy for getting respect.

In Italian, a Mafia member is called a "man of respect" (*uomo di rispetto*). Henry Hill grows up watching people defer to local mobsters the way baboons defer to their alpha. Young Henry's mirror neurons respond to the pleasure in that. At home he is violently dominated by his parents, so we can understand his urge to get out of the house and apprentice himself to the mob at age eleven. Soon, he starts getting respect.

The everybody-does-it attitude toward violence is brilliantly illuminated in a scene where Henry and friends stop for a snack at Mamma's house in the midst of committing murder. In an Academy Award-winning role, Joe Pesci invites the gang to his house to get shovels to bury the body and some home-cooked meatballs. In a stunning mammalian moment, Mamma is so thrilled by the company of these nice young men that she doesn't ask nosy questions about the blood all over them. They politely wash their hands and enjoy the meatballs without fear of her sauce staining their shirts. Scorsese cast his own mother in the role.

Henry becomes attractive to women as he rises in his chosen profession. He desires a nice Jewish girl from the other side of the tracks (played by a young Lorraine Bracco, the therapist in the *Sopranos*). Ordinarily she wouldn't look twice at him, but she sees *maitre d*'s fawn over him at top nightclubs, and she sees his brute-strength protectiveness when she's harassed by the boy next door. He seduces her with so much stuff that she quickly stops asking where the money cam from. He abuses her, and she submits to protect her own safety. It could easily be a case study from a primatology textbook.

Henry Hill gets the world to submit to his domination, over and over. He kills and steals with impunity. He brazenly defies the Mafia, first with drugs and then by testifying against them in court. Even the US Department of Justice submits to Henry. The Federal Witness Protection Program saves his life with a new identity, and he flagrantly returns to drugs and crime while under their protection. He blows his cover and they give him a second new identity, and then a third. This part of the story in taken up in another Hollywood movie, *My Blue Heaven*. Steve Martin is cast as a Henry Hill who's too hip for the suburban life the Feds have foisted on him. The FBI agents assigned to protect him are portrayed as bumblers who eagerly submit to his dominance. The *uomo di rispetto* is the good guy in Nora Ephron's screen adaptation of her husband's book *Wiseguy*.

Why would movie makers and audiences empathize with a brutal dominator rather than with his countless victims? Because the mammal brain is so impressed by social dominance that it can skim over horrific means to that end.

Remorse has not impeded Henry Hill's quest for status. He is still leveraging his story to pay the bills. He developed a Mafia cookbook, a website, and other marketing tie-ins to supplement his income from royalties and drug-dealing. His career as a celebrity is still gaining traction – consult YouTube for the dismaying details.

The Bicycle Thief (originally, Bicycle Thieves)

This movie has become a classic for its depiction of the crushing struggle for survival in post-war Rome. Young mammals learn their survival skills from their parents, and *The Bicycle Thief* keeps reminding us that the child is watching.

We see an unemployed father thrilled to hear of a job pasting posters around Rome. Unfortunately, a bicycle is required for the job. He and his wife decide to sell their last possession, their bed linens, to buy a bicycle. All too soon, street toughs steal the bike and the father searches for it desperately. The 1948 footage of Rome filled with bicycles rather than cars is intriguing despite the somber tone.

The young son joins his father on the search. They find the thief but can't get justice from the police. Feeling wronged, the father decides to steal a bicycle himself. He is quickly caught and arrested in front of his son. The son explodes with grief, which moves the victim to not to press charges. The victim's empathy for the child makes this a truly mammalian moment. Mammals nurture their young longer than other species. The victim was deprived of his bicycle as much as the father, yet his urge to nurture the young is stronger than his own self interest.

In the end, father and son return home with an air of hopelessness about their quest for survival. Hopelessness is a neural circuit that makes it easy to find facts that fit. Some historical context helps us see that things are less hopeless than the movie suggests.

Lawlessness spun out of control in Italy after World War II, especially in the South. A mass outbreak of theft and violence came with the end of fascism. The police tried to respond, and were vilified for jailing fathers who were allegedly "just feeding their families." *The Bicycle Thief* portrays the hypocrisy that perpetuates the problem: the father wanted law enforcement when he was the victim but reviled law enforcement when he was the perpetrator. A man who was anti-theft when he was the victim is pro-theft when he is the beneficiary.

Humans can overlook contradictions in their logical positions because their mammal brain's perspective feels more real. To the mammal brain, what promotes my survival is good and what hinders it is bad.

Policing cannot keep order when large numbers of people decide to put themselves above the law. When parents think this way, children learn from watching. In many places, children watch a lot of disrespect for the law. In Southern Italy, order was re-established by organized crime because they got respect where the formal system did not. When people only respect force, violent dominators rise to the top of the status hierarchy.

A hungry father has no other choice, people often say. That view is reinforced by the lack of hope presented at the end of this film. It is called a "neo-realist" film, which implies that hopelessness is realistic. But the fact is, Italy's GDP pulled ahead of England's four decades after this movie. Life does improve. We live better than our ancestors. We don't realize it because our mammal brains still feel insecure and frustrated. They're just doing the job they evolved to do: staying alert for risks and focusing on problems rather than accomplishments. Our problem-focused minds improve our lives and quickly shift focus to the next problem. We hardly notice our past successes as we rush to solve the next problem.

Some days are a total bust, and movies reflect that. But some days hold breakthroughs. If you lean toward "neo-realism," you can build a mental model of the world that only includes the disappointment and frustration. Such a film festival of despair would include *La Terra Trema* (The Earth Trembles), which is even bleaker than the Bicycle Thief. This Visconti saga portrays an impoverished Sicilian fisherman trying to better his life by buying his own boat. His family risks everything to eliminate the middleman instead of being a cog in the wheel of Big Fishing. Everything goes wrong, and they end up with even bigger holes in their rags, and more emaciated bones showing through. Worst of all, they are shunned by their peers. A viewer could easily conclude that no one has ever bought a boat and improved their life, and that everyone will always be a hopeless victim of big business. Or a person could choose different movies.

A wonderful choice would be the Chinese re-make of this movie, called *Beijing Bicycle*. It revolves around a poor boy who needs the bike to make a living and a rich boy who bought the bike from a used-bike street market. This movie astutely avoids oversimplifying things. It show the social frustrations of both the rich and the poor boy - frustrations universal to group-living mammals.

Ninotchka / Silk Stockings

Ninotchka is a female Soviet functionary visiting Paris on business. Greta Garbo plays her in the 1939 movie, and Cole Porter scored her in the 1955 Broadway musical *Silk Stockings*. Fred Astaire plays her suitor in the movie based on the musical. Beneath the fluffy trimmings lies a classic mammalian story.

Ninotchka has high status as a Soviet official, though she speaks in the rhetoric of self-sacrifice. In Paris she sees the bourgeois self-indulgence that she equates with the imminent collapse of the West. Lovers in Paris represent bourgeois sentimentalism to Ninotchka. Her inner Stalinist is soon challenged by a persistent suitor. She tells him what her communist teachers told her: sex is a physiological necessity but personal attachment is weak and decadent.

The suitor pursues Ninotchka doggedly. Both are caricatures. She is absurdly stiff and the suitor is implausibly smooth. But the conflict between them dramatizes the perennial mammalian conflict between the urge to meet one's needs and the urge to defer to more powerful individuals in order to protect one's self. The Cold War came and went but this conflict will always be with us.

Ninotchka expresses her disapproval in romance by telling her suitor: "We're tiny cogs in the great wheel of evolution." He's an experienced Parisian boulevardier and refuses to give up on the apparatchik. She tells him, "You're a product of a doomed culture; your type will soon be extinct." Finally she warms up to him, but the only way she can express herself is in ideological terms: "Let's form our own party." I found this hilarious because I have known many such ideologues in my life.

Cole Porter transforms the socialist theory of sexuality into the brilliant song *It's A Chemical Attraction, That's All*. Physical attraction is purely electrochemical, Ninotchka asserts. She quotes Soviet scientists who "proved" that electro-magnetism is all there is to the decadent capitalist phenomenon of romantic love. Their debate continues in the song *Paris Loves Lovers*. Cole Porter's counterpoint is the perfect vehicle for this debate. Fred Astaire flirts, and Ninotchka rebuffs each overture with the rhyming "imperialistic," "militaristic," "individualistic," "not collectivistic." When he says lovers are "in heaven," she retorts "they should be atheistic." It is rare to hear human nature debated with such perfect rhythm and rhyme.

The memorable mammalian moment revolves around Ninotchka's love for a hat. At first, she scoffs at the excessive ornamentation of 1939 Paris. A pouffy hat on sale in the lobby of her hotel is clear proof to her that capitalism is crumbling. "How can such a civilization survive which permits their women to put things like that on their heads? It won't be long now, comrades." But in the end, she buys the hat and even acknowledges her insecurity about her looks. She subtly acknowledges that her insecurity comes from her own desire for approval rather than from outside forces - a significant insight that not everyone achieves.

The point of the movie is not to celebrate pouffy hats, silk stockings, and seedy French boulevardiers. The point is that Ninotchka's desire for status in the Communist Party hierarchy is the same as romantic desire - just a mammal brain's quest for opportunities to improve its own survival prospects. The indulgences that Ninotchka saw as corruption ultimately make her less corrupt. The "before" Ninotchka had no regard for others except as it helped her pursuit of status in the Soviet hierarchy. Her answer to a request for news from Moscow was: "The latest mass trials were a great success. There are going to be fewer Russians but better Russians." The "after" Ninotchka learns to feed her inner mammal with small pleasures rather than with grandiose schemes for controlling her fellow mammal. It's amazing to see such deep issues depicted in song and dance routines.

Mrs. Brown

Queen Victoria was in a deep depression after the early death of her husband Albert, and she only came out of it when she formed an attachment to a servant. Her relationship with John Brown was not sexual, but it so outraged polite society that they took to calling her "Mrs. Brown."

Victoria's huge staff of retainers and sycophants could not understand what she saw in the lowly Scottish horse groomer. But it's clear that he satisfied her mammal brain's desire for protection. John Brown was a primal-type alpha male: big and aggressive. He had low status in British society, but he focused all of his energy on protecting Victoria. An alpha female like Victoria could have her pick of the males. Like any female ape, she wanted an effective protector more than a toadying twit from high society.

Some women prefer a toadying twit with money, but Victoria did not need money. She needed someone she could trust to keep her safe. She got that oxytocin feeling around John Brown for the first time since her husband died. That trust was based on his ability to dominate.

John Brown tackled a prowler who tried to attack the Queen. Then he dominated the other servants who tried to keep him away from the Queen. These servants were well-born courtiers, as is typical of royal households. Brown lowered their status by capturing the Queen's attention, so they united to resist him, as apes unite to eliminate a rival. John Brown's status plummets from bodyguard with benefits to back-office security clerk.

To be fair to the twits, it must be explained that John Brown is a drunken lout. In a brilliant mammalian moment, the courtiers convey their disdain for him with synchronized eye rolls that barely ruffle the extreme decorum they maintain in front of the Queen. We see the Queen strolling with her ladies-in-waiting, and we see the ladies give each other "the look" that says "we don't respect him." But we also see that these ladies have low status. They walk in lock-step with the Queen, pausing whenever she pauses, with their hands primly folded. They do not move a muscle without permission for fear of losing their status in the royal household, while John Brown freely acts on every impulse.

These upper crust ladies choose this life of servitude because it raises their status. The Queen feels trapped by them and longs to be free of her retinue. But the retainers cling so relentlessly to their alliance with the alpha that the Queen lacks the power to free herself. Primatologists often note that individuals in the second tier, just below the alpha, have the most relentless drive for status. Baboon-expert Robert Sapolsky discovered the highest stress levels, as measured by blood cortisol, among the high but not top-ranking individuals – the alpha's cronies as it were. It makes sense because they have the most to lose. They've invested a lot of effort to reach the top, and their mammal brain goads them to keep trying. The slogan *We're #2, We try harder* came from an ad for the second-ranking car-rental company, but it reflects a ubiquitous mammalian attitude.

If a royal courtier departs from prescribed convention in the smallest degree, they can lose the status their families spent generations accumulating. The other wannabes make sure of it. High status does not guarantee happiness, but the brain seeks it anyway.

When Prince Albert was alive, the Queen wanted to avoid the fishbowl court and be alone with her husband. But Albert insisted they make nice with courtiers for the sake of their legacy. Their main goal in life was establishing their children in monarchies, so they did everything they could to preserve the institution. Albert knew that what keeps a monarchy going is courtiers striving to raise their status. The reflected glory of associating with the royal family is what motivates elite support for the institution of royalty. If monarchs just kept to themselves, or cavorted with whatever Scottish louts amused them, support would soon dwindle. So Victoria kept letting retainers groom her the way alpha apes lets their underlings groom them. And she succeeded in marrying her children into royal families and producing lots of high-status grandchildren. Victoria wanted reproductive success more than she wanted to be free to do what she pleased on a moment-to-moment basis. Alphas and wannabes are as trapped by the status hierarchy as everyone below them. Each person traps themselves, as their mammal brain strives for happy chemicals.

Creation: How Darwin Saw the World and Changed It Forever

Charles Darwin was a mammal. He created two great legacies: the theory he's known for today, and the ten children he fathered. His scientific legacy gets most of the attention, but this movie shows how intensely his brain was focused on the reproductive side of his life. On the day that his theory was finally presented to the public, Darwin was home grieving the death of another child. The torment Darwin experienced on the road to his great accomplishments is vividly recreated in this movie. That torment came not from the system but from the mammalian challenges that frustrate everyone.

Darwin did not want to lose the goodwill of his wife. She was a religious woman who believed Darwin would go to hell for his blasphemy. She agonized over the thought of being separated from her husband in eternity, and that forced Darwin to agonize over it. In truth, Mrs. Darwin also seemed concerned about what the neighbors would think if one blasphemed. Charles hated to cause her pain, so he hesitated to publish his findings without her support.

Darwin also suffered greatly over the health of his children. The death of his favorite daughter is the focus of the movie, but the overall sickliness of his children is the real issue. In a painful mammalian moment, Darwin realizes that marrying his first cousin may be the cause of his children's sickliness. This insight is more significant than it seems today, with our molecular understanding of genetics. In Darwin's time, the dangers of inbreeding were only understood through experience with animal breeding, a popular activity among country gentlemen. People were not accustomed to taking responsibility for their genetic choices – Victoria and Albert's first-cousin marriage was celebrated at this time. Darwin's advanced scientific intuition forced him to confront the likelihood that his choice to marry within the confines of his high-status family caused the suffering of his children. Today, most of us have not watched a child die, so it's hard for us to imagine him doing it three times.

Darwin suffered from chronic abdominal pain, and this guilt made it worse. The movie shows how he finally overcomes his anxiety and presents his new paradigm to the world. It condenses the facts to add drama. A fuller account of Darwin's inner turmoil can be found in a highly-readable book called *The Reluctant Mr. Darwin*.

Darwin was a modest man, not known as a status seeker. But his mammalian motives are obvious if you look deeper. First, Darwin grew up with a father who called him a loser in no uncertain terms ("you will be a disgrace to yourself and all your family"). Charles came from an extremely accomplished family and he needed to do something to distinguish himself. He was pressured to be a doctor like his father and grandfather, but found the blood revolting. He considered other careers, but felt no calling to anything but observing nature. The only respectable way to do that was to be a country parson. He escaped that ironic double-bind when the opportunity to be a naturalist on the Beagle arose.

But twenty years after the voyage of the Beagle, he was still kicking tires. He hadn't assembled his scientific data into a new paradigm he felt was persuasive. Only the threat of a competitor provoked him to publish his work. Rivals provoke mammals to take the risks necessary to triumph. Darwin had never proven himself, and without that urge for status he may never have taken the risk of presenting his ideas to the world.

The mammalian quest for a legacy shaped Darwin in an even more significant way. It is not widely known that Charles's grandfather, Erasmus Darwin, had already thought of evolution. Darwin gave scientific form to ideas he had picked up at the dinner table. Though Erasmus died before Charles was born, each generation   is deeply shaped by the ideas they're exposed to during the formative years of their brain. The writings of Erasmus were public, so anyone could have built on their legacy. But not everyone would think it was worth the reward. To Charles, building on the legacy of his grandfather was his best shot at winning the respect of his father.

Early experience shapes our understanding of the natural world. Max Planck said that "science advances one funeral at a time." In other words, the brain has trouble seeing scientific data in any but the way it first wires itself for. Thomas Kuhn highlighted this quirk of history in *The Structure of Scientific Revolutions*. He said that new facts are seen as errors until a new generation grows up with the conflicting data. Kuhn left out the status part. New scientists need new paradigms to raise their status. Old scientists see new paradigms as threats to their status, and from a career perspective this is patently true. Young scientists are not more "objective" or "honest." They are simply mammals who build careers on new paradigms and the grant money and titles that go with it. Then they go on protect their new paradigm like generation before them. They too dismiss conflicting evidence, thus creating opportunity for the next generation of thinkers to make a place for themselves. Truth is not a finite set of facts. Truth is a social process that evolves.

Bibliography

Adler, Alfred
Understanding Human Nature
    1927, 2009 One World Publications

Allee, W. C.
The Social Life of Animals
    1938, 1958 Beacon Press

Andreski, Stanislav
Social Sciences as Sorcery
    1973 St. Martin's Press

Ardrey, Robert
The Territorial Imperative
    1966 Dell Publishing

Ardrey, Robert
*African Genesis: A Personal Investigation
    into the Animal Origins and Nature of Man*
    1961, 1977 Bantam Books

Bettman, Otto
The Good Old Days: They Were Terrible!
    1974 Random House

Bronson, Po
Nurture Shock: New Thinking About Children
   2009 Twelve Books

Cheney, Dorothy and Seyfarth, Robert
Baboon Metaphysics: The Evolution of a Social Mind
   2007 University of Chicago Press

Cheney, Dorothy and Seyfarth, Robert
How Monkeys See the World
   1990 University of Chicago Press

Conniff, Richard
A Natural History of the Rich
   2003 W.W. Norton

Conniff, Richard
The Ape in the Corner Office
   2005 Crown Publishing

Coyle, Daniel
The Talent Code: Greatness Isn't Born, It's Grown
   2009 Bantam Books

Darwin, Charles
The Expression of Emotions in Man and Animals
   1872, 2009 Oxford University Press

deBoton, Alain
Status Anxiety
   2004 Penguin Books

deWaal, Frans
Chimpanzee Politics: Power and Sex Among Apes
    1982, 1998 Johns Hopkins University Press

deWaal, Frans
*Our Inner Ape: A Leading Primatologist Explains Why We Are
    Who We Are*
    2006 Riverhead Books

deToqueville, Alexander
Democracy in America
    1831, 2002 University of Chicago Press

Dunbar, Robin; Barrett, Louise; and Lycett, John
Evolutionary Psychology
    2005, 2009 Oneworld Publications

Edgerton, Robert
Sick Societies: Challenging the Myth of Primitive Harmony
    1992 The Free Press

Epstein, Joseph
Snobbery: The American Version
    2002 Houghton Mifflin

Fisher, Helen
Why We Love: The Nature and Chemistry of Romantic Love
    2004   Henry Holt

Gilbert, Daniel
Stumbling on Happiness
    2007 Vintage

Grandin, Temple
Animals in Translation
    2006   Mariner Books

Greenberg, Gary and Haraway, Maury
Principles of Comparative Psychology
    2002   Allyn and Bacon

Klein, Stefan
*The Science of Happiness: How Our Brains Make Us Happy—
    and What We Can Do to Get Happier*
    2002, 2006 Da Capo Press

Kuegler, Sabine
Jungle Child
    2005 Virago Press (UK)

Le Blanc, Steven
Constant Battles: The Myth of the Peaceful Noble Savage
    2003 St. Martin's Press

LeDoux, Joseph
The Emotional Brain: Mysterious Underpinnings of Emotional Life
    1998 Simon and Schuster

Lehrer, Jonah
How We Decide
    2010 Mariner Books

Maestripieri, Dario
Macachiavellian Intelligence: How Rhesus Macaques and Humans Have Conquered the World
   2007 University of Chicago Press

Marais, Eugene
The Soul of the Ape
   1969, 1973 Penguin Books

Millan, Cesar
Cesar's Way: The Natural, Everyday Guide to Understanding and Correcting Common Dog Problems
   2007 Three Rivers Press

Morgan, Elaine
The Descent of the Child
   1995 Oxford University Press

Packard, Vance
The Human Side of Animals
   1950 Dial Press

Palmer, Jack, and Palmer, Linda
Evolutionary Psychology: The Ultimate Origins of Human Behavior
   2002 Allyn and Bacon

Pert, Candace
Molecules of Emotion: The Science Behind Mind-Body Medicine
   1999 Simon and Schuster

Pinker, Steven
The Blank Slate: The Modern Denial of Human Nature
    2002 Viking

Pinker, Steven
How the Mind Works
    1997, 2009 W.W. Norton

Robb, Peter
Midnight in Sicily
    1996, 2007 Farrar, Straus and Giroux

Russell, Robert Jay
The Lemurs' Legacy: The Evolution of Power, Sex and Love
    1993 Tarcher/Putnam

Sagan, Carl
The Dragons of Eden: Speculations on the Evolution of
    Human Intelligence
    1977 Random House

Sapolsky, Robert
A Primate's Memoir: A Neuroscientist's Unconventional Life
    Among the Baboons
    2001 Scribner

Sapolsky, Robert
Monkeyluv: And Other Essays on Our Lives as Animals
    2005 Scribner

Shubin, Neil
Your Inner Fish: A Journey Into the 3.5-Billion-Year History of the Human Body
    2008 Pantheon Books

Trivers, Robert
Social Evolution
    1985 Benjamin-Cummings Publishing

Washington, Booker T.
The Man Farthest Down: A Record of Observation and Study in Europe
    1912, 2010 BiblioLife

Whitaker, Robert
Anatomy of An Epidemic: Magic Bullets, Psychiatric Drugs, and the Astonishing Rise of Mental Illness in America
    2010 Crown Publishing

Wrangham, Richard
Catching Fire: How Cooking Made Us Human
    2009 Basic Books

Wrangham, Richard and Peterson, Dale
Demonic Males: Apes and the Origins of Human Violence
    1996 Houghton Mifflin

Index

addiction, 67, 73, 161-64, 172, 177, 273

aggression, 1, 14-15, 36, 45, 64, 78-80, 91-92, 99-103, 121-23, 227-30, 251, 255-57, 272-73, 275

Albert, Prince Consort of England, 233-35, 254-55, 264, 265

alliances, 4, 40, 42, 45, 65, 95-99, 127, 139, 205, 206

alphas, x, 3, 5, 42, 44, 49, 61, 64, 97-100, 106-7, 109, 112-13, 117, 120, 123, 158, 182-53, 193, 200, 217, 224, 236, 240-41, 246, 248, 250, 253-54

amygdala, 23 (illustration), 271, 278

appetite, 62, 189, 192-98

attention, *of others*: 26, 43, 70, 135-36, 138, 152
　　　　internal focus: 6, 19, 42, 68, 129-31, 138-39, 180, 185

baboons, 5-6, 61, 89, 96-97, 99, 110-12, 118, 177, 268, 271

big man system, 179

bonobos, 30, 85, 107, 121-22, 269

bribery, iv-xi, 203

bullying, 100-102

childhood, 35, 87-89, 94-95, 142-56, 258, 276-77

children, 9, 28, 50-51, 60, 72, 92, 117, 125, 126, 168, 171, 199-200, 205-207, 242, 255, 247-49, 265-66, 276-77

chimpanzees, 12, 22 (illustration), 29, 61, 75, 93, 97, 99, 110, 117, 120, 151, 228, 246, 247, 269

chronocentrism, 223, 279

college, iv-xi, 38-39, 43, 158, 206, 212, 218-19, 228-30, 278

conflict, 40, 41, 61, 65, 78-80, 93, 97, 112, 116, 118, 119, 122-26, 190-91, 237, 242, 274

contrast, 137-38, 217

cooperation, 30, 42, 46-47, 89, 151, 250, 255

cortex, ii, 3, 7, 21-24, 35, 55, 75, 79, 86-87, 103, 116, 136, 149, 153, 160, 167, 180, 231

cows, 1-2, 59, 81-83, 234, 274

criminality, x, 45, 65, 184-85, 255-59

culture, 41, 124-25, 132-33, 135, 165, 199-200, 227, 272

de Tocqueville, 13

Darwin, 78, 105, 264-67, 271

dogs, 90-92, 110, 185-86, 275, 276

dominance, 3-4, 33-34, 47, 61, 63-66, 78-102, 135, 158, 179-82, 199-200, 256-57

dopamine, 66-73, 120, 145, 155, 170-71, 187

endorphins, 56-58

ego, 16-17

expectations, 67-73, 75, 80, 90, 129-159, 175, 197, 217, 220, 224, 231-36

equality, 1, 12, 92-93, 200

free will, 10, 128-29, 218, 272

gorillas, 97, 122-24, 244

grooming, 4-5, 60, 74, 96, 118

habits, 17, 73, 156-63, 177, 180-86, 199, 201, 205

herd behavior, vii, 37, 59-61, 63, 82, 147-150, 199-200, 205

infanticide, 94, 97-99, 113, 124

inherited status, 83-85, 125

junk learning, 166-67, 171-77, 196

junk status, 201-205, 235

learning, 57, 69, 83, 85-88, 133-34, 139-146, 152-55, 171-77, 206-207, 213, 279

limbic system, 7, 21-24 (illustration on 23)

looks, 37, 114-16, 135, 261

love, 52,71-72, 119-120, 234, 243, 247, 260-62, 268

macaque monkeys, 83-88, 93-94, 100-102, 269-270

mating, 50-51, 88, 96-97, 104-126, 234, 247-49, 253, 255, 260-62

Mafia, viii-x, 238, 256-57

mirror neurons, 29-30, 85-87, 149, 191, 196, 199, 210, 211, 225, 237

money, 44

neuroplasticity, 129-134, 139-146, 175, 201, 251-52, 279

news, 49, 230, 278

opiates, 57, 275

oppositionalism, 36, 42, 48, 184

oxytocin, 33, 59-61, 72, 119-21, 147, 155, 171, 187, 263

politics, 41-43

popularity, 41, 134-37, 163, 241

puberty, 29-31, 109, 113, 124-25, 133-34, 175

Queen Victoria, 233-35, 253-55, 262-65

reptiles, 6, 23, 57-59, 77-78, 95, 173, 277, 278

reproductive success xi, 3, 6-11, 21, 25-30, 33-35, 48-52, 70, 89, 104-26, 161-62, 165-66, 168-71, 206, 225, 247, 253, 264, 271

rewards, 46, 52, 67-73, 126, 133-34, 139, 158, 175-76, 180, 231-36, 276

risk, 19, 29, 47-48, 167-70, 177-81, 192, 196

satisfaction, 192-98, 201, 224, 231

status anxiety, 128, 224-31, 270

serotonin, 61-66, 72, 75-76, 155, 170-71, 187

sex, 9-10, 28, 51-52, 60, 104-26, 166, 188-89, 192, 223, 260-62, 269

sexy son hypothesis, 106

Sicilians, viii-x, 5, 227, 260

social comparison, 12, 35-36, 44, 47, 137-39

submission, 1, 33-34, 36, 44, 63-64, 78, 123, 200, 203, 257

success, (see also winning, satisfaction, reproductive success) 49-52, 198-99

trust, x, 33, 47, 59-61, 64, 72, 74, 75, 87, 117, 139, 149, 155, 174, 187, 204, 254, 260-63

unhappiness, 7-8, 11, 13-14, 26-29, 32, 57, 128, 134-35, 162, 171, 172, 176, 188, 200, 207, 209, 223-31, 251-52

vervet monkey, 64, 272

violence (see aggression)

Washington, Booker T., ix, 227

winning, 26, 72, 108, 172, 183-213, 251-52

work, vii, 40, 182, 258, 276

I, Mammal: How to make peace with the animal urge for social power